European Patent Litigation in the Shadow of the Unified Patent Court

This book is dedicated to Rothna Begum.

European Patent Litigation in the Shadow of the Unified Patent Court

Luke McDonagh

City Law School, City University of London, UK

Edward Elgar
PUBLISHING

Cheltenham, UK • Northampton, MA, USA

Published by
Edward Elgar Publishing Limited
The Lypiatts
15 Lansdown Road
Cheltenham
Glos GL50 2JA
UK

Edward Elgar Publishing, Inc.
William Pratt House
9 Dewey Court
Northampton
Massachusetts 01060
USA

A catalogue record for this book
is available from the British Library

Library of Congress Control Number: 2016935774

This book is available electronically in the **Elgar**online
Law subject collection
DOI 10.4337/9781784714741

FSC
www.fsc.org
MIX
Paper from
responsible sources
FSC® C013056

ISBN 978 1 78471 473 4 (cased)
ISBN 978 1 78471 474 1 (eBook)

Typeset by Columns Design XML Ltd, Reading

Printed and bound in Great Britain by
TJ International Ltd, Padstow, Cornwall

Contents

Acknowledgements

I am grateful to a number of people who assisted me in the creation of this book. First and foremost, I would like to thank Christian Helmers for contacting me in 2011 and offering me the chance to collaborate with him on an interdisciplinary patent litigation project with Katrin Cremers, Max Ernicke, Fabian Gaessler, Dietmar Harhoff, Paula Schliessler, and Nicolas van Zeebroeck. The work that came out of that project, which to some extent anticipated the current EU patent reforms, proved invaluable when considering the Unified Patent Court over the course of this book.

A large number of academics have encouraged and supported me since my days as an PhD student at Queen Mary. University of London, through my time as a post-doctoral fellow at the London School of Economics (LSE), my lectureships at Cardiff University and The City Law School, and my visiting fellowship at Waseda University. In this, there are simply too many to mention, but I feel I must thank Jonathan Griffiths, Dev Gangjee, Alain Pottage, Tatiana Flessas, Siva Thambisetty, Andrew Murray, Marc Mimler, Noam Shemtov, Duncan Matthews, Guido Westkamp, Uma Suthersanen, Gaetano Dimita, Leslie Lansman, Georg von Graevenitz, Ian Walden, Malcolm Langley, Johanna Gibson, Phillip Johnson, Tim Press, Enrico Bonadio, Mara Malagodi, Tatsuhiro Ueno and Kazuhiro Ando.

I am grateful to the UK Intellectual Property Office, who supported the underlying research of this book with funding during 2014.

I would like to give special thanks to Rothna Begum in London and the McDonagh family in Galway – Thomas, Bridget, Sarah, Nicholas and Paul.

Luke McDonagh, January 2016

Table of cases

EUROPEAN UNION CASE LAW

GERMAN CASE LAW

DUTCH CASE LAW

UK CASE LAW

Table of legislation

EUROPEAN LEGISLATION

DUTCH LEGISLATION

FRENCH LEGISLATION

GERMAN LEGISLATION

UK LEGISLATION

1. Introduction

A NEW BEGINNING FOR THE EUROPEAN PATENT SYSTEM?

Until recently, only scant data were publicly available on the subject of patent litigation in EU member states, and as a result it was difficult to accurately examine how prevalent patent litigation was from state to state, how costly it was and how significant the divergences were between the various systems. However, in recent years a number of major studies – based on analysis of carefully gathered empirical patent case data – have been published.[1] These studies have shed new light on the subject of patent litigation in EU member states, particularly in the major jurisdictions of the UK, Germany, France and the Netherlands, where the vast majority of

[1] The most prominent study is K. Cremers, M. Ernicke, D. Harhoff, C. Helmers, G. Licht, L. McDonagh, et al. 'Patent litigation in Europe', *ZEW Discussion Paper* No. 13-07 (2013), 1 (hereafter known as Cremers), available at http://ftp.zew.de/pub/zew-docs/dp/dp13072.pdf. This study attempts to analyse all patent cases filed in the various jurisdictions during the period 2000–2008 (though cases may have been decided post-2008 since case lengths can span a number of years post-filing). The Cremers data collection took place during 2010–2012. The German and UK data are for the most part accurate reflections of cases filed, but the data for the Netherlands and France do not cover all cases filed, and are largely restricted to cases that were adjudicated. Nonetheless, the Cremers paper represents the first authoritative account of patent litigation in these four jurisdictions. See also the following country-specific studies: P. Véron, 'Patent infringement litigation in France', *Mitteilungen der deutschen Patentanwälte* 93 (2002), 386; C. Helmers and L. McDonagh, 'Patent litigation in the UK: an empirical survey 2000–2008', *Journal of Intellectual Property Law & Practice* 8 (2013), 846; T. Bouvet, 'France', in M.C. Elmer and C.G. Gramaenopoulos (eds), *Global Patent Litigation* (Virginia: Bloomberg BNA, 2014), 546–89; and the European overview given in N. Van Zeebroeck and S. Graham, 'Comparing patent litigation across Europe: a first look', *Stanford Technology Law Review* 17 (2014), 655.

European patent ligation takes place. This leads us to the first rationale for the writing of this book – it is now, for the first time, possible to paint an accurate, detailed picture of the patent litigation system in Europe. The first part of this book aims to paint that picture, setting the scene by analysing and summing up the current state of patent litigation in Europe's major patent jurisdictions.

This brings us to the second rationale for the writing of this book – the need to take account of the seismic shift represented by the coming into force of the EU-driven European patent reform package. On 19 February 2013, the UK and 24 other countries signed an intergovernmental agreement (the Agreement) to create a Unified Patent Court (UPC), which will be a new specialist patents court common to participating states.[2] The provision of a new Unitary Patent (UP) – known officially as the 'European Patent with Unitary Effect' – is the other key aspect of the reforms. Overall, the package of measures is designed to establish and enforce unitary patent protection within the European Union, with the ultimate ambition of unifying the European patent system as much as possible.[3] Moreover, a central aim of the establishment of the UPC

---

[2] Agreement on a Unified Patent Court (The UPC Agreement), C 175/01 (2013), accessible at http://eur-lex.europa.eu/LexUriServ/LexUriServ.do?uri=OJ:C:2013:175:0001:0040:EN:PDF.

[3] Regulation (EU) No. 1257/2012 of the European Parliament and of the Council of 17 December 2012 implementing enhanced cooperation in the area of the creation of unitary patent protection (UP Regulation), OJ L 361/1 (2012) and Council Regulation (EU) No. 1260/2012 of 17 December 2012 implementing enhanced cooperation in the area of the creation of unitary patent protection with regard to the applicable translation arrangements (Translation Regulation), OJ L 361/89 (2012) – both documents accessible at http://ec.europa.eu/internal_market/indprop/patent/documents/index_en.htm. For a further explanation of the changes, see the EPO website: www.epo.org/law-practice/unitary.html.

See also R. Romandini and A. Klicznik, 'The territoriality principle and transnational use of patented inventions: the wider reach of a unitary patent and the role of the CJEU', *International Review of Intellectual Property and Competition Law* 44 (2013), 524; and M. Brandi-Dohrn, 'Some critical observations on competence and procedure of the unified patent court', *International Review of Intellectual Property and Competition Law* 43 (2012), 372.

and the UP is to offer inventors and businesses a more streamlined and easy-to-use system that is also cost-effective. The second part of this book gives academic consideration to all relevant aspects of the reforms, and evaluates what the impact of the UPC and the UP is likely to be on patent litigation in Europe in the short term and in the long term.

Thus, over the course of this book I ask and answer a series of questions: first, what is the current state of patent litigation in Europe? Second, what are the aims and crucial features of the reforms? Third, in practice will these reforms likely succeed at achieving their overall aims; and, finally, what will the overall picture of European patent litigation look like in the decades following the coming into being of the new system? As explained further on, one of the novel things about this book is the use of interview data – gathered from patent experts in the legal and business communities – to answer questions concerning the challenges facing patent litigants and their legal representatives in Europe over the coming decades.

Following this introductory Chapter 1, Chapter 2 examines the current state of European patent litigation, which, although it is framed by the European Patent Convention (EPC), is actually undertaken on a largely national basis.[4] European Patents (EPs) granted by the European Patent Office (EPO) must be validated – and, subsequently, litigated – within national jurisdictions.[5] National courts have the ability to issue binding rulings concerning patent infringement within their national territories, and they may

[4] Text of the European Patent Convention, of 5 October 1973, as revised by the Act revising Article 63 EPC of 17 December 1991, and the Act revising the EPC of 29 November 2000, available at http://documents.epo.org/projects/babylon/eponet.nsf/0/00E0CD7FD461C0D5C1257C060050C376/$File/EPC_15th_edition_2013.pdf, also accessible at www.epo.org/law-practice/legal-texts/html/epc/2010/d/index.html.

[5] See also The Agreement on the application of Article 65 of the Convention on the Grant of European Patents agreed on 17 October 2000 (see OJ EPO 549 (2001)) (hereafter known as the London Agreement), available at http://documents.epo.org/projects/babylon/eponet.nsf/0/7FD20618D28E9FBFC125743900678657/$File/London_Agreement.pdf.

also consider questions of patent validity – although the EPO retains the final say on validity via its patent opposition service.[6] Indeed, it is not uncommon for national patent litigation to take place at the same time as parallel EPO opposition proceedings; and the lengthy backlog at the EPO means that national courts sometimes rule on questions of validity and infringement before the EPO Board of Appeals has reached a final decision regarding validity.[7] Moreover, due to the fact that national courts have the ability under the EPC to make decisions based on their own jurisprudence, the courts in one EPC member state (e.g. the UK) may reach different conclusions to the courts of another EPC member state (e.g. Germany) when resolving the central questions of patent litigation: what amounts to infringement of a patent in suit? Is the patent in suit valid or invalid? In what circumstances is it appropriate to grant a preliminary injunction to a patentee? And if EPO proceedings are ongoing, should a stay of national proceedings be granted?

The precise intricacies of the way this system works are examined in Chapter 2 by assessing the state of patent litigation within Europe‘s four key patent litigation venues: the UK (London), Germany (Dusseldorf, Mannheim and Munich), France (Paris) and the Netherlands (The Hague).[8] As noted at the outset, until recently there was a lack of empirical evidence concerning patent litigation within these four major jurisdictions; in light of recently published studies, this chapter explores litigation at an in-depth level in each of the above territories.[9] It is shown that each of these four major jurisdictions has developed its own unique characteristics in the

---

[6] See generally EPO, *Patent Litigation in Europe: An overview of national law and practice in the EPC contracting states* (2013), www.epo.org/learning-events/materials/litigation.html.

[7] K. Cremers, M. Ernicke, D. Harhoff, C. Helmers, G. Licht, L. McDonagh, et al. ‘Patent litigation in Europe’, *ZEW Discussion Paper* No. 13-07 (2013), 1, 1–3.

[8] As discussed further in Chapter 2, between them these four jurisdictions handle the majority of European patent cases, with Germany by far the most popular venue.

[9] K. Cremers, M. Ernicke, D. Harhoff, C. Helmers, G. Licht, L. McDonagh, et al. ‘Patent litigation in Europe’, *ZEW Discussion Paper* No. 13-07 (2013), 1. See also European Patent Office (EPO), *Patent Litigation in Europe:*

field of patent litigation: the UK's courts possess a well-earned reputation for requiring broad disclosure on the part of both parties, making use of a great deal of expert evidence, and conducting lengthy and detailed (and, consequently, expensive) hearings on the issues of patent validity and infringement; the German courts, meanwhile, represent the most popular patent litigation venues in Europe, and are often commended for providing parties with relatively cost-effective and speedy infringement hearings, though they are sometimes criticized for the complexities which can arise due to the system of bifurcation – a process required by the German Federal Constitution that is not present in any of the other three jurisdictions – whereby the issues of infringement and validity are resolved by separate courts in separate hearings; by contrast, the French courts are admired for the unique set of *saisie* procedures that enable a party to gain access to another company's premises to speedily and efficiently collect evidence on allegedly infringing acts; and, finally, while for a long time the advantage to filing suit in the Netherlands was the availability of cross-border injunctions – now less common – in more recent years, the Dutch courts have been praised for the speed and cost-effectiveness of their proceedings, and the technical expertise of their judges. In Chapter 2 each of these jurisdictions is examined in detail with respect to the key aspects of the litigation process and the volume and nature of the cases taken in the jurisdiction. The final part of this chapter sums up the various commonalities and differences present in the key jurisdictions of European patent litigation, shedding light on the advantages and disadvantages of the patent litigation system as it is currently framed.

Following this assessment of the current state of patent litigation in Europe, Chapter 3 outlines the motivation behind the reforms – the perceived need to provide a more efficient, cost-effective, harmonious litigation system – as well as the structure of the proposed reforms, i.e. the UPC and the UP. The key EU reformative innovations – the Intergovernmental Agreement on a Unified Patent Court[10] and the two EU Regulations implementing enhanced cooperation with regards to the creation of unitary patent protection

---

An overview of national law and practice in the EPC contracting states (2013), available at www.epo.org/learning-events/materials/litigation.html.

[10] UPC Agreement.

and facilitating translations of such patents as granted[11] – are discussed. The fact that Spain has, thus far, refused to sign up to any part of the 'reform package' is noted here, as is the fact that Poland has decided not to participate in the UPC; while Italy has, having wavered, agreed to sign up to both the new UP and the UPC.[12] Croatia, an EU member state as of 2013, did not join until after the above agreements/regulations had already been signed/passed. At the time of writing, Croatia had not yet decided whether to participate in the UPC or the UP.

This third chapter goes on to analyse the background of the EU-driven patent reform package, including the questions of why reforms were thought necessary and why these particular reforms (UPC, UP) were chosen. The key legal aspects of the UPC and the UP are then discussed.

The UPC is examined with regards to the court's key institutional architecture: its sources of law; its jurisdiction; the substantive law to be utilized by the court; the UPC's relationship with the Court of Justice of the European Union; issues of standing and legal representation; the court's structure and competence; the practicalities and procedures of filing a UPC case; the way bifurcation is likely to operate within the UPC; the process of making appeals; the availability of the opt-out from the UPC's jurisdiction; the UPC's enforcement powers; the make-up of its judiciary; and, finally, the transitional period that will see national courts and the UPC share jurisdiction for at least 7 years. Throughout the chapter, reference is made to the UPC Rules of Procedure, where relevant. The fees for using the UPC are also discussed in this part of the chapter and are further outlined in the conclusion of this book.

Regarding the UP, this chapter explores its central features: the processes of application and grant; its territorial scope; the consequences of unitary effect; the property considerations involved in holding a UP; translation requirements; and the various fees involved, including the annual UP renewal fees. The third chapter concludes with a summary of the most significant elements of the

---

[11] UP Regulation and Translation Regulation.

[12] See, generally, T. Cook, 'The progress to date on the Unitary European Patent and the Unified Patent Court for Europe', *Journal of Intellectual Property Rights* 18 (2013), 584.

UPC and the UP, with a view to the empirical study featured in Chapter 4.

At this point of the book, a crucial question is posed: in light of the underlying rationale for the reforms – the need to provide a more efficient, cost-effective and harmonious litigation system – what features of the new system will be particularly crucial to achieving these aims? A number of potential positives and negatives of the reforms are outlined here, including the impact of the fees/costs of the new system (given the aim to reduce overall litigation costs); the availability of centralized enforcement via the grant of patent injunctions and revocations spanning 25 UPC Signatory States (regarding the aim to create more legal harmony and certainty); the possibility that forum shopping will occur within the UPC and the associated risk of 'patent troll' litigation (given the need for an efficient and fair litigation system); and, finally, the lack of uniformity of patent enforcement across all 28 EU member states (MS) (in light of the fact that Spain, Poland and Croatia are, as yet, not parties to the UPC).

Chapter 4 – the penultimate chapter of this book – is framed around a UK IPO-commissioned empirical study, carried out by the author, that examines the perspectives of those within the business and legal communities concerning the UPC and the UP.[13] This piece of research had the specific aim of discovering at a qualitative level the answer to the following question: what are the most important issues for the stakeholders who will potentially use the new system?[14] For instance, is it likely that inventors and businesses will seek patent protection via the new UP route, rather than through the existing system of obtaining EPs or national patents? If so, why (and if not, why not)? Moreover, is the proposed UPC likely to prove to be a popular venue for companies/litigants? What makes the UPC attractive to litigants (or unattractive, as the case may be)? Are patentees likely to opt out of the UPC during the

---

[13] This study was undertaken from January to May 2014 – see further L. McDonagh, 'Exploring perspectives of the Unified Patent Court and the Unitary Patent within the business and legal communities', *A Report Commissioned by the UK Intellectual Property Office* (July 2014), available at www.gov.uk/government/publications/exploring-perspectives-of-the-up-and-upc.

[14] J. Pagenberg, 'Unitary patent and Unified Court: what lies ahead?', *Journal of Intellectual Property Law & Practice* 8 (2013), 480.

transition period? What is the likely impact of the fact that the UPC central divisions will be divided between three cities – Paris, Munich and London? For instance, do those in the Pharma/ Chemicals sector favour the location of the proposed London-based court?

Thus, following on from the examination of the reforms in Chapter 3, Chapter 4 explores what the most important issues are for those within the business and legal communities, i.e. the potential users of the UPC and the UP. This chapter assesses a large amount of empirical data gathered from interviews with 28 participants from the legal and business communities. The interview data shows that stakeholders are carefully considering what the impact of pan-25 EU MS injunctions and pan-25 EU MS revocations might be; are cautiously assessing the legal costs of using the new system viz. the current system; and are trying to evaluate whether the existence of bifurcation at the UPC, the possibility of forum shopping and the possible growth in 'patent troll' litigation are causes for concern.

As detailed in Chapter 4, although this was a UK IPO-funded study, in terms of its (anonymous) participants the survey's remit includes not only in-house counsel working at businesses based in the UK, but also at businesses that operate internally and externally to the wider EU, including companies based in Germany, the United States, Canada and Japan. Interview participants were also drawn from the legal community – primarily solicitors and patent attorneys – working in both the UK and Germany, two important EU and EPC member states with large, embedded patent litigation systems – as examined in Chapter 2 – that will no doubt be affected by the establishment of the UPC.

Then Chapter 5 – the conclusion of this book – takes the key concerns identified by the empirical study and considers how both the setting up of and the organization of the UPC and the UP have moved on since 2014, looking further ahead to 2017 and beyond. Several observations are made by the author with respect to the remaining key concerns of those within the business and legal communities about the UPC and the UP, including the establishment and maintenance of a high quality judicial system across the UPC, and the maintenance of appropriate fee levels for the UP and the UPC. Additionally, it is considered how the seismic changes brought about by the UPC and the UP may end up altering litigant behaviours within Europe. Overall, taking into account empirical data concerning both the current state of patent litigation in Europe and the views of the potential users of the new system, this chapter considers what European patent litigation is likely to look like in the years following the coming into being of the UPC and the UP – a perspective taken at this crucial time, with the new system steadily emerging, but not yet fully in view.

The title of this book suggests that the UPC currently casts a shadow over patenting in Europe; indeed, my concluding argument is that it is likely this shadow will continue to be observable for some time – for, with the arrival of the UPC and the UP, we have surely come to the end of one phase of the European patent project, and are at the beginning of another.

At time of writing, the UK's membership of the EU is not certain – much will depend on the outcome of the June 2016 referendum on EU membership. If the UK remains an EU member state, then the UPC and UP will proceed as planned. However, if the UK does exit the EU, it will likely no longer be able to participate in the UPC or UP; indeed, the UPC itself may need be to redesigned to take account of a UK exit, given that the UK is currently expected to host one of the UPC's central divisions. Although this book is written with the status quo in mind, i.e. with the expectation that the UK will remain an EU member state and thus a participant in the UPC, ultimately the analysis of European patent litigation undertaken over the course of this book remains valuable even in the case that the UK does not participate in the UPC, for it highlights both the current state of patent litigation in the UK, Germany, France and the Netherlands, and anticipates expected and possible future reforms that will undoubtedly have an impact both on the continued fragmentation of litigation at the national levels and on the uniformity of patent jurisdiction at the UPC level.

Indeed, the long-term impact of the UPC is likely to be so profound that whatever the new dawn looks like, it will be substantially different from what came before. Thus, what I wish to present with this book is an in-depth exploration of European patent litigation in the context of the new court system – a work that sums up the current state of European patent litigation while simultaneously looking ahead to upcoming and future reforms.

2. European patent litigation under the European Patent Convention (EPC)

EUROPEAN PATENT LITIGATION: FROM THE EPC TO THE UPC

The trend in Europe since the advent of the Treaty of Rome in 1957 has been towards legal harmonization within the European Union (EU), something that is particularly evident in regulatory areas where the law has a significant economic impact on the workings of the single market, such as in the areas of free movement (of goods, capital, services and people), competition and consumer protection.[1] Yet, despite its economic importance, patenting in Europe has stubbornly remained a fragmented and complex process, both in application and in enforcement.[2]

One clear reason for the lack of harmony within the current European patent system is the longstanding failure – despite many attempts – of the EU to agree on a uniform, harmonized 'Community Patent' system, similar to that which has long existed within the EU for Community trade marks (recently renamed EU trade

[1] Treaty establishing the European Economic Community, Mar. 25, 1957, 298 U.N.T.S. 3 (Treaty of Rome). See also Consolidated version of the Treaty on European Union OJ C115/13 (2008) and Consolidated version of the Treaty of the Functioning of the European Union (TFEU) OJ C326/61 (2012), available at http://eur-lex.europa.eu/legal-content/EN/TXT/?uri=celex:12012E/TXT. Note also the reference to the protection of intellectual property in Article 17 of the Charter of Fundamental Rights of the European Union OJ C83/389 (2010).

[2] D. Harhoff, 'Economic cost-benefit analysis of a unified and integrated European patent litigation system', *EU Final Report Tender No. MARKT/2008/06/D* (2009), 1, 31, available at http://ec.europa.eu/internal_market/indprop/docs/patent/studies/litigation_system_en.pdfHarhoff.

marks).[3] Unlike in the area of trade mark law, for patents the language issue has been a major stumbling block in negotiations.[4]

Despite this failure, in addition to the national patent systems of each European country, a non-EU based, pan-European patent system of a kind has actually existed since 1973 under the terms of the European Patent Convention (EPC).[5] Notably, however, because the EPC is not an EU agreement it lacks the administrative and judicial mechanisms – such as the EU Commission and the CJEU, so commonly utilized in the fields of trade mark law and competition law – that might bring harmony to European patent law. Nonetheless, the EPC's impact has been substantial, and understanding the way the EPC works remains the key to unlocking the European patent system as it is currently designed.

European Patents: Application and Enforcement

Since the coming into force of the EPC, individuals or businesses seeking to protect their inventions across Europe have had the option of either (i) making – under national law – separate applications to each national patent office for a national patent of that territory – for example, a UK patent (GB), a French patent (FR), a German patent (DE) or a Dutch patent (NL); or (ii) making – via the EPC – a single application to the Munich-based European Patent Office (EPO) for a European patent (EP),[6] which in fact,

---

[3] J. Pila, 'The European patent: an old and vexing problem', *International & Comparative Law Quarterly* 62 (2013), 917, 917–921.

[4] Hoffmann-Eitle, *The EU Patents Package Handbook: A Practioner's Guide* (Munich: Hoffmann-Eitle, 2014), 46.

[5] Text of the European Patent Convention (EPC), of 5 October 1973, as revised by the Act revising Article 63 EPC of 17 December 1991, and the Act revising the EPC of 29 November 2000, available at http://documents.epo.org/projects/babylon/eponet.nsf/0/00E0CD7FD461C0D5C1257C060050C376/$File/EPC_15th_edition_2013.pdf. Interestingly, in Switzerland/Liechtenstein a type of 'supra-national' EP has existed since the coming into force of the EPC – a patent granted by, or validated by, the Swiss Patent Office is in legal force in Liechtenstein as well.

[6] At the EPO, the key patenting concepts, e.g. subject matter, novelty, obviousness (inventive step), industrial character, are interpreted in line with the EPC. Examining these subjects in detail is beyond the remit of this book –

as one or more of the three largest EU markets: Germany, France and the UK.[12]

Crucially, when litigation takes place in multiple arenas national jurisprudential variances may have a significant impact on the course of a legal dispute. The various national courts may differ in their approaches to procedural issues (disclosure, preliminary enforcement) as well as in regards to substantive matters, such as the question of whether patent infringement has occurred.[13] Similarly, on the subject matter of validity, although the EPO gives guidance to national courts on how validity-related concepts ought to be applied, the national courts retain the ability under the EPC to interpret the key concepts – subject matter, novelty, obviousness, industrial character, etc. – as they see fit. National courts may issue decisions that are, in general, effective and enforceable only within their own national territories. Therefore, the fragmented nature of the litigation system can lead to an inconsistency in decision making between national courts – for example, even with the same set of facts/parties, a patent found to have been infringed by a defendant in one jurisdiction may not be found to have been infringed in another jurisdiction; moreover, an EP invalidated by a court in one national jurisdiction remains in force in other national jurisdictions where it has been validated.[14]

Nonetheless, the EPO does retain the ultimate say on validity via its post-grant opposition proceedings – not a process of litigation as such, but rather an administrative procedure whereby other parties, such as competitors, may challenge the validity of an EP. In theory,

---

[12] T. Bouvet, 'France', in M.C. Elmer and C.G. Gramaenopoulos (eds), *Global Patent Litigation* (Arlington, VA: Bloomberg BNA, 2014), 546–89, 588.

[13] K. Cremers, M. Ernicke, D. Harhoff, C. Helmers, G. Licht, L. McDonagh, et al. 'Patent litigation in Europe', *ZEW Discussion Paper* No. 13-07 (2013), 1, 1–5.

[14] See, for instance, the divergence between decisions concerning the same patent in the UK (England and Wales) and the Netherlands in the case of *Novartis AG v Sun Pharmaceutical Industries BV* [2013] EWCA Civ 1663 as reported on the IPKat weblog – http://ipkitten.blogspot.co.uk/2015/01/dutch-diverge-with-english-as-novartis.html. See also K. Cremers, M. Ernicke, D. Harhoff, C. Helmers, G. Licht, L. McDonagh, et al. 'Patent litigation in Europe', *ZEW Discussion Paper* No. 13-07 (2013), 1, 1–5.

this should prevent serious inconsistency problems occurring concerning the issue of patent validity, because the effect of an EPO opposition finding is immediate in all relevant EPC territories (e.g. an EPO decision that the EP is, in fact, invalid is effective in all territories where the patent had previously been validated). However, an initial EPO opposition decision can be appealed to the EPO Technical Board of Appeals, where it can take several years before a final decision on validity is made.[15]

In the meantime, national litigation may still go ahead, meaning that national litigation and EPO opposition proceedings can sometimes occur in parallel, leaving open the possibility of conflicting rulings being issued at the national and EPO levels. In other words, during this often lengthy interim period national courts around Europe can issue findings concerning validity and infringement of a patent that the EPO may later decide to invalidate. This highly unfortunate and deeply unsatisfactory scenario sometimes involves the successful national assertion of EPs that are actually invalid (and, thus, should never have been granted in the first place).[16]

Thus, there are two potential scenarios where inconsistency can occur: (i) courts in different national jurisdictions may make inconsistent decisions concerning infringement and/or validity – for example, a patent held to be valid and infringed in Germany may be found invalid and not infringed in the UK; and (ii) a national court may rule on validity (and, consequently, infringement) and the EPO opposition finding may later contradict this decision – for example, the UK may hold that a patent is valid, but the EPO may find that it is in fact invalid.

This problem of inconsistency in decision making – including the existence of duplicative, and even contradictory, patent enforcement decisions across EU member states – is discussed further below in the comparative analysis of the jurisdictions of the UK, Germany, France and the Netherlands. For now it is simply necessary to note a few key points about the current fragmented litigation system: first, inconsistent national decision making concerning EPs creates legal uncertainty and unnecessary complexities; second, EU intra-Community trade is impacted because inconsistent legal decisions

[15] See Article 99 EPC seq.

[16] *Unilin Beheer BV v Berry Floor NV* [2007] EWCA Civ 364; [2007] FSR 25, comments of Jacob LJ at para. 17.

between EU MS effectively fragment the single market (e.g. a product covered by a competitor's patent found valid in one MS but invalid in another may be seized in one EU MS but marketed legally in the other);[17] and third, the existence of a splintered European patent system often leads to (much) greater costs of patenting and undertaking litigation compared to other economic territories covering large markets, with the USA the primary case in point.[18]

Dissatisfaction with the current costly and fragmented system is longstanding, and negotiations for a unified system were ongoing across Europe for 40 years.[19] Eventually, on 19 February 2013 the UK and 24 other countries signed an intergovernmental agreement (the Agreement) to create a Unified Patent Court (UPC) – a new specialist patents court common to participating states.[20] The Agreement is part of a package of measures designed to establish and enforce unitary patent protection within Europe with the ambition of unifying the European patent system as much as possible.[21]

---

[17] Sir David Kitchen, 'Introductory Remarks: A Judicial Perspective', in J. Pila and C. Wadlow (eds), *The Unitary EU Patent System* (Oxford: Hart, 2015), 1–8.

[18] B. van Pottelsberghe, *Lost Property: The European patent system and why it doesn't work* (Brussels: Bruegel Blueprint Series, 2009), available at http://bruegel.org/wp-content/uploads/imported/publications/patents_BP_050609.pdf.

[19] K. Cremers, M. Ernicke, D. Harhoff, C. Helmers, G. Licht, L. McDonagh, et al. 'Patent litigation in Europe', *ZEW Discussion Paper* No. 13-07 (2013), 1, 1–3.

[20] Agreement on a Unified Patent Court (UPC Agreement), OJ C 175/01 (2013), available at http://eur- http://eur-lex.europa.eu/LexUriServ/LexUriServ.do?uri=OJ:C:2013:175:0001:0040:EN:PDF.

[21] Regulation (EU) No. 1257/2012 of the European Parliament and of the Council of 17 December 2012 implementing enhanced cooperation in the area of the creation of unitary patent protection (UP Regulation), OJ L 361/1 (2012) and Council Regulation (EU) No. 1260/2012 of 17 December 2012 implementing enhanced cooperation in the area of the creation of unitary patent protection with regard to the applicable translation arrangements (Translation Regulation) OJ L 361/89 (2012) – both documents available at http://ec.europa.eu/internal_market/indprop/patent/documents/index_en.htm. For a further explanation of the changes, see the EPO website – www.epo.org/law-practice/unitary.html. See also R. Romandini and A. Klicznik, 'The territoriality principle and transnational use of patented inventions: the wider

The major elements of the UPC/UP reforms are detailed in the chapter which follows this one. However, before the effects of the reforms can be assessed at an in-depth level it is first necessary to undertake analysis of the current state of European patent litigation, and in particular to analyse the key jurisdictions of the UK, Germany, France and the Netherlands.

COMPARATIVE ANALYSIS OF THE JURISDICTIONS OF THE UK, GERMANY, FRANCE AND THE NETHERLANDS

As noted earlier, within the EPC system the EPO has the ultimate competence to issue decisions with respect to the validity of EPs – decisions that have immediate effect within all 38 contracting states of the EPC. The usefulness of this, however, is undermined by the fact that the primary EPO mechanism for evaluating the validity of granted EPs – the patent opposition procedure – is currently marred by delays, something which has resulted in a considerable backlog as well as the potential for inconsistent European patent enforcement decisions.

The specific problem of inconsistency of European decisions concerning patent validity and infringement is difficult to analyse without access to reliable pan-European patent litigation statistics. Thankfully, over the past few years several authoritative studies have been published in this regard.[22] By making use of recently

reach of a unitary patent and the role of the CJEU', *International Review of Intellectual Property and Competition Law (IIC)* 44 (2013), 524; A. West, S. Kusumakar and T. Powell, 'Unitary Patents and the Unified Patent Court', *Computer and Telecommunications Law Review* 19 (2013), 105; and M. Brandi-Dohrn, 'Some critical observations on competence and procedure of the Unified Patent Court', *International Review of Intellectual Property and Competition Law (IIC)* 43 (2012), 372.

[22] The most prominent study is K. Cremers, M. Ernicke, D. Harhoff, C. Helmers, G. Licht, L. McDonagh, et al. 'Patent litigation in Europe', *ZEW Discussion Paper* No. 13-07 (2013), 1. See also the following country-specific studies – P. Véron, 'Patent infringement litigation in France', *Mitteilungen der deutschen Patentanwälte* 93 (2002), 386; C. Helmers and L. McDonagh, 'Patent litigation in the UK: an empirical survey 2000–2008', *Journal of Intellectual Property Law & Practice* 8 (2013), 846; T. Bouvet, 'France', in

published data, the remainder of this chapter attempts to shed light on the current state of European patent litigation by focusing primarily on four legal jurisdictions – the UK, Germany, France and the Netherlands.

The reasons for concentrating on these four jurisdictions are as follows: first, they are acknowledged as the most prominent sites of patent litigation in Europe;[23] second, all four states have signed up as full participants with respect to the UPC and the UP, and as such will be directly affected by the jurisdiction of the new court; and third, there is now a wealth of recent publications that analyse these four jurisdictions and which provide reliable quantitative litigation data – data that are, in general, not available for other European jurisdictions.[24]

The United Kingdom (UK)

Assessing the applicable law and competent courts in the UK

The primary piece of UK patent legislation is the Patents Act 1977, which brought the provisions of the EPC into national law.[25] Regarding patent litigation in the UK, the first point to note is that the UK is not a unified legal system – there are in fact three separate legal/court systems in the UK: England and Wales, Scotland and Northern Ireland. Notably, the enforcement system of England and Wales – based in London at the Patents Court (PHC) and the Intellectual Property Enterprise Court (IPEC) – is, by an

---

M.C. Elmer and C.G. Gramaenopoulos (eds), *Global Patent Litigation* (Arlington, VA: Bloomberg BNA, 2014), 546–89; and the European overview given in N. Van Zeebroeck and S. Graham, 'Comparing patent litigation across Europe: a first look', *Stanford Technology Law Review* 17 (2014), 655.

[23] J. Radcliffe and M. Brown, *European Patent Litigation Strategy* (Arlington, VA: Bloomberg BMA, 2014) 1, 2–3, available at www.bna.com/uploadedFiles/Content/Web_Forms/Real_Magnet_Form/European_Patent_Litigation/WIPR0813_whitepaper_eu-patent-lit.pdf.

[24] K. Cremers, M. Ernicke, D. Harhoff, C. Helmers, G. Licht, L. McDonagh, et al. 'Patent litigation in Europe', *ZEW Discussion Paper* No. 13-07 (2013), 1, 1–4.

[25] Patents Act 1977 (UK), available at www.ipo.gov.uk/patentsact1977.pdf.

overwhelming margin, the most important of the three UK jurisdictions with respect to patent litigation, and for that reason it is the only one discussed in detail here.[26]

The litigation procedures of the courts of England and Wales, including the PHC and the IPEC, are guided by the Civil Procedure Rules (CPR).[27] Patent proprietors – including joint owners – have automatic standing to bring infringement claims; meanwhile, exclusive licensees also have standing to bring proceedings, but only regarding alleged infringements which are within the scope of the licence and which take place post-licence agreement.[28]

Of the two courts relevant to the analysis in this chapter, the IPEC – a specialist court within the Chancery Division of the High Court of Justice of England and Wales – generally deals with low-value claims; while the PHC – also a specialist court of the Chancery Division of the High Court (HC) of Justice of England and Wales – hears cases of a higher value and complexity.[29] At both the IPEC and the PHC, each case is tried by a single judge who possesses patent expertise.[30] Where leave is granted, appeals are made to the Court of Appeal (CA) (though appeals from the IPEC can, in some circumstances, be heard at the PHC). The appeal is decided by a three-person panel at the Court of Appeal (generally not entirely composed of IP specialists, although usually containing at least one such specialist). Where leave is given, a decision of the CA can be challenged on a significant point of law at the UK Supreme Court (SC) (formerly the House of Lords). SC patent cases are quite rare with an average of less than one per calendar

---

[26] C. Helmers, Y. Lefouili and L. McDonagh, 'Examining Patent Cases at the Patents Court and Intellectual Property Enterprise Court 2007–2013', *A Report Commissioned by the UK Intellectual Property Office* (March 2015), 1, available at www.gov.uk/government/publications/examining-patent-cases-at-the-patents-court-and-ipec-2007-2013.

[27] Civil Procedure Rules 1998 (CPR) (SI 1998/3132), available at www.legislation.gov.uk/uksi/1998/3132/contents/made.

[28] Ss 60 and 67 Patents Act 1977 (UK).

[29] G. Kamstra, 'United Kingdom', in Global Legal Group (eds), *The International Comparative Legal Guide to: Patents* (4th edn, Global Legal Group Ltd, 2014), 194–200, 194–5, available at www.twobirds.com/~/media/PDFs/News/Articles/2013/An%20update%20on%20Patents%20in%20the%20United%20Kingdom.pdf.

[30] R. Arnold, 'Case management, judicial specialisation and intellectual property litigation', *Civil Justice Quarterly* 29 (2010), 478.

year.[31] Issues of EU law – such as those concerning biotechnology or supplementary protection certificates (SPCs) – may lead to a reference being made by a UK court (typically the HC, CA or SC) to the Court of Justice of the European Union (CJEU) under the Article 267 TFEU procedure.[32]

With respect to the IPEC, from 2010 to 2013 the court was subjected to a substantial reform process.[33] Post-reform, there has been a large increase in patent cases filed and heard at the IPEC, with many large businesses and SMEs taking advantage of the IPEC's procedural rules to achieve a speedier, less costly outcome than that which would occur at the PHC.[34]

Assessing the procedural structure and typical length of proceedings in the UK

Every claim at the PHC or the IPEC begins with the issuance of a claim form. Following the serving of the claim, an acknowledgement of service and, subsequently, the defence will be filed.[35] The

---

[31] C. Helmers and L. McDonagh, 'Patent litigation in the UK: an empirical survey 2000–2008', *Journal of Intellectual Property Law & Practice* 8 (2013), 846, 846–9. A recent example of SC patent case is *Virgin Atlantic Airways Ltd v Zodiac Seats UK Ltd (formerly known as Contour Aerospace Ltd)* [2013] UKSC 46.

[32] Article 267 of the Consolidated version of the Treaty of the Functioning of the European Union (TFEU), OJ C326/61 (2012), available at http://eur-lex.europa.eu/legal-content/EN/TXT/?uri=celex:12012E/TXT.

[33] The IPEC was, until October 2013, known as the Patents County Court (PCC) (even thought its remit included other IP rights). Before the onset of the reforms in October 2010, patents were the least litigated right at the PCC, with most cases involving other IP rights such as copyright or trade marks – see C. Helmers, Y. Lefouili and L. McDonagh, 'Evaluation of the reforms of the Intellectual Property Enterprise Court 2010–2013', *A Report Commissioned by the UK Intellectual Property Office* (July 2015), 1, available at www.gov.uk/government/news/independent-review-finds-ipec-reforms-have-improved-access-to-justice.

[34] C. Helmers, Y. Lefouili and L. McDonagh, 'Examining Patent Cases at the Patents Court and Intellectual Property Enterprise Court 2007–2013', *A Report Commissioned by the UK Intellectual Property Office* (March 2015), 1, www.gov.uk/government/uploads/system/uploads/attachment_data/file/413693/Examing_Patent_Cases_at_the_Patents_Court_and_IP_Enterprise_Court_2007-2___.pdf.

[35] CPR parts 7.2, 7.4 and 7.5.

claimant then typically applies for a case management conference (CMC) where the further progress of the action will be outlined.[36]

At both the PHC and the IPEC, patent infringement and revocation (invalidity) claims may be filed simultaneously at the same court. This means that the PHC and the IPEC have jurisdiction to determine issues concerning both the infringement of and validity of the UK-validated segment of an EP as well as, of course, any UK-granted patent (GB).[37] In addition to the claims for infringement and/or invalidity of the patent, other common claims include filing for a declaration of non-infringement and claiming groundless threats of infringement.[38]

Disclosure and evidence gathering With respect to the gathering of evidence at the PHC level, there is a wide responsibility of disclosure.[39] At the CMC, the PHC judge can order the disclosure of internal documents, the preparation of a detailed product or process description, the inspection of factory premises (and of the processes which occur there), the provision of samples or ingredients, and for experiments to be undertaken (to be repeated in the presence of the other party).[40] By contrast, there are strict limits imposed by the IPEC judge at the CMC regarding the claims that can be made, the availability of disclosure and the use of expert evidence and testimony. In addition, at the IPEC CMC, if the parties wish, the judge can offer an initial opinion as to where he/she thinks the case is heading, something that tends to push parties closer to a settlement position.[41]

---

[36] CPR part 63, Practice Direction 5.3.

[37] S 72 Patents Act 1977 (UK). The validity of a UK national patent (GB) may also be challenged at the UK IPO, e.g. via its patent opinion service.

[38] Ss 70 and 71 Patents Act 1977 (UK).

[39] See CPR Part 63, Practice Direction 6.

[40] J. Radcliffe and M. Brown, *European Patent Litigation Strategy* (Arlington, VA: Bloomberg BMA, 2014), 1, 4–5. See also S. Thambisetty, 'Patent litigation in the United Kingdom: solutions in search of a problem?', *European Intellectual Property Review* 32 (2010), 238, 239–46.

[41] C. Helmers, Y. Lefouili and L. McDonagh, 'Evaluation of the reforms of the Intellectual Property Enterprise Court 2010–2013', *A Report Commissioned by the UK Intellectual Property Office* (July 2015) 1, 7–9, available at www.gov.uk/government/news/independent-review-finds-ipec-reforms-have-improved-access-to-justice.

The trial hearing At the PHC trial, barristers for both parties outline their claims in detail, referring to evidence gathered via disclosure, and making use of examination (and cross-examination) of witnesses/experts, before final arguments are made. PHC trials can vary considerably in length – from around two days to several weeks, depending on case complexity and the amount of witnesses/experts who must be cross-examined.[42] The PHC judgment will usually be handed down between two weeks and three months after the trial has ended. Meanwhile, applications for summary judgment can be made in circumstances where the claimant believes that there is no realistic prospect of a reasonable defence being mounted. Nevertheless, due to the complexities involved in patent claims concerning the issues of validity and infringement, the issuance of summary judgments is rare at the PHC.[43]

Unlike PHC hearings, which can be quite lengthy, the remit of the IPEC as a venue for smaller-scale claims means that its trials typically last for no more than 1–2 days.[44] For this reason, complex patent cases are not suitable to be heard at the IPEC – they belong at the PHC (cases are occasionally transferred between the two courts).[45]

Interim injunctions and post-trial enforcement While the IPEC and the PHC have the power to grant interim injunctions – in order to prevent a defendant from carrying out the (allegedly) infringing act until a full hearing on the facts can be undertaken – in practice,

---

[42] N. Beckett and J. Morton, 'United Kingdom', in N. Beckett and J. Morton (eds), *CMS International Patent Litigation Guide* (CMS, 2013), 95–100, 96.

[43] C. Helmers and L. McDonagh, 'Patent litigation in the UK: an empirical survey 2000–2008', *Journal of Intellectual Property Law & Practice* 8 (2013), 846, 846–9. See also Freshfields Bruckhaus Deringer, *A Guide to Patent Litigation in Europe: England and Wales* (Freshfields, 2011), 1, 10, available at www.lexology.com/library/detail.aspx?g=6bd0f5bc-df2c-4578-8102-02c6d3c9946f.

[44] C. Helmers and L. McDonagh, 'Patent litigation in the UK: an empirical survey 2000–2008', *Journal of Intellectual Property Law & Practice* 8 (2013), 846, 846–9.

[45] C. Helmers, Y. Lefouili and L. McDonagh, 'Examining Patent Cases at the Patents Court and Intellectual Property Enterprise Court 2007–2013', *A Report Commissioned by the UK Intellectual Property Office* (March 2015) 1, 1–4.

interim injunctions are rarely granted.[46] One key reason for this is the existence of the doctrine of 'clearing the way', whereby if a company knows that there is a possibility that their upcoming product may infringe a competitor's patent, such potential infringers are encouraged to file a claim to 'clear the way' by seeking either to revoke the competitor's patent, or to gain a declaration that their product does not infringe their competitor's patent (a declaration of non-infringement).[47] If a competitor does not do this, it is more likely that the PHC will grant a preliminary injunction preventing the sale of the potentially infringing product on the commencement of infringement proceedings.[48] The existence of the 'clear the way' doctrine is one of the reasons for the relatively high proportion of revocation actions filed as initial claims at the IPEC and the PHC when compared to the relevant courts in Germany, France and the Netherlands (something that is highlighted further below in the comparative summary of the four jurisdictions). At the PHC, in the rare circumstance where an interim injunction is granted, a cross-undertaking will typically be made so that the defendant can later get compensation from the claimant if it is held that the preliminary injunction ought not to have been granted after all.[49]

With respect to enforcement post-PHC judgment on the merits – which usually comes several weeks after the trial has ended – a

---

[46] N. Beckett and J. Morton, 'United Kingdom', in N. Beckett and J. Morton (eds), *CMS International Patent Litigation Guide* (CMS, 2013), 95–100, 99, noting that it is possible for a PHC judge to expedite the trial rather than grant an interim injunction.

[47] *SmithKline Beecham & Anor v Apotex Europe Ltd & Ors* [2002] EWHC 2556; [2003] EWCA (Civ) 137; *Cephalon & Ors v Orchid & Anor* [2010] EWHC 2945 (Pat); *Merck Sharp Dohme Corp v Teva Pharma BV* [2012] EWHC 627 (Pat).

[48] C. Helmers and L. McDonagh, 'Patent litigation in the UK: an empirical survey 2000–2008', *Journal of Intellectual Property Law & Practice* 8 (2013), 846, 846–9. See also consideration of interim patent injunctions in *Warner-Lambert Company, LLC v Actavis Group Ptc EHF & Others* [2015] EWHC 72 (Pat).

[49] N. Beckett and J. Morton, 'United Kingdom', in N. Beckett and J. Morton (eds), *CMS International Patent Litigation Guide* (CMS, 2013), 95–100, 99.

separate hearing takes place where the consequences of the judgment are discussed.[50] A permanent injunction is the typical remedy sought by, and granted to, the claimant in an infringement case.[51] Delivery or destruction of infringing items may also be sought.

With regard to damages (or accounts of profits), the court takes various factors – such as lost profits and unfairly gained profits – into account when compensating the successful claimant.[52] At the IPEC, there is a cap of £500,000 on damages; at the PHC, there is no specific damages limit. However, since separate proceedings are typically required to approximate damages awards, these issues are generally settled between the parties once substantive liability is determined on the facts, and/or once a final injunction has been handed down, as this is usually the primary remedy sought in a patent case.[53]

One final thing is worth noting concerning enforcement – it is possible for the PHC to grant a cross-border injunction but only in very limited circumstances. Such an injunction may be granted at the PHC where the validity of the EP is not in question in any of the relevant EPC jurisdictions, such as France, Germany and the Netherlands.[54]

The relationship between EPO opposition decisions and UK enforcement The question of whether EPO opposition proceedings are pending at the time of a PHC or an IPEC hearing will not necessarily affect the UK court's willingness to hear validity challenges. In practice, this means that the PHC and the IPEC can issue rulings, which are then operative and binding within the UK, concerning the validity (or invalidity) of an EP, even while EPO proceedings are ongoing. Nonetheless, as an alternative to issuing a

---

[50] S 62 Patents Act 1977 (UK).

[51] C. Helmers, Y. Lefouili and L. McDonagh, 'Evaluation of the reforms of the Intellectual Property Enterprise Court 2010–2013', *A Report Commissioned by the UK Intellectual Property Office* (July 2015) 1, 7–10.

[52] N. Beckett and J. Morton, 'United Kingdom', in N. Beckett and J. Morton (eds), *CMS International Patent Litigation Guide* (CMS, 2013), 95–100, 99.

[53] Freshfields Bruckhaus Deringer, *A Guide to Patent Litigation in Europe: England and Wales* (Freshfields, 2011), 1, 2, available at www.lexology.com/library/detail.aspx?g=6bd0f5bc-df2c-4578-8102-02c6d3c9946f.

[54] *Actavis Group HF v Eli Lilly & Co* [2012] EWHC 3316 (Pat).

decision on validity, both the PHC and the IPEC have the option to stay the proceedings until the EPO has come to a final decision regarding ongoing opposition proceedings concerning the EP as granted.[55] For the most part, however, the PHC rarely grants such stays – though it is worth noting that a recent decision of the UK Supreme Court has led the lower courts to partially revise this policy in favour of granting a stay in certain circumstances.[56]

It is worth noting that problems sometimes arise in the UK as a result of EPO opposition delays. For example, in *Unilin Beheer v Berry Floor* and *Virgin v Zodiac* the UK courts had to grapple with the aftermath of a situation where in *Unilin Beheer* the precursor court to the IPEC – the Patents County Court (PCC) – and in *Virgin* the PHC – and subsequently, the CA – held EPs to be valid and infringed; yet later – at the end of opposition proceedings – the EPO retrospectively amended the EPs, limiting their claims to the extent that infringement could no longer be said to have taken place.[57] In *Unilin Beheer*, the defendant – the alleged infringer of the now amended patent – argued that the damages should not be payable in light of the ongoing EPO proceedings; however, the UK CA held that under the doctrine of *res judicta* the defendant must pay the damages that arose from the original UK decision (notwithstanding the EPO proceedings).[58] As noted earlier, this kind of inconsistency is highly problematic and can lead to clear cases of injustice. However, some comfort for defendants came in the later UK SC case of *Virgin v Zodiac*, where it was held that the

---

[55] Mewburn Ellis, 'Stays of UK patent litigation proceedings pending the outcome of EPO opposition proceedings' (2014), available at http://mewburn.com/zh-hans/stays-of-uk-patent-litigation-proceedings-pending-the-outcome-of-epo-opposition-proceedings/.

[56] *Virgin Atlantic Airways Ltd v Zodiac Seats UK Ltd (formerly known as Contour Aerospace Ltd)* [2013] UKSC 46; [2013] 3 WLR 299.

[57] *Unilin Beheer BV v Berry Floor NV* [2007] EWCA Civ 364; [2007] FSR 25, comments of Jacob LJ at para. 17; *Virgin Atlantic Airways Ltd v Zodiac Seats UK Ltd* [2013] UKSC 46; [2013] 3 WLR 299.

[58] *Unilin Beheer BV v Berry Floor NV* [2007] EWCA Civ 364; [2007] FSR 25, comments of Jacob LJ at para. 17. See also *Glaxo Group Ltd v Genentech Inc & Anor* [2008] EWCA Civ 23; [2008] Bus LR 888.

defendant could rely on the EPO's amendment of the patent in answer to Virgin's claim for damages.[59]

Length of proceedings Recently published data suggest that cases at the PHC take, on average, slightly less than a year to reach a first-instance decision.[60] However, depending on the nature of the proceedings, the time spent gathering evidence and the number of applications filed, in some cases it can take longer, even up to 18 months, before a first-instance decision is reached.[61] As noted earlier, cases are decided much more quickly at the IPEC, but this venue is only suitable for straightforward, non-complex patent cases.

The award of costs in the UK

Until very recently, the court fees at the IPEC and the PHC were set at a very low level when compared with other European jurisdictions such as Germany. However, in spring 2015 civil court claim fees – including fees for IP cases – were increased substantially by the UK government.[62] For the IPEC and the PHC, there is now a value-based fee system – for claims in the range of £10,000–200,000 a fee of 5% of the value is payable, and for claims above £200,000 a fee of £10,000 is payable.[63]

Nonetheless, even taking into account the new higher fee level, it is the private legal costs of taking a patent case through to a full PHC trial that make the PHC an expensive litigation venue: these

---

[59] *Virgin Atlantic Airways Ltd v Zodiac Seats UK Ltd* [2013] UKSC 46; [2013] 3 WLR 299.

[60] C. Helmers and L. McDonagh, 'Patent litigation in the UK: an empirical survey 2000–2008', *Journal of Intellectual Property Law & Practice* 8 (2013), 846, 846–50.

[61] N. Beckett and J. Morton, 'United Kingdom', in N. Beckett and J. Morton (eds), *CMS International Patent Litigation Guide* (CMS, 2013), 95–100, 96, available at www.cmslegal.com/relatedsites/patentswithoutborders/Documents/CMS-International-Patent-Litigation-Guide-2013.PDF. See also Freshfields Bruckhaus Deringer, *A Guide to Patent Litigation in Europe: England and Wales* (Freshfields, 2011), 1–19, 6, available at www.lexology.com/library/detail.aspx?g=6bd0f5bc-df2c-4578-8102-02c6d3c9946f.

[62] Civil Proceedings and Family Proceedings Fees (Amendment) Order 2015 (SI 2015/576).

[63] The current list of fees is available at www.gov.uk/guidance/take-a-case-to-the-intellectual-property-enterprise-court.

costs can often amount to £1–1.5 million for each side.[64] Moreover, in complex cases costs at the PHC can reach £2–3 million per side, and very occasionally even higher figures are spent by one side or the other.[65]

The main reasons for the existence of high private legal costs at the PHC are as follows: (i) complying with the PHC's broad disclosure requirement is often expensive for litigants; (ii) the carrying out of experiments and inspections often proves costly; (iii) for PHC cases, it is virtually always necessary to hire both solicitors and barristers in assembling a legal team, which adds to the expense; and (iv) the trial hearings tend to be lengthy, largely because they include the cross-examination of expert witnesses by barristers, which can prove costly.

With respect to the award of costs post-trial, the system of costs allocation in the UK is known as 'loser pays', i.e. 'fee shifting'. This system differs substantially from the system in the USA, where parties in patent cases pay their own costs unless there are exceptional circumstances.[66] In practice, what 'loser pays' means is that the party who loses a PHC case must pay not only its own costs, but also the costs of the other side.

The reality at the PHC is a little more complicated: typically the 'losing party' will not have to pay the entire costs of the other side on a blanket basis – instead, the allocation of costs is determined by the judge on an issue-by-issue approach. In other words, the number of grounds and issues claimed and argued at trial are considered with respect to how much of the court's time each issue took to resolve, and in which party's favour each issue was decided. The judge then allocates the costs to each side on a proportionate

---

[64] L. McDonagh and C. Helmers, 'Patent litigation in England and Wales and the issue-based approach to costs', *Civil Justice Quarterly* 32 (2013) 369, 384.

[65] L. McDonagh and C. Helmers, 'Patent litigation in England and Wales and the issue-based approach to costs', *Civil Justice Quarterly* 32 (2013) 369, 384.

[66] C. Helmers, B. Love and L. McDonagh, 'Is there a patent troll problem in the UK?', *Fordham Intellectual Property, Media and Entertainment Law Journal* 24 (2014), 509, 509–11.

basis (also taking into account the overall reasonableness of each party's overall costs).[67]

Examining empirical research on patent litigation in the UK

As noted by the UK Strategic Advisory Board for Intellectual Property (SABIP) in 2009, the available empirical evidence on patent litigation in the UK was, up until recently, fairly limited.[68] Since 2009, however, the amount and quality of patent litigation data has increased considerably, largely due to work done by legal researchers and academics.

In 2010, Moss et al. examined the outcomes of 47 validity and infringement cases heard between January 2008 and August 2009 by the Patents County Court (PCC) (the precursor to the IPEC), the PHC, the Court of Appeal (CA) and the House of Lords (now the UK Supreme Court). The Moss et al. data show that the patentee won – in the sense that the patent was held to be valid and/or infringed – in only 18 out of these 47 cases (a 38% success rate).[69]

In 2013, the most comprehensive quantitative survey yet undertaken of UK patent litigation was published.[70] The study – undertaken by Christian Helmers and the author – provides quantitative data analysis of all patent cases filed at the PHC 2000–2008 for which online records are available – a total of 256 cases, of which 125 resulted in a judgment. Data on appeals from cases filed during that period heard at the CA and the House of Lords/Supreme Court were also analysed.[71] About 50% of these 256 patent cases were filed at the PHC as infringement claims, while around 37% of filed

---

67 *Research in Motion UK Ltd v Visto Corp* [2008] EWHC 819 (Pat); (2008) 31(5) I.P.D. 31033.

68 K. Weatherall, E. Webster and L. Bently, *IP Enforcement in the UK and Beyond: A Literature Review – SABIP Report* Number EC001, SABIP (2009), 1, 5.

69 G. Moss, M. Jones and R. Lundie-Smith, 'Just how "anti-patent" are the UK courts?', *Journal of Intellectual Property Law & Practice* 5 (2010), 148, 148–50.

70 C. Helmers and L. McDonagh, 'Patent litigation in the UK: an empirical survey 2000–2008', *Journal of Intellectual Property Law & Practice* 8 (2013), 846.

71 C. Helmers and L. McDonagh, 'Patent litigation in the UK: an empirical survey 2000–2008', *Journal of Intellectual Property Law & Practice* 8 (2013), 846.

cases sought the revocation of a patent.[72] Importantly, on the subject of the 125 judgments out of the 256 cases filed in 2000–2008 for which some online records were available, the data show that revocation was the most likely judicial outcome, regardless of the initial claim. In other words, even if the initial claim was filed by the patentee for infringement, in most cases the patent was nonetheless invalidated by the PHC, showing how seriously the question of patent validity is taken at the venue.[73] Meanwhile, 33% of cases that were filed initially as infringement claims resulted in a settlement.[74]

During this period, the majority of litigant companies were in the chemical and pharmaceutical industries; and, consequently, the majority of litigated patents in 2000–2008 were chemical and/or pharmaceutical inventions. This demonstrates the UK's reputation as a centre of chemical, pharmaceutical and legal expertise.

In a 2014 companion paper, Helmers et al. examined litigation involving so-called 'patent trolls', or non-practicing entities (NPEs), at the PHC.[75] Helmers et al. found that during 2000–2010 NPE litigation was relatively uncommon in the UK when compared to other jurisdictions such as the USA – in fact, only 11% of patent cases filed during 2000–2010 involved a NPE, and a substantial number of these cases occurred between the same parties. Furthermore, in most of these PHC cases, the NPEs did not initiate the case by issuing an infringement claim; rather, it was more often the

---

[72] In 61% of the infringement actions, the defendants filed a counterclaim for revocation and in around 41% of revocation actions, the defendants filed a counterclaim for infringement. Aside from the infringement and revocation claims, other types of cases included ownership and licensing disputes – C. Helmers and L. McDonagh, 'Patent litigation in the UK: an empirical survey 2000–2008', *Journal of Intellectual Property Law & Practice* 8 (2013), 846, 854–61.

[73] C. Helmers and L. McDonagh, 'Patent litigation in the UK: an empirical survey 2000–2008', *Journal of Intellectual Property Law & Practice* 8 (2013), 846, 854–61.

[74] K. Cremers, M. Ernicke, D. Harhoff, C. Helmers, G. Licht, L. McDonagh, et al. 'Patent litigation in Europe', *ZEW Discussion Paper* No. 13-07 (2013), 47.

[75] C. Helmers, B. Love and L. McDonagh, 'Is there a patent troll problem in the UK?', *Fordham Intellectual Property, Media and Entertainment Law Journal* 24 (2014), 509, 509–11.

case that manufacturers sought to 'clear the way' of the NPE-held patent by filing a revocation case at the PHC.

The lack of UK NPE litigation makes sense when one considers that the 2013 Helmers and McDonagh article shows that revocation of the patent was by far the most likely outcome of a judgment for cases filed in 2000–2008. In this vein, it seems logical that NPEs would seek to avoid litigation at the PHC; while, on the other hand, companies that are sued by NPEs in other jurisdictions may find it advantageous to challenge the validity of the NPE patent at the PHC,[76] a point recently cited in the House of Commons.[77]

A more recent study, by Helmers, Lefouili and McDonagh, found that a total of 445 patent cases were filed at the PHC during 2007–2013, whereas a total of 96 patent cases were filed at the IPEC during the same 7-year period.[78] This greater total reflects the fact that the number of patent cases in the UK has increased substantially over time, and particularly following the IPEC reforms, which encouraged more patent claims at the venue. It also reflects the fact that the authors of the later study had direct access to the paper court files and, thus, had access to the complete range of cases for the examined period. For 2007–2013, infringement was the most common initial claim at both the PHC and the IPEC, though revocation was a frequent claim at the PHC and a frequent counterclaim at both courts. With respect to litigant-level data, the 2007–2013 data show that more SMEs (106) were involved in PHC litigation than were involved in IPEC litigation (41) over the same period, a fact which shows that despite the increasing popularity of

---

[76] C. Helmers and L. McDonagh, 'Patent litigation in the UK: an empirical survey 2000–2008', *Journal of Intellectual Property Law & Practice* 8 (2013), 846, at Table 12.

[77] Reference was made in this debate to C. Helmers and L. McDonagh, 'Trolls at the High Court?', *LSE Law, Society and Economy Working Paper* No. 13 (2012), available at http://papers.ssrn.com/sol3/papers.cfm?abstract_id=2154958. This discussion was reported in the UK Parliamentary record (Hansard) on 20 March 2014, available at www.publications.parliament.uk/pa/cm201314/cmhansrd/cm140320/text/140320w0002.htm#14032098000031.

[78] C. Helmers, Y. Lefouili and L. McDonagh, 'Examining Patent Cases at the Patents Court and Intellectual Property Enterprise Court 2007–2013', *A Report Commissioned by the UK Intellectual Property Office* (March 2015), 1, available at www.gov.uk/government/publications/examining-patent-cases-at-the-patents-court-and-ipec-2007-2013.

the IPEC, a large proportion of litigant SMEs are familiar with the PHC, something which may enter into their UPC preparations. A very large number of the PHC patent cases – 372 – concerned an EP, while at the IPEC 47 out of 96 patent cases centred on an EP. In other words, EPs tend to be the subject of PHC litigation much more frequently than GBs, but there is a more even split at the IPEC.

One final thing is worth noting – recent data gathered by Helmers, Lefouili and McDonagh show that in recent years – cases filed in 2007–2013 – the PHC has begun to invalidate a slightly lower proportion of patents than for cases filed during 2000–2008.[79] If this trend continues, we may see the UK's longstanding reputation as an 'anti-patent' jurisdiction change to one that is seen as being more patent-friendly.[80]

Germany

Assessing the applicable law and competent courts in Germany

With respect to the procedural aspects of litigation in Germany, patent issues are dealt with in the German Patent Code[81] as well as in the Law on International Patent Treaties.[82] Meanwhile, matters of legal practice and ligation are regulated in accordance with the German Code for Civil Procedures (*Zivilprozessordnung* (ZPO)),[83]

---

[79] Statistics on file with author – they were gathered during the process of preparing C. Helmers, Y. Lefouili and L. McDonagh, 'Evaluation of the reforms of the Intellectual Property Enterprise Court 2010–2013', *A Report Commissioned by the UK Intellectual Property Office* (July 2015), 1.

[80] G. Moss, M. Jones and R. Lundie-Smith, 'Just how "anti-patent" are the UK courts?', *Journal of Intellectual Property Law & Practice* 5 (2010), 148, 148–50.

[81] *Patentgesetz* (PatG) (German Patent Law) (as amended by the Law of 31 July 2009); English translation available at www.wipo.int/wipolex/en/details.jsp?id=6128; see also T. Kühnen, *Patent Litigation Proceedings in Germany: A Handbook for Practitioners* (6th edn, Cologne: Heymanns, 2013) and P. Mes, *Kommentar: Patentgesetz, Gebrauchsmustergesetz* (4th edn, Munich: Beck, 2015).

[82] *Gesetz über internationale Patentübereinkommen* (IntPatÜG) (German Civil Code); English translation available at www.gesetze-im-internet.de/englisch_bgb/index.html.

[83] *Zivilprozessordnung* (ZPO); English translation available at www.gesetze-im-internet.de/englisch_zpo/index.html.

the Remuneration Code for Lawyers' Costs (*Rechtsanwalts-vergütungsgesetz* (RVG))[84] and the German Code for Court Costs (*Gerichtskostengesetz*).[85] Patent proprietors – including joint owners – have standing to initiate infringement proceedings, as do exclusive licensees, and even non-exclusive licensees can have standing where this is granted to them by the licensor.[86]

As with the UK, in addition to their jurisdiction to rule on German national patents (DEs), in line with Article 2 and 64 of the EPC, national courts in Germany also have the right to consider and issue decisions in cases concerning the infringement and/or validity of a German element of an EP.[87] However, in a crucial distinction with the UK, German courts do not deal with infringement and validity via unified proceedings – for constitutional reasons, the German legal system provides for bifurcation of infringement and validity decisions, with separate courts deciding these issues, an important feature of the German system that is explored further below.[88] It is also worth noting that, in addition to patent protection, Germany provides a system of protection of 'utility models' (*Gebrauchsmuster*) in line with the German Utility Model Code – a type of protection that is not available in the UK or the Netherlands.[89]

With respect to infringement, there are a total of 12 regional courts in Germany that feature chambers (*Kammern*) which are

---

[84] *Rechtsanwalts-vergütungsgesetz* (RVG); English translation available at www.gesetze-im-internet.de/englisch_rvg/englisch_rvg.html.

[85] *Gerichtskostengesetz* (GKG); German version available at www.gesetze-im-internet.de/bundesrecht/gkg_2004/gesamt.pdf and English translation partly available at www.gesetze-im-internet.de/Teilliste_translations.html.

[86] G. Schoenen, M. Deck and M. Eck, 'Germany', in N. Beckett and J. Morton (eds), *CMS International Patent Litigation Guide* (CMS, 2013), 45–50, 45, available at www.cmslegal.com/relatedsites/patentswithoutborders/Documents/CMS-International-Patent-Litigation-Guide-2013.PDF.

[87] H. Marshall, 'The enforcement of patent rights in Germany', *International Review of Intellectual Property and Competition Law (IIC)* 31 (2000), 646, 646–9.

[88] H. Marshall, 'The enforcement of patent rights in Germany', *International Review of Intellectual Property and Competition Law (IIC)* 31 (2000), 646, 665. See also T. Kühnen, *Patent Litigation Proceedings in Germany: A Handbook for Practitioners* (6th edn, Cologne: Heymanns, 2013).

[89] *Gebrauchsmustergesetz* (GebrMG); English machine translation at www.wipo.int/wipolex/en/details.jsp?id=10002.

competent to hear patent and utility model infringement cases.[90] It is also possible to file for a declaration of non-infringement, as long as patent infringement proceedings have not already been initiated.[91] The relevant courts are known as *Landgerichte* (LG). They are located in the cities of Berlin, Braunschweig, Düsseldorf, Erfurt, Frankfurt, Hamburg, Leipzig, Magdeburg, Mannheim, Munich, Nuremberg-Fürth and Saarbrücken. Despite the existence of 12 possible venues, the vast majority of German patent litigation actually takes place at one of only three of these courts – Düsseldorf, Mannheim and Munich – where a panel of three judges sits with the competence to hear patent cases.[92] Questions of validity are decided separately at the *Bundespatentgericht* (BPatG).[93] German patent judges are known for their technical expertise.[94]

An appeal against an LG infringement decision may be heard by one of the higher German regional courts – *Oberlandesgericht* (OLG).[95] Following this, a subsequent appeal can be brought before the German Federal Court of Justice – *Bundesgerichtshof* (BGH). Unlike appeals to one of the OLG – at which leave to appeal is not required – leave to appeal is required for a subsequent appeal to the

---

[90] H. Marshall, 'The enforcement of patent rights in Germany', *International Review of Intellectual Property and Competition Law (IIC)* 31 (2000), 646, 665.

[91] G. Schoenen, M. Deck and M. Eck, 'Germany', in N. Beckett and J. Morton (eds), *CMS International Patent Litigation Guide* (CMS, 2013), 45–50, 46, available at www.cmslegal.com/relatedsites/patentswithoutborders/Documents/CMS-International-Patent-Litigation-Guide-2013.PDF.

[92] K. Cremers, M. Ernicke, D. Harhoff, C. Helmers, G. Licht, L. McDonagh, et al. 'Patent litigation in Europe', *ZEW Discussion Paper* No. 13-07 (2013), 12, referring to §§ 253 ZPO seq.

[93] G. Schoenen, M. Deck and M. Eck, 'Germany', in N. Beckett and J. Morton (eds), *CMS International Patent Litigation Guide* (CMS, 2013), 45–50, 46. For DE national patents, validity opposition issues may also be decided by the *Deutsches Patent-und Markenamt* (DPMA).

[94] Taylor Wessing, *Global Intellectual Property Index* (2013), 1, 26, available at http://united-kingdom.taylorwessing.com/ipindex/.

[95] K. Cremers, M. Ernicke, D. Harhoff, C. Helmers, G. Licht, L. McDonagh, et al. 'Patent litigation in Europe', *ZEW Discussion Paper* No. 13-07 (2013), 1, 12, referring to §§ 511 ZPO seq.

BGH. Such leave can be granted by either the OLG or the BGH.[96] Regarding validity, a BPatG decision can be appealed to the BGH.[97]

Assessing the procedural structure and typical length of proceedings in Germany

Each infringement action in Germany begins with the filing, at one of the courts (LG), of a complaint, setting out the details of the alleged patent infringement, which is then served on the defendant. As noted earlier, there are 12 competent courts (LG), with the vast majority of claims being initiated at Düsseldorf, Mannheim and Munich. Generally, a claimant may choose which court to file at.

Due to bifurcation, the courts (LG) with the jurisdiction to hear patent infringement cases – most prominently, Düsseldorf, Mannheim and Munich – do not have the jurisdiction to rule that a patent is either valid or invalid.[98] Of course, if validity is not questioned by the potential infringer then there is no issue of bifurcation, as the case will be determined by the relevant LG purely in relation to the infringement question.

Nevertheless, if the question of validity of the patent is raised as a counterclaim (or as part of a defence filing to an infringement claim), the validity issue must be decided at a different venue to the LG, i.e. at the *Deutsches Patent und Markenamt* (DPMA) and/or the *Bundespatentgericht* (BPatG).[99] In such cases, a stay on the patent infringement proceedings may be granted by the relevant LG pending the outcome of the invalidity proceedings at the DPMA

---

[96] K. Cremers, M. Ernicke, D. Harhoff, C. Helmers, G. Licht, L. McDonagh, et al. 'Patent litigation in Europe', *ZEW Discussion Paper* No. 13-07 (2013), 1, 13, referring to §§ 542 ZPO seq.

[97] K. Cremers, M. Ernicke, D. Harhoff, C. Helmers, G. Licht, L. McDonagh, et al. 'Patent litigation in Europe', *ZEW Discussion Paper* No. 13-07 (2013), 1, 12.

[98] H. Marshall, 'The enforcement of patent rights in Germany', *International Review of Intellectual Property and Competition Law (IIC)* 31 (2000), 646, 665.

[99] K. Cremers, M. Ernicke, D. Harhoff, C. Helmers, G. Licht, L. McDonagh, et al. 'Patent litigation in Europe', *ZEW Discussion Paper* No. 13-07 (2013), 1, 13, referring to § 148 ZPO.

and/or the BPatG – but the LG does not have to grant the stay, and if the LG considers there is no serious validity question, it is unlikely a stay will be granted.[100] This issue of bifurcation is discussed in detail later on in this chapter.

Disclosure and evidence gathering Until relatively recently, it was typically the case in Germany that only limited disclosure and inspections were allowed by courts in patent proceedings.[101] However, as a result of the coming into force of the EU Enforcement Directive in 2008,[102] it is now possible for German courts to consider wide-ranging applications for disclosure and inspection;[103] moreover, such an application can be initiated prior to – or in parallel with – the first-instance proceedings via a preliminary application, without the need to give prior notice to the defendant.[104]

The trial hearing Concerning first-instance patent infringement proceedings, the caseload dominance of Düsseldorf, Mannheim and Munich means that it is worth considering these three courts in

---

[100] Bardehle Pagenberg, *Patent Infringement Proceedings* (2013), 1, 9, available at www.bardehle.com/fileadmin/contentdocuments/broschures/Patent_Infringement_Proceedings.pdf.

[101] K. Cremers, M. Ernicke, D. Harhoff, C. Helmers, G. Licht, L. McDonagh, et al. 'Patent litigation in Europe', *ZEW Discussion Paper* No. 13-07 (2013), 1, 14, referring to the fact that although § 142 ZPO and § 809 BGB allowed for inspections and the exchange of written evidence, the German courts were 'hesitant' to apply these rules.

[102] Directive 2004/48/EC of the European Parliament and of the Council of 29 April 2004 on the enforcement of intellectual property rights, OJ L 195 (2004), available at http://ec.europa.eu/internal_market/iprenforcement/directive/index_en.htm.

See also the German implementing law: Gesetz zur Verbesserung der Durchsetzung der Rechte des Geistigen Eigentums, BGB part I dated 11 July 2008, 1119–211.

[103] J. Radcliffe and M. Brown, *European Patent Litigation Strategy* (Arlington, VA: Bloomberg BMA, 2014), 1–48, 3–4.

[104] K. Cremers, M. Ernicke, D. Harhoff, C. Helmers, G. Licht, L. McDonagh, et al. 'Patent litigation in Europe', *ZEW Discussion Paper* No. 13-07 (2013), 1, 14, referring to § 140 c PatG and 24 c GebrMG.

detail.[105] Interestingly, each one of these three courts provides a different judicial model with respect to the timing of – and number of – oral hearings, as well as in terms of how substantive and procedural legal claims are dealt with.

Nonetheless, regardless of whether the claim is filed in Düsseldorf, Mannheim or Munich, the legal action proceeds on a mostly written basis – rather than on an oral one like in the UK – with legal matters requiring 'substantiation' (*Substantiierungspflichten*). Prior to the oral hearing, arguments are submitted to the court and exchanged between the parties, including the initial plea by the claimant, the defendant's filing of a defence, the counter-plea by the claimant, and the defendant's rejoinder. With respect to both written and oral procedures, German patent lawyers are often assisted by German patent attorneys.[106] Unlike in the UK, in Germany the hearing of expert opinions is rare and only acceptable in exceptional circumstances.[107] The emphasis on written submissions means that LG trial hearings typically last only 1–4 hours – a real and substantial difference when compared to the lengthy oral hearings found at the PHC in the UK.[108]

German judges are known for taking 'a very active role in structuring the hearing based on the written arguments filed by the parties'.[109] The presiding judge usually begins the trial by outlining the court's preliminary opinion on the infringement question based

---

[105] J. Herr and M. Grunwald, 'Speedy patent infringement proceedings in Germany: pros and cons of the go-to courts', *Journal of Intellectual Property Law & Practice* 7 (2012), 44, 44–7.

[106] G. Schoenen, M. Deck and M. Eck, 'Germany', in N. Beckett and J. Morton (eds), *CMS International Patent Litigation Guide* (CMS, 2013), 45–50, 46, available at www.cmslegal.com/relatedsites/patentswithoutborders/Documents/CMS-International-Patent-Litigation-Guide-2013.PDF.

[107] G. Schoenen, M. Deck and M. Eck, 'Germany', in N. Beckett and J. Morton (eds), *CMS International Patent Litigation Guide* (CMS, 2013), 45–50, 45.

[108] K. Cremers, M. Ernicke, D. Harhoff, C. Helmers, G. Licht, L. McDonagh, et al. 'Patent litigation in Europe', *ZEW Discussion Paper* No. 13-07 (2013), 1, 14, referring to § 138 ZPO. See also generally T. Kühnen, *Patent Litigation Proceedings in Germany: A Handbook for Practitioners* (6th edn, Cologne: Heymanns, 2013).

[109] G. Schoenen, M. Deck and M. Eck, 'Germany', in N. Beckett and J. Morton (eds), *CMS International Patent Litigation Guide* (CMS, 2013), 45–50, 46.

on the written submissions exchanged between the parties and received by the court prior to the hearing.[110] Following this, the rest of the trial proceeds with the presiding judge directing specific questions to each party's lawyers regarding the key issues.

Interim injunctions and post-trial enforcement In Germany, applications for a preliminary injunction during an infringement case are possible,[111] but in practice the granting of such injunctions is relatively rare due to the overall speed of the regular patent infringement proceedings.[112] Following a first-instance infringement decision, the patentee whose patent has been infringed must start enforcement proceedings in order to, for example, obtain an injunction with respect to the claims which succeeded in court.

Due to the system of bifurcation, a patent invalidity claim is typically filed at the BPatG by a litigant who is already involved (as a defendant) in separate but parallel patent infringement litigation at one of the LG. Notably, the process for obtaining a judgment on the validity question from the BPatG often takes much longer than it does to obtain an infringement judgment from one of the LG.[113] Crucially, for this reason, unless the LG agrees to grant a stay on the infringement proceedings, a decision on infringement may be granted by the LG before the BPatG issues a judgment concerning validity. This leads us to an oft-made critical point about the German system: if a later BPatG judgment invalidates a patent which the prior LG already held was infringed, the bifurcated proceedings result in the dreaded 'invalid but infringed' scenario.[114]

---

[110] K. Cremers, M. Ernicke, D. Harhoff, C. Helmers, G. Licht, L. McDonagh, et al. 'Patent litigation in Europe', *ZEW Discussion Paper* No. 13-07 (2013), 1, 14.

[111] Bardehle Pagenberg, *Patent Infringement Proceedings* (2013), 9, available at www.bardehle.com/fileadmin/contentdocuments/broschures/Patent_Infringement_Proceedings.pdf.

[112] K. Cremers, M. Ernicke, D. Harhoff, C. Helmers, G. Licht, L. McDonagh, et al. 'Patent litigation in Europe', *ZEW Discussion Paper* No. 13-07 (2013), 1, 15

[113] K. Cremers, M. Ernicke, D. Harhoff, C. Helmers, G. Licht, L. McDonagh, et al. 'Patent litigation in Europe', *ZEW Discussion Paper* No. 13-07 (2013), at Table 18.

[114] K. Cremers, F. Gaessler, D. Harhoff and C. Helmers, 'Invalid but infringed? An analysis of Germany's bifurcated patent litigation system', *Max*

On this point, it is worth stressing two things: first, the LG typically only grants a stay pending an invalidity decision if – on preliminary assessment – the LG believes that the challenge to the patent's validity at the BPatG is 'predominantly likely' to succeed;[115] second, although this 'invalid but infringed' scenario can lead to injustice, in practice the patentee typically has to offer a security/indemnity in circumstances where an infringement decision is granted while the invalidity question is still pending, something which lessens the impact of – though does not entirely eliminate – the 'invalid but infringed' problem.[116]

Thus, post-trial, the initiation of enforcement usually occurs via the submission of a formal letter and a security – typically in the form of a bank guarantee – to the court. Cremers et al. state:

> In most cases the winner chooses to enforce only the claim for rendering of accounts and waits with the enforcement of the injunction until the validity has been confirmed or the judgement of the second instance has been handed down. If the winning party enforces a first instance judgment and the patent is later revoked, the patentee is liable for the damages it has caused to the defendant.[117]

Planck Institute for Innovation & Competition Research Paper No. 14-14 (2014), 1, available at http://papers.ssrn.com/sol3/papers.cfm?abstract_id=2504507.

[115] G. Schoenen, M. Deck and M. Eck, 'Germany', in N. Beckett and J. Morton (eds), *CMS International Patent Litigation Guide* (CMS, 2013), 45–50, 46. Generally, a less stringent standard is used by the OLG in the case of an appeal – it is sufficient for the OLG to consider that the invalidity challenge is likely to succeed for a stay to be granted. For further discussion of the German litigation appeals process, see T. Kühnen, *Patent Litigation Proceedings in Germany: A Handbook for Practitioners* (6th edn, Cologne: Heymanns, 2013).

[116] This indemnity makes it possible for the defendant to recover damages if a later/second-instance decision – by e.g. the BPatG – holds that the patent is invalid and/or not infringed. No security is required with respect to the second-instance decision. K. Cremers, M. Ernicke, D. Harhoff, C. Helmers, G. Licht, L. McDonagh, et al. 'Patent litigation in Europe', *ZEW Discussion Paper* No. 13-07 (2013), 1, 14, referring to §§ 704, 708, 709 and 717 (2) ZPO.

[117] K. Cremers, M. Ernicke, D. Harhoff, C. Helmers, G. Licht, L. McDonagh, et al. 'Patent litigation in Europe', *ZEW Discussion Paper* No. 13-07 (2013), 1, 14, referring to § 717 (2) ZPO.

The amount of damages to be paid in award to the patentee by an infringer is considered in a separate action subsequent to the infringement decision.[118]

The relationship between EPO opposition and German enforcement

As with the UK, in Germany in addition to validity actions undertaken at the national level an EP's validity may be challenged via the patent opposition proceedings at the EPO; and where the same patent is the subject of both opposition proceedings and German patent infringement proceedings, the LG has the power to stay the German patent infringement proceedings pending the outcome of the EPO opposition.[119]

Nonetheless, it is important to note that in Germany an invalidity action at the BPatG – against either a DE or an EP – can only be filed once the deadlines for filing an opposition against the DE or EP have lapsed, and all relevant pending oppositions and/or appeals against the granting of the patent have been terminated.[120] In other words, if EPO opposition proceedings are still pending, no German patent validity challenge may be brought to the BPatG.[121] Following the BPatG decision on validity, an appeal can be brought before the BGH.[122]

---

[118] G. Schoenen, M. Deck and M. Eck, 'Germany', in N. Beckett and J. Morton (eds), *CMS International Patent Litigation Guide* (CMS, 2013), 45–50, 48.

[119] Regarding national patents, the validity of a German national patent (DE) or utility model may be challenged by filing an opposition at the DPMA – K. Cremers, M. Ernicke, D. Harhoff, C. Helmers, G. Licht, L. McDonagh, et al. 'Patent litigation in Europe', *ZEW Discussion Paper* No. 13-07 (2013), 1, 12, referring to §§ 21 and 59 PatG seq, as well as § 25 GebrMG seq.

[120] K. Cremers, M. Ernicke, D. Harhoff, C. Helmers, G. Licht, L. McDonagh, et al. 'Patent litigation in Europe', *ZEW Discussion Paper* No. 13-07 (2013), 1, 12, referring to §§ 65, 81 PatG seq. and Article II § 2 IntPatÜG.

[121] G. Schoenen, M. Deck and M. Eck, 'Germany', in N. Beckett and J. Morton (eds), *CMS International Patent Litigation Guide* (CMS, 2013), 45–50, available at www.cmslegal.com/relatedsites/patentswithoutborders/Documents/CMS-International-Patent-Litigation-Guide-2013.PDF.

[122] K. Cremers, M. Ernicke, D. Harhoff, C. Helmers, G. Licht, L. McDonagh, et al. 'Patent litigation in Europe', *ZEW Discussion Paper* No. 13-07 (2013), 1, 12.

Length of proceedings Regarding length of infringement proceedings, generally in Germany a first-instance action at one of the LG proceeds quite quickly, with a first hearing scheduled within 6–12 months.[123] For instance, in Düsseldorf – the most popular court venue in Europe for patent infringement claims – the procedures are highly streamlined, so that 'proceedings from first filing to the oral hearing take between eight to twelve months', with oral hearings typically lasting 1–2 hours in a single day.[124] Moreover, a decision on patent infringement is usually handed down 1–3 months after the hearing. However, the average duration of a validity action in Germany, from filing to judgment at the BPatG, is 18 months.[125]

The award of costs in Germany

As with the UK – and unlike the USA – the German courts system utilizes a 'loser pays' system of fee shifting. Moreover, in Germany a value-based fee system is in operation – something which, as noted above, until 2015 marked a crucial distinction between the German and UK systems. Furthermore, the court fees in Germany are typically higher, on average, than the fees in other jurisdictions such as the UK, France and the Netherlands (though the UK fees have recently been increased in line with the 2015 switch to a value-based fee system).[126] Taking into account the value of the

---

123 G. Schoenen, M. Deck and M. Eck, 'Germany', in N. Beckett and J. Morton (eds), *CMS International Patent Litigation Guide* (CMS, 2013), 45–50, 46.

124 G. Schoenen, M. Deck and M. Eck, 'Germany', in N. Beckett and J. Morton (eds), *CMS International Patent Litigation Guide* (CMS, 2013), 45–50, 46.

125 K. Cremers, M. Ernicke, D. Harhoff, C. Helmers, G. Licht, L. McDonagh, et al. 'Patent litigation in Europe', *ZEW Discussion Paper* No. 13-07 (2013), at Table 18.

126 C. Helmers, Y. Lefouili and L. McDonagh, 'Evaluation of the reforms of the Intellectual Property Enterprise Court 2010–2013', *A Report Commissioned by the UK Intellectual Property Office* (July 2015), 1. In Dusseldorf, the use of per patent court fees differentiates this LG from Mannheim and Munich, as well as from other European legal systems (in the UK, for instance, the number of patents cited in a case filing has no impact on the overall court fee – it is the value of the overall claim that affects the level of fee).

dispute, German court fees often exceed €10,000, and can even sometimes fall into a range of €100,000–200,000 in high-value cases.[127]

The overall costs of taking a first-instance patent infringement case in Germany have been estimated by Schoenen et al. as ranging from '€40,000 in a simple case, to €100,000 in a more complex case'; while in a very technical and/or highly valuable case the costs may be 'significantly more' than this; with the costs of appeals also potentially falling within this range, depending on case complexity.[128] This chimes with the Cremers study which states that the private legal costs of patent litigation in Germany often range 'between €40,000 and €100,000 per party'.[129]

This is significantly less than the private fees in the UK, where each side's costs can easily reach £1 million. The reasons for this include lack of a wide, pre-trial disclosure requirement in Germany, coupled with the fact that German oral hearings are, by comparison with the UK, very short, with less expert testimony and cross-examination.

Overall, the value-based fee system used in Germany means that both the court fees and the recoverable private legal fees are calculated based on a formula centring on the dispute's estimated value, and following the judgment the value of the case is used as the basis for the apportioning of costs between the winner and the loser.[130] Effectively, therefore, the presence of the value-based system places limits on recoverable costs, meaning that the winning party is unlikely to get back all of its legal costs. For this reason, it can be said that in Germany the legal costs 'often are not fully shifted to the loser'; instead, the winner ends up with a portion

---

[127] Bardehle Pagenberg, *Patent Infringement Proceedings* (2013), 12, available at www.bardehle.com/fileadmin/contentdocuments/broschures/Patent_Infringement_Proceedings.pdf.

[128] G. Schoenen, M. Deck and M. Eck, 'Germany', in N. Beckett and J. Morton (eds), *CMS International Patent Litigation Guide* (CMS, 2013), 45–50, 47.

[129] K. Cremers, M. Ernicke, D. Harhoff, C. Helmers, G. Licht, L. McDonagh, et al. 'Patent litigation in Europe', ZEW Discussion Paper No. 13-07 (2013), 1, 16.

[130] Bardehle Pagenberg, *Patent Infringement Proceedings* (2013), 12, available at www.bardehle.com/fileadmin/contentdocuments/broschures/Patent_Infringement_Proceedings.pdf.

determined by a calculation based on the value of the case and the associated costs.[131]

Exploring empirical research on patent litigation in Germany

The exact overall amount of patent cases filed at the LG and OLG each year is difficult to ascertain as these statistics officially go unpublished. By contrast, summary statistics for the BPatG and the BGH are made available on an annual basis.[132] This means that it is less easy to collect data on outcomes of patent infringement cases at LG than it is for patent validity cases at the BPatG. As a result of this, to a great extent what is known about German patent infringement cases comes from data-gathering projects carried out by patent experts and academics.[133]

In 2007, Cremers published data gathered from court archives at the IP chambers in Düsseldorf and Mannheim for cases filed in 1993–1995.[134] Cremers' data show that a total of 715 patent cases were filed, referring to a total of 910 patents and/or utility models; and by comparing the patents litigated in 1993–1995 to a control

[131] K. Cremers, M. Ernicke, D. Harhoff, C. Helmers, G. Licht, L. McDonagh, et al. 'Patent litigation in Europe', *ZEW Discussion Paper* No. 13-07 (2013), 1, 16.

[132] See BGH statistics, available at www.bundesgerichtshof.de/DE/BGH/Statistik/statistik_node.html; see also BPatG statistics published in the journal *Blatt für Patent-, Muster- und Zeichenwesen* – http://dpma.de/service/veroeffentlichungen/blattfuerpmz/index.html.

[133] K. Cremers, M. Ernicke, D. Harhoff, C. Helmers, G. Licht, L. McDonagh, et al. 'Patent litigation in Europe', *ZEW Discussion Paper* No. 13-07 (2013), 1, 6, noting that during the 1980s Stauder collected data on German patent and utility model cases filed in 1971–1973, examining litigation patterns, case outcomes and case duration, referring to D. Stauder, 'Die tatsächliche Bedeutung von Verletzungen- und Nichtigkeitsverfahren in der Bundesrepublik Deutschland, Frankreich, Großbritannien und Italien: Ergebnisse einer statistisch-empirischen Untersuchung', *GRUR: Gewerblicher Rechtsschutz und Urheberrecht international (GRUR Int.)* (1983), 233, 233–42 and D. Stauder, *Patent- und Gebrauchsmusterverletzungsverfahren in der Bundesrepublik Deutschland, Großbritannien, Frankreich und Italien* (Cologne: Heymanns, 1989).

[134] K. Cremers, *Incidence, Settlement and Resolution of Patent Litigation Suits in Germany*, doctoral dissertation, University of Mannheim (2007), http://ub-madoc.bib.uni-mannheim.de/1405/1/Diss_cremers.pdf.

sample of relevant non-litigated patents, Cremers shows that – as is perhaps logical – it is the most valuable patents that are more frequently litigated. Then, in a 2009 paper based on the same data set, Cremers shows that the settlement rates can vary significantly between the two regional courts – the most likely cause being the variances in the interpretation of procedures between the LG in Düsseldorf and Mannheim.[135] Moreover, she notes that where an invalidity case concerning the allegedly infringed patent is started during the latter stages of the LG infringement action, the parties are more likely to settle. Again, this seems logical from the perspective of both parties given the additional costs and complexity of pursuing an additional trial on validity. Interestingly, Cremers also shows that if a patent survives an opposition challenge, this increases the likelihood that there will be a settlement (in a case featuring that patent), perhaps because it gives the patentee a strong hand in negotiations.

In 2013, Kühnen and Claessen published a paper based on data gathered from undertaking case counts at the LGs in Düsseldorf and Mannheim for the period 2009–2011. Kühnen and Claessen's data demonstrate that the LG in Düsseldorf and Mannheim are ranked 1 and 2 in terms of their importance to the overall volume of patent litigation in Germany – almost 40% of all patent infringement cases in Germany in 2011 took place in one of these two regional jurisdictions. Kühnen and Claessen suggest that 475 cases were filed at the Düsseldorf court in 2011.[136] This is a modest increase (9%) in the caseload of prior years. Meanwhile, the increase at the LG Mannheim for this period is more substantial (27%).

---

[135] K. Cremers, 'Settlement during patent litigation trials: an empirical analysis for Germany', *The Journal of Technology Transfer* 34 (2009), 182, 182–7.

[136] T. Kühnen and R. Claessen, 'Die Durchsetzung von Patenten in der EU', *Gewerblicher Rechtsschutz und Urheberrecht international (GRUR Int.)* (2013), 592, 593.

Finally, in the 2013 Cremers et al. study, a wide survey of German patent litigation data was analysed.[137] Due to the bifurcation system, Cremers et al. had to collect the data on infringement and revocation cases separately. The infringement case data were collected from the paper court records at the LG in Düsseldorf, Mannheim and Munich, where the vast majority – an estimated 80% – of patent litigation in Germany takes place. The validity case data were collected from the available information published by the BPatG and its appeal court, the BGH, as well as from the German Patent and Trademark Office (DPMA), which holds statistics on cases withdrawn quickly after filing. A total of 5,121 patent cases filed at the LG in Düsseldorf, Mannheim and Munich were examined; as were 1,618 validity actions filed at the BPatG. This brings the total number of examined patent cases – including infringement and validity actions – for 2000–2008 to 6,739. This proves beyond any doubt that by far the greatest proportion of patent litigation in Europe takes place in Germany, with infringement being by far the most common claim and the most likely outcome of a dispute that reaches a first-instance decision. Of cases filed in Germany during 2000–2008 as infringement actions, 22% reached a judgment of infringement, a higher proportion than in the UK and France; furthermore, a very high proportion – 46.1% – of patent infringement cases settled.[138]

The Cremers et al. data set was then used in a 2014 paper by Cremers, Gaessler, Harhoff, Helmers and Lefouili examining German bifurcation, including the dreaded 'invalid, but infringed' scenario (where a patent is found to have been infringed, yet it is later invalidated at the Federal level).[139] Cremers et al. show that in Germany the share of patents involved in an infringement suit that are ultimately revoked by the BPatG is a mere 9.2%, reflecting to

[137] K. Cremers, M. Ernicke, D. Harhoff, C. Helmers, G. Licht, L. McDonagh, et al. 'Patent litigation in Europe', *ZEW Discussion Paper* No. 13-07 (2013), 1.

[138] K. Cremers, M. Ernicke, D. Harhoff, C. Helmers, G. Licht, L. McDonagh, et al. 'Patent litigation in Europe', *ZEW Discussion Paper* No. 13-07 (2013), 1, 47.

[139] K. Cremers, F. Gaessler, D. Harhoff, C. Helmers and Y. Lefouili, 'Invalid but infringed? An analysis of Germany's bifurcated patent ligitation system', *Max Planck Institute for Innovation & Competition Research Paper* No. 14-14 (2014), 1, 1–6.

some extent the fact that only in around a third of infringement cases filed in 2000–2008 did the defendant to a patent infringement case file a revocation claim at the BPatG. Moreover, only a low share of invalidity challenges are actually decided by the BPatG, something that indicates that bifurcation may create an incentive for the parties to settle patent disputes before the later validity hearing. On the subject of settlements, a 2012 paper by Cremers and Schliessler based on the same 2000–2008 data set notes that where 'new information' is revealed during trial, this also tends to prompt settlements.[140]

France

Assessing the applicable law and competent courts in France

As with the UK and Germany, France is a party to the EPC.[141] In France, the EPC is enshrined in law by the French Intellectual Property Code – *Code de la propriété intellectuelle* (CPI) – which governs patent matters, including the French validations of EPs.[142] With regard to litigation, the French Code of Civil Procedure (*Code de la procédure civile* – CPC)[143] and the Judicial Organisational Code (*Code de l'organisation judiciaire*) set out the relevant procedural rules for litigation in France.[144]

Patent proprietors – including joint owners – have standing to initiate patent infringement claims and licensees are entitled to

140 K. Cremers and P. Schliessler, 'Patent litigation settlement in Germany: why parties settle during trial', *ZEW Discussion Paper* No. 12-084 (2012), 1.

141 Text of the European Patent Convention (EPC), of 5 October 1973, as revised by the Act revising Article 63 EPC of 17 December 1991, and the Act revising the EPC of 29 November 2000, available at http://documents.epo.org/projects/babylon/eponet.nsf/0/00E0CD7FD461C0D5C1257C060050C376/$File/EPC_15th_edition_2013.pdf.

142 *Code de la propriété intellectuelle* (CPI) version consolidée au 8 août 2015 (French Code of intellectual property), available at http://legifrance.gouv.fr/affichCode.do?cidTexte=LEGITEXT000006069414&dateTexte=20150920.

143 *Code de la procédure civile* (CPC) – English translation available at www.legifrance.gouv.fr/Traductions/en-English/Legifrance-translations.

144 *Code de l'organisation judiciaire* – French version available at http://legifrance.gouv.fr/affichCode.do?cidTexte=LEGITEXT000006071164 (English translation not available).

participate where they have suffered a loss.[145] Furthermore, unless the specific licence states otherwise, beneficiaries of exclusive – or even compulsory – licences can initiate proceedings where, having notified the patent proprietor of the alleged infringement, the patent proprietor has failed to file a claim.[146]

The *Tribunal de Grande Instance* (TGI), located in Paris, possesses the exclusive jurisdiction to hear all patent cases in France.[147] At the TGI there are four judicial panels that can hear IP cases, with each panel comprising of three judges.[148] Unlike in Germany, there is no bifurcation of infringement and validity issues – both infringement and invalidity are considered at the TGI. In general, the TGI judges are not technical experts.[149] Technical evidence by experts can, however, be presented to the court, usually in written form.[150]

A first-instance decision of the TGI can be appealed before the Court of Appeal (*Cour d'Appel* – CdA) in Paris.[151] The appeal court consists of a panel of experienced judges with IP expertise within Division 5 of the CdA in Paris. Appeals made with respect to preliminary injunction rulings are heard by Division 1 of the Paris CdA. However, where a preliminary injunction is granted by a

---

[145] Article L 615-2 CPI.

[146] J.-G. Moninand and S. Vilfeu, 'France', in N. Beckett and J. Morton (eds), *CMS International Patent Litigation Guide* (CMS, 2013), 39–44, 39.

[147] K. Cremers, M. Ernicke, D. Harhoff, C. Helmers, G. Licht, L. McDonagh, et al. 'Patent litigation in Europe', *ZEW Discussion Paper* No. 13-07 (2013), 1, 22, noting that this exclusive jurisdiction has existed since 2009, and referring to Articles L615-17 CPI and D211-6 COJ (decree dated 9 October 2009).

[148] J.-G. Moninand and S. Vilfeu, 'France', in N. Beckett and J. Morton (eds), *CMS International Patent Litigation Guide* (CMS, 2013), 39–44, 39.

[149] J.-G. Moninand and S. Vilfeu, 'France', in N. Beckett and J. Morton (eds), *CMS International Patent Litigation Guide* (CMS, 2013), 39–44, 40.

[150] J.-G. Moninand and S. Vilfeu, 'France', in N. Beckett and J. Morton (eds), *CMS International Patent Litigation Guide* (CMS, 2013), 39–44, 40, referring to Article 282 of the French Code of Civil Procedure.

[151] K. Cremers, M. Ernicke, D. Harhoff, C. Helmers, G. Licht, L. McDonagh, et al. 'Patent litigation in Europe', *ZEW Discussion Paper* No. 13-07 (2013), 1, 22, referring to Article R 211-1 COJ.

judge in charge of a pending case on the merits, this cannot be appealed before the judgment on the merits is issued.[152]

There is no need to seek leave to appeal, and making an appeal usually suspends the enforceability of the first-instance decision, pending the appeal outcome, unless – as often happens – the TGI has ruled that the decision ought to be enforceable notwithstanding an appeal.[153] Finally, the decisions of a CdA can be appealed on an exact issue of law to the Commercial Chamber (*Chambre Commerciale*) of France's Supreme Court – the *Cour de Cassation* (CC).[154] Again, no leave is required. Like the UK and German courts, French courts may refer questions to the CJEU in line with the Article 267 procedure, though Bouvet notes that this is quite rare in patent matters.[155]

Assessing the procedural structure and typical length of proceedings in France

Both infringement and validity claims can be filed at the TGI. However, as discussed further below with respect to empirical data, it is known that patent infringement is by far the most common initial claim for FRs and EPs; whereas, a patent invalidity challenge is typically only raised as a counterclaim, or as a defence, to a prior infringement claim.[156] Thus, although it is possible in France to file

---

[152] T. Bouvet, 'France', in M.C. Elmer and C.G. Gramaenopoulos (eds), *Global Patent Litigation* (Arlington, VA: Bloomberg BNA, 2014), 546–89, 548.

[153] T. Bouvet, 'France', in M.C. Elmer and C.G. Gramaenopoulos (eds), *Global Patent Litigation* (Arlington, VA: Bloomberg BNA, 2014), 546–89, 548.

[154] K. Cremers, M. Ernicke, D. Harhoff, C. Helmers, G. Licht, L. McDonagh, et al. 'Patent litigation in Europe', *ZEW Discussion Paper* No. 13-07 (2013), 1, 23, referring to Article L 111-2 COJ.

[155] T. Bouvet, 'France', in M.C. Elmer and C.G. Gramaenopoulos (eds), *Global Patent Litigation* (Arlington, VA: Bloomberg BNA, 2014), 546–89, 548.

[156] P. Véron, 'Patent infringement litigation in France', *Mitteilungen der deutschen Patentanwälte* 93 (2002), 386, 387 notes that in France there is an important distinction between citing patent invalidity as a defence and making a counterclaim for revocation: the counterclaim constitutes a claim of the defendant and results, when it is admitted, in the revocation of the patent, whereas the defence of patent invalidity results only in the dismissal of the claim for infringement and the patent itself remains in force.

a standalone initial action alleging patent invalidity at the TGI – rather than as a response to an infringement claim – in practice this does not occur that often.[157] If the patent is declared invalid by the court, the effect is immediate within the jurisdiction.

In addition to filing initial claims for infringement or invalidity, it is possible to seek a declaration of non-infringement from the TGI via the following procedure: first, the owner of the relevant patent(s) is invited by another party to provide an opinion as to whether the relevant product/process constitutes an infringement; then, if the other party disagrees with the patentee's position, that party can bring the case before the TGI, which can give an opinion regarding the possibility of infringement – and the TGI can at this stage issue a binding declaration of non-infringement.[158]

Disclosure and evidence gathering One of the key – and from the point of view of patentees, most highly valued – elements of the French patent litigation system is the possibility of making an application for search and seizure of evidence (*saisie contrefaçon*), a process which can even precede the full patent infringement case filing at the TGI.[159] The *saisie* rules are quite strict and unique to France – the TGI president cannot refuse to give the authorization for search and seizure if a legally granted patent, which is still in force, is at issue in the case, although the TGI president has the power to legally determine the extent of the search and seizure.[160] In addition to providing evidence for French patent cases, the *saisie* procedure is well regarded by patentees because evidence gathered

---

[157] K. Cremers, M. Ernicke, D. Harhoff, C. Helmers, G. Licht, L. McDonagh, et al. 'Patent litigation in Europe', *ZEW Discussion Paper* No. 13-07 (2013), 1, 23, referring to Articles L613-25 and L614-12 CPI.

[158] J.-G. Moninand and S. Vilfeu, 'France', in N. Beckett and J. Morton (eds), *CMS International Patent Litigation Guide* (CMS, 2013), 39–44, 39.

[159] Article L 615-5 CPI. See also P. Véron, 'Patent infringement litigation in France', *Mitteilungen der deutschen Patentanwälte* 93 (2002), 386, 392.

[160] K. Cremers, M. Ernicke, D. Harhoff, C. Helmers, G. Licht, L. McDonagh, et al. 'Patent litigation in Europe', *ZEW Discussion Paper* No. 13-07 (2013), 1, 23, referring to Article L 615-5 CPI, noting that the president might grant the *saisie* with a considerably smaller scope than applied for by the patentee.

in France may be of relevance to parallel litigation between the same parties in other jurisdictions.[161]

In practice, a bailiff (*huissier de justice*) – chosen by the plaintiff – carries out the *saisie* (search and seizure) order, typically accompanied by a 'person skilled in the art' and/or any person whose technical skills would be useful to the search – often the plaintiff's patent attorney (*conseil en propriété industrielle*).[162] A police officer is also present during the search, and in practical terms, the bailiff, policeman and accompanying skilled person(s) have wide powers: they are allowed to enter into the alleged infringer's premises to examine any allegedly infringing products, devices or ongoing processes therein, as well as to obtain a number of examples thereof, and/or to make copies of the relevant technical and financial documents (even where such documents are marked confidential).[163]

Of course, the fact that the *saisie* may take place before an actual case filing against the alleged infringer means that without safeguards the process could be open to serious abuse. To try to avoid this, there is a requirement on the prospective plaintiff/claimant to serve a writ of summons on the alleged infringer within two weeks of the carrying out of the order for *saisie*.[164] It is the serving of the writ of summons on the alleged infringer – setting out the plaintiff's claims – that is the beginning of the formal, substantive patent infringement proceedings. If the plaintiff fails to serve the writ of summons within the two-week period, the *saisie* will be declared effectively invalid; and, crucially, the patentee may be held liable for any damage or cost caused to the alleged infringer by the

---

[161] J. Radcliffe and M. Brown, *European Patent Litigation Strategy* (Arlington, VA: Bloomberg BNA, 2014), 1–48, 5. See also T. Bouvet, 'France', in M.C. Elmer and C.G. Gramaenopoulos (eds), *Global Patent Litigation* (Arlington, VA: Bloomberg BNA, 2014), 546–89, 588.

[162] P. Véron, 'Patent infringement litigation in France', *Mitteilungen der deutschen Patentanwälte* 93 (2002), 386, 393.

[163] P. Véron, 'Patent infringement litigation in France', *Mitteilungen der deutschen Patentanwälte* 93 (2002), 386, 393.

[164] K. Cremers, M. Ernicke, D. Harhoff, C. Helmers, G. Licht, L. McDonagh, et al. 'Patent litigation in Europe', *ZEW Discussion Paper* No. 13-07 (2013), 1, 23–4.

carrying out of the *saisie*.[165] The plaintiff must also have the writ ascribed on the register of pending cases at the TGI office (*placer l'affaire*).[166]

The trial hearing The substantive patent infringement case proceeds largely on the basis of a written, rather than an oral, procedure. In French patent infringement cases, it is common for three or four written pleadings to be exchanged between the parties as the proceedings progress.[167] Parties are allowed to conduct experiments, and there is no need to obtain prior agreement from the other party or from the court to do this.[168] The exchange of written pleadings is followed by an oral hearing at the TGI, heard by the three-judge panel. Witness testimonies are usually recorded in writing and submitted to the court in advance – meaning there is very little oral testimony. Moreover, unlike in Germany, in patent cases at the TGI the judges typically do not present a preliminary opinion.[169] The lawyers' pleadings during this process typically take between 1 and 3 hours, and only on very rare occasions do they take up more than one day of the court's time.[170] In other words, this 'paper-based' system is quite unlike that of the UK, and is closer to the system found in Germany and the Netherlands.

Interim injunctions and post-trial enforcement Preliminary proceedings are also possible at the TGI. Proceedings for preliminary injunctions are handled by the presiding judge of the relevant judicial panel, or where a case is already pending, by the judge in

---

165 P. Véron, 'Patent infringement litigation in France', *Mitteilungen der deutschen Patentanwälte* 93 (2002), 386, 393.

166 P. Véron, 'Patent infringement litigation in France', *Mitteilungen der deutschen Patentanwälte* 93 (2002), 386, 394.

167 P. Véron, 'Patent infringement litigation in France', *Mitteilungen der deutschen Patentanwälte* 93 (2002), 386, 397.

168 J.-G. Moninand and S. Vilfeu, 'France', in N. Beckett and J. Morton (eds), *CMS International Patent Litigation Guide* (CMS, 2013), 39–44, 40.

169 P. Véron, 'Patent infringement litigation in France', *Mitteilungen der deutschen Patentanwälte* 93 (2002), 386, 399.

170 J.-G. Moninand and S. Vilfeu, 'France', in N. Beckett and J. Morton (eds), *CMS International Patent Litigation Guide* (CMS, 2013), 39–44, 40.

charge of that case.[171] Where infringement is an imminent risk or already taking place, the patentee (or exclusive licensee/patent right holder) can ask the President of the Court to grant a preliminary/ interlocutory injunction. This can be granted *inter partes* or on an *ex parte* basis, but *ex parte* injunctions are only granted where irreparable harm would otherwise be called to the patent right holder (and can be later contested by the defendant).[172] Where the patent's validity cannot seriously be challenged, the issuance of a preliminary injunction is more likely. However, although following the filing of an infringement claim it is possible for a preliminary injunction to be granted by the president of the TGI, in practice Cremers et al. note that such interlocutory injunctions are very rarely granted.[173]

Remedies available include damages; a recall and/or destruction of the infringing goods and publication of the infringement finding; and, most crucially, an injunction. Following a judgment on the merits of the case, the provisional enforcement of a decision – for example, via the granting of an injunction – occurs where this is requested by the winning party, so long as the court considers this to be justified in the circumstances. Unlike in Germany, in France it is not usually necessary for the party who has won the substantive decision to provide a security/indemnity for its provisional enforcement.[174]

Nonetheless, in the context of preliminary proceedings, a TGI judge can make the provision of an indemnity by the plaintiff a condition of the grant of a preliminary injunction, so that any

---

[171] T. Bouvet, 'France', in M.C. Elmer and C.G. Gramaenopoulos (eds), *Global Patent Litigation* (Arlington, VA: Bloomberg BNA, 2014), 546–89, 548.

[172] J.-G. Moninand and S. Vilfeu, 'France', in N. Beckett and J. Morton (eds), *CMS International Patent Litigation Guide* (CMS, 2013), 39–44, 42.

[173] K. Cremers, M. Ernicke, D. Harhoff, C. Helmers, G. Licht, L. McDonagh, et al. 'Patent litigation in Europe', *ZEW Discussion Paper* No. 13-07 (2013), 1, 23, referring to L615-3 CPI and noting that according to P. Véron, 'Patent infringement litigation in France', *Mitteilungen der deutschen Patentanwälte* 93 (2002), 386, 386–403, less than five preliminary injunctions are handed out each year compared to 300–500 infringement cases on the merits.

[174] P. Véron, 'Patent infringement litigation in France', *Mitteilungen der deutschen Patentanwälte* 93 (2002), 386, 400.

potential losses felt by the defendant are recoverable if the infringement action is found to have no foundation.[175] Similarly, rather than granting the preliminary injunction to the plaintiff, the court may instead require the defendant to provide an indemnity to the plaintiff against possible damages suffered, if infringement is later shown to have taken place.

Damages are usually calculated on the basis of loss of profit to the patentee and/or benefit gained to the infringer.[176] Materials seized during the *saisie* procedure may be useful to the process of calculating lost profits/infringer benefits, etc. After a decision on the merits, an expert may be appointed to determine the appropriate level of damages, with a further hearing taking place for the court to evaluate the damages report.[177]

The relationship between EPO opposition and French enforcement

As with the UK and Germany, EPs can be challenged via the EPO opposition service, while the validity of EPs (with French validations) can also be contested at the TGI.[178] Like other EPC MS courts, the TGI has discretion concerning whether to stay ongoing French court proceedings pending parallel EPO opposition proceedings; in practice, however, the TGI will do so only if the court considers that there is a high likelihood of opposition success and if it is in the overall balance of the parties' interests.[179]

---

[175] J.-G. Moninand and S. Vilfeu, 'France', in N. Beckett and J. Morton (eds), *CMS International Patent Litigation Guide* (CMS, 2013), 39–44, 40.

[176] J.-G. Moninand and S. Vilfeu, 'France', in N. Beckett and J. Morton (eds), *CMS International Patent Litigation Guide* (CMS, 2013), 39–44, 41.

[177] T. Bouvet, 'France', in M.C. Elmer and C.G. Gramaenopoulos (eds), *Global Patent Litigation* (Arlington, VA: Bloomberg BNA, 2014), 546–89, 548.

[178] Unlike in e.g. Germany there is no opposition procedure to challenge French national patents (FRs) at the *Institut National de la Propriété Industrielle* (INPI).

[179] Hogan Lovells, *Patent Litigation Guide: Jurisdictions (France)* (2013), 1, 1, available at http://limegreenip.hoganlovells.com/patents/patentlitigation/Pages/default.aspx.

Length of proceedings The TGI usually makes its first-instance decision within 4–6 weeks of the hearing.[180] In total, it usually takes 18–22 months from filing the writ of summons to the first-instance decision, though in urgent cases 'the president of the Court may permit the plaintiff, upon his petition, to summon the defendant to an earlier fixed date'.[181]

Assessing the award of costs and fee shifting in France

Unlike in the UK and Germany, there is no charge in France for the administrative work of the court with respect to patent proceedings.[182] That, of course, does not mean that there is no overall cost for taking proceedings in France. One estimate states that the private legal costs arising from a patent case – from case filing to full judgment – typically range between €50,000 and €200,000 per party.[183] Another estimate for the private legal costs of first-instance proceedings gives a range of €40,000–150,000 per party, though it is noted that the costs can potentially be higher in technical cases.[184] Regardless of the precise range, it is clear that the costs in France are relatively low in comparison with the UK due to the limited use of witnesses and experts, and the existence of relatively short, largely paper-based, trials.[185] The lack of court fees is also notable, and contrasts with the high value-based fees in the UK and Germany.

---

[180] J.-G. Moninand and S. Vilfeu, 'France', in N. Beckett and J. Morton (eds), *CMS International Patent Litigation Guide* (CMS, 2013), 39–44, 40. See also P. Véron, 'Patent infringement litigation in France', *Mitteilungen der deutschen Patentanwälte* 93 (2002), 386, 399.

[181] J.-G. Moninand and S. Vilfeu, 'France', in N. Beckett and J. Morton (eds), *CMS International Patent Litigation Guide* (CMS, 2013), 39–44, 40.

[182] K. Cremers, M. Ernicke, D. Harhoff, C. Helmers, G. Licht, L. McDonagh, et al. 'Patent litigation in Europe', *ZEW Discussion Paper* No. 13-07 (2013), 1, 23, referring to Article L. 111-2 *Code de l'organisation judiciaire* (COJ). See also P. Véron, 'Patent infringement litigation in France', *Mitteilungen der deutschen Patentanwälte* 93 (2002), 386–403, 400.

[183] B. van Pottelsberghe, *Lost Property: The European patent system and why it doesn't work* (Bruegel Blueprint Series, 2009), available at http://bruegel.org/wp-content/uploads/imported/publications/patents_BP_050609.pdf.

[184] J.-G. Moninand and S. Vilfeu, 'France', in N. Beckett and J. Morton (eds), *CMS International Patent Litigation Guide* (CMS, 2013), 39–44, 41.

[185] T. Bouvet, 'France', in M.C. Elmer and C.G. Gramaenopoulos (eds), *Global Patent Litigation* (Arlington, VA: Bloomberg BNA, 2014), 546–89.

As with the UK and Germany, in France there is a system of fee shifting from 'loser' to 'winner' – but in terms of the amount of costs typically awarded, the awards tend to be much more limited than the cost totals awarded in the UK and Germany.[186] For instance, Cremers et al. estimate that the total recoverable costs awarded to the winning party by the French courts tend to be at around the €3000–3500 level.[187] Thus, the award rarely covers the winning party's full costs or even a large proportion; but the TGI can sometimes award higher amounts to successful parties, including costs within the range of €150,000–300,000.[188] The costs of an appeal are broadly the same as for the first-instance trial.

Exploring empirical data on patent litigation in France

A key study of French patent litigation was undertaken by the experienced litigator Pierre Véron in 2001, whereby he examined patent case data for cases undertaken during the period 1990–1999.[189] The data show that around half of all French patent cases taken during 1990–1999 were heard by the TGI in Paris, showing the dominance of the Paris court even before it gained exclusive jurisdiction for patent cases in 2009. Furthermore, according to Véron's study 82% of the patent cases filed in Paris were infringement claims, with the remaining cases mainly relating to employee inventions and breach of contract, illustrating that standalone validity challenges are very rare in France. Indeed, infringement proceedings in France are viewed as highly patentee-friendly.[190]

Véron's data also show that, at least for French patent cases undertaken during his survey period of 1990–1999, the vast majority – almost three quarters – of patent litigants were local, i.e. based

---

[186] K. Cremers, M. Ernicke, D. Harhoff, C. Helmers, G. Licht, L. McDonagh, et al. 'Patent litigation in Europe', *ZEW Discussion Paper* No. 13-07 (2013), 1, 25, referring to Articles 696 and 700 CPC.

[187] P. Véron, 'Patent infringement litigation in France', *Mitteilungen der deutschen Patentanwälte* 93 (2002), 386, 401.

[188] J.-G. Moninand and S. Vilfeu, 'France', in N. Beckett and J. Morton (eds), *CMS International Patent Litigation Guide* (CMS, 2013), 39–44, 41.

[189] P. Véron, 'Le contentieux des brevets d'invention en France Étude statistique 1990–1999' (2001), available at www.veron.com/publications/Colloques/Le_contentieux_des_brevets_invention_1990_1999_en_couleurs.pdf.

[190] Taylor Wessing, *Global Intellectual Property Index* (2013), 1, 29, available at http://united-kingdom.taylorwessing.com/ipindex/.

in France, with most of the remaining quarter based either in Germany or the USA. Véron also demonstrates that the vast majority of patents litigated in Paris at the TGI concern electronics and technical instruments. This contrasts, for example, with Germany, which features a large proportion of mechanical and engineering patents; and the UK, where a large proportion of patent cases involve pharmaceutical and chemical inventions.[191]

With respect to outcomes, Véron's data show that in around half of all patent cases heard during 1990–1999 the patent was held both valid and infringed. Interestingly, revocation occurred only in 23% of cases involving French national patents and in only 15% of cases involving the French validation of an EP – a relatively low rate when compared with the UK.

Véron's study also demonstrated that the majority of damages awards in cases taken in 1990–1999 fell below the €80,000 level. Very occasionally, however, higher damage awards were handed down in French patent cases, with some even rising above the €1,000,000 level.

More recently, in 2010, Véron published a range of data for the period between 2000 and 2009. In terms of case counts, on average Véron found that for the period 2004–2009 335 patent cases were filed per year across all courts in France (i.e. before 2009 when all patent cases were moved to Paris).[192]

With respect to types of claims filed, in the more recent study Véron found that, like the earlier period, during the later period a very similar percentage – 81% to the earlier 82% – of all patent claims filed were for infringement, showing a remarkable level of consistency over time. The remaining 19% of claims included invalidity claims or claims relating to employee inventions and related ownership disputes with employers.

Looking closely at the data from the TGI in Paris – now the exclusive court – Véron observed that infringement of a valid patent

---

191 K. Cremers, M. Ernicke, D. Harhoff, C. Helmers, G. Licht, L. McDonagh, et al. 'Patent litigation in Europe', *ZEW Discussion Paper* No. 13-07 (2013), 1, 3.

192 P. Véron, 'Le contentieux des brevets d'invention en France Étude statistique 2000–2009' (2010) – available at http://www.veron.com/publications/Colloques/Stats_contentieux_brevets_France_2000–2009_Veron_et_Associes.pdf.

was judged to have occurred in 33% of all cases. For the same court over the same period, in 40% of all cases even though the patent was upheld as being valid, it was nonetheless held not to have been infringed. Only in just over a quarter of all cases – 27% – was the patent held to be invalid. As with the figures for 1990–1999, for 2000–2009 there was a higher probability that a French national patent would be found invalid when compared to an EP (31% v 21%). Thus, it is evident from the most recent Véron study that since the 1990s there has been an increase in invalidity findings, as well as in decisions that found the patent valid though not infringed. As with the UK, shifting trends across the realm of judicial decision making may play a role in this change.

Thomas Bouvet states that in 2006–2011 only around 18% of patent case filings resulted in a full decision on the merits.[193] The TGI in Paris issues rulings in an average of 80 patent cases per year, and, according to Bouvet, more than 50% of first-instance decisions (around 45 cases) are appealed to the CdA, with the CC subsequently hearing around 20 patent cases per year.[194] From 2006 to 2011, Bouvet notes that patentees had a win rate of 41% in patent cases in France.[195]

The 2013 Cremers et al. study used data collected for cases filed in 2000–2008 at the TGI in Paris. The data were collected by Darts-IP. The data show a total of 1,002 patent cases at the TGI for this period. The data demonstrate that patent infringement was the most common initial claim for FRs and EPs; meanwhile, a patent invalidity challenge was typically only raised as a counterclaim, or as a defence, to a prior infringement claim; and on this point, Cremers et al. note that more than 90% of validity challenges were raised as a counterclaim/defence to an earlier infringement action

---

[193] T. Bouvet, 'France', in M.C. Elmer and C.G. Gramaenopoulos (eds), *Global Patent Litigation* (Arlington, VA: Bloomberg BNA, 2014), 546–89, 548.

[194] T. Bouvet, 'France', in M.C. Elmer and C.G. Gramaenopoulos (eds), *Global Patent Litigation* (Arlington, VA: Bloomberg BNA, 2014), 546–89, 549.

[195] T. Bouvet, 'France', in M.C. Elmer and C.G. Gramaenopoulos (eds), *Global Patent Litigation* (Arlington, VA: Bloomberg BNA, 2014), 546–89, 546.

rather than as separate individual actions.[196] Furthermore, 16.3% of patent infringement cases filed in France were settled.

Overall, the comparative lack of standalone invalidity challenges in France marks a clear distinction from the German system, where validity actions must be filed separately. Furthermore, in the UK initial validity challenges are common due in large part to the doctrine of 'clearing the way'. However, there is no French equivalent of this doctrine; in fact, with regard to France, Bouvet states that there is 'no specific advantage to a possible infringer taking the initiative of starting revocation proceedings or actions for the declaration of non-infringement'.[197] Nonetheless – as is the case in other jurisdictions – challenging the validity of the patentee's patent(s) at the EPO via opposition proceedings remains a useful strategy for potential infringers/competitors.

The Netherlands

Assessing the applicable law and competent courts in the Netherlands

Like the UK, Germany and France, the Netherlands is a party to the EPC. The Patent Act of 1995 (PA 1995) – *Rijkswet van 15 december 1994, houdende regels met betrekking tot octrooien* – regulates Dutch patents, including national patents (NLs) and the national validations of EPs, and sets out the options for filing infringement cases and validity challenges before the Dutch courts.[198] Meanwhile, the Code of Civil Procedure – *Wetboek van Burgerlijke Rechtsvordering* (Rv) – provides the procedural rules

[196] K. Cremers, M. Ernicke, D. Harhoff, C. Helmers, G. Licht, L. McDonagh, et al. 'Patent litigation in Europe', *ZEW Discussion Paper* No. 13-07 (2013), 1, 23, referring to P. Véron, 'Patent infringement litigation in France', *Mitteilungen der deutschen Patentanwälte* 93 (2002), 386, 387, who estimates inter alia that only 5% of the actions are isolated actions.

[197] T. Bouvet, 'France', in M.C. Elmer and C.G. Gramaenopoulos (eds), *Global Patent Litigation* (Arlington, VA: Bloomberg BNA, 2014), 546, 589.

[198] *Rijkswet van 15 december 1994, houdende regels met betrekking tot octrooien* – Patent Act 1995 (Netherlands). An English translation is available at: http://english.rvo.nl/sites/default/files/2013/12/ROW95_ENG_niet_officiele_vertaling_0.pdf.

for civil litigation in the Netherlands.[199] Patent proprietors have standing to initiate patent infringement proceedings before the Dutch courts; meanwhile, licensees can join these proprietor-led proceedings, or they can even initiate proceedings themselves if this right is included within the licence agreement.[200]

Notably, in the Netherlands the system of patent enforcement is highly centralized; it is based at courts in The Hague which hold exclusive jurisdiction to hear patent cases.[201] Although the Netherlands shares some similarities with the German courts system – primarily the front-loaded paper-based style of proceedings – it is important to emphasize that in the Netherlands there is no German-style bifurcation between the issues of validity and infringement – these issues are considered by the same court. There are two streams of patent proceedings – accelerated and regular.[202]

At The Hague, first-instance court filings are undertaken at the District Court (*Rechtbank*) Civil Chamber, which hears patent cases. Regarding patent case appeals, the Civil Chamber of the Court of Appeals (*Gerechtshof*) has jurisdiction to hear challenges to first-instance decisions. The judges at both the first instance and the appeal level possess a great deal of technical and legal expertise.[203] In patent cases, it is also possible to file a final appeal on a point of law at the Supreme Court of the Netherlands (*Hoge Raad*).

---

199 *Wetboek van Burgerlijke Rechtsvordering* (Rv) – Code of Civil Procedure. An English translation is available at www1.umn.edu/humanrts/research/Civil%20Procedure%20Code%20(English).pdf

200 S 70 (1-6) Patents Act 1995 (Netherlands).

201 S 80 Patents Act 1995 (Netherlands). See also J. Brinkhoff, 'The enforcement of patent rights in the Netherlands', *International Review of Intellectual Property and Competition Law (IIC)* 31 (2000), 706, 707, noting that prior to 1987 19 Dutch district courts had the ability to hear patent infringement cases, but now The Hague is the sole venue.

202 W. Hoorneman, 'The Netherlands', in N. Beckett and J. Morton (eds), *CMS International Patent Litigation Guide* (CMS, 2013), 61–6, 61–2.

203 Taylor Wessing, *Global Intellectual Property Index* (2013), 1, 26, available at http://united-kingdom.taylorwessing.com/ipindex/.

Assessing the procedural structure and typical length of proceedings in the Netherlands
Interestingly, in the Netherlands there is no need for a court filing to kick off legal action – it can be initiated via the serving of a writ of summons upon the defendant, with the court merely being informed of this having occurred at a subsequent date.[204] In other words, once the writ has been served, the defendant is considered to have been put on notice that full litigation proceedings are pending/forthcoming. The served writ must contain a statement of the plaintiff's case, indicating the evidence that the plaintiff seeks to rely on. The defendant must then issue a statement detailing the basis of the defence and the potential evidence relied on.[205] A counterclaim, for example, alleging invalidity of the patent may be filed at this stage. Following this, the plaintiff may submit a statement of defence to the defendant's counterclaim.

In the Netherlands, if the first-instance claim is for infringement, patent invalidity may be raised by the defendant either as a defence, or as an invalidity counterclaim, to the infringement filing. Alternatively, the validity of a patent may be challenged in a 'stand-alone' first-instance revocation claim.[206] Regardless of how the challenge is brought, the validity issue will be determined at the same court as the infringement claim. It is also possible for a party – for example, a competitor of the patentee – to seek a declaration of non-infringement of the patent(s) from the District Court at The Hague.[207]

Disclosure and evidence gathering In the Netherlands prior to 2007, it was the case that neither applications for UK-style broad disclosure orders, nor actions seeking French-style *saisie* (search

[204] W. Hoorneman, 'The Netherlands', in N. Beckett and J. Morton (eds), *CMS International Patent Litigation Guide* (CMS, 2013), 61–6, 61.
[205] W. Hoorneman, 'The Netherlands', in N. Beckett and J. Morton (eds), *CMS International Patent Litigation Guide* (CMS, 2013), 61–6, 61.
[206] W. Hoorneman, 'The Netherlands', in N. Beckett and J. Morton (eds), *CMS International Patent Litigation Guide* (CMS, 2013), 61–6, 61.
[207] W. Hoorneman, 'The Netherlands', in N. Beckett and J. Morton (eds), *CMS International Patent Litigation Guide* (CMS, 2013), 61–6, 61.

and seizure) orders, were possible.[208] However, although there is still no specific disclosure requirement, since the implementation of the EU Enforcement Directive in 2007 the Netherlands has provided for a new set of procedures aimed at enabling patentees to secure evidence of possible patent infringement.[209] To avail of these procedures, the patentee is required to make a written request to the Preliminary Relief Judge who usually conducts the proceedings on an *ex parte* basis.[210]

The trial hearing As noted earlier, patent proceedings in the Netherlands follow a largely paper-based litigation system, whereby the claims and evidence are largely set out, pre-trial, in writs that are filed at the court and passed between the various parties. In regular proceedings – but not in accelerated proceedings – the parties may be required by the court to appear, pre-trial hearing, in person, for a less formal outline of the key issues, with the aim of reaching a settlement.[211] In accelerated proceedings, no filings after the initial exchanges of writs/statements/defences by the parties are allowed.

During the trial hearing itself, limited oral arguments are typically heard from both sides. If necessary, an independent technical expert may be appointed by the court to provide an opinion and the presentation of experiment-based evidence is permissible.[212] However, it is rare for Dutch courts to seek to rely on an independent expert's testimony.[213] One reason for this is the high level of

---

[208] J. Brinkhoff, 'The enforcement of patent rights in the Netherlands', *International Review of Intellectual Property and Competition Law (IIC)* 31 (2000), 706, 716.

[209] K. Cremers, M. Ernicke, D. Harhoff, C. Helmers, G. Licht, L. McDonagh, et al. 'Patent litigation in Europe', *ZEW Discussion Paper* No. 13-07 (2013), 1, 27, referring to Articles 1019(a)–1019(i) Rv.

[210] O. Swens, 'Patent litigation in the Netherlands and recent developments', presentation delivered in Munich (February, 2011), slide 12, available at www.vondst-law.com/v2/files/Recent%20developments%20in%20Dutch%20patent%20law%20-%20February%202011.pdf.

[211] W. Hoorneman, 'The Netherlands', in N. Beckett and J. Morton (eds), *CMS International Patent Litigation Guide* (CMS, 2013), 61–6, 62.

[212] W. Hoorneman, 'The Netherlands', in N. Beckett and J. Morton (eds), *CMS International Patent Litigation Guide* (CMS, 2013), 61–6, 62.

[213] W. Hoorneman, 'The Netherlands', in N. Beckett and J. Morton (eds), *CMS International Patent Litigation Guide* (CMS, 2013), 61–6, 61–2.

technical expertise that Dutch patent judges have.[214] The official language of the courts in The Hague is Dutch, and all filings must be in Dutch. Nonetheless, written supporting evidence may additionally be submitted in English, and exceptionally in German or French.[215]

Interim injunctions and post-trial enforcement Within the legal system of the Netherlands, preliminary relief proceedings (*Kort-Geding*) are available if the court decides the urgency of the case justifies it.[216] In such proceedings, a writ of summons is served upon the defendant by the plaintiff, requiring the defendant to appear before the president of the court. This writ of summons contains the primary claim as well as some details of its legal and evidentiary basis. At the preliminary hearing, the plaintiff and the defendant have the chance to provide oral arguments and the court's decision is made swiftly.[217] Following the enactment of the EU Enforcement Directive and its implementation in the Netherlands in 2007, it is possible for a Dutch court to grant an *ex parte* injunction, but only in circumstances of urgency – for example, in a case involving repeat infringers or involving distributers of goods where manufacturers have already been shown to have infringed.[218]

During the late 1990s, a somewhat unique characteristic of patent litigation in the Netherlands was the willingness of Dutch judges to impose cross-border injunctions to prevent patent infringement in

---

[214] Taylor Wessing, *Global Intellectual Property Index* (2013), 26, available at http://united-kingdom.taylorwessing.com/ipindex/.

[215] W. Hoorneman, 'The Netherlands', in N. Beckett and J. Morton (eds), *CMS International Patent Litigation Guide* (CMS, 2013), 61–6, 61–2.

[216] W. Hoorneman, 'The Netherlands', in N. Beckett and J. Morton (eds), *CMS International Patent Litigation Guide* (CMS, 2013), 61–6, 63–4.

[217] J. Brinkhoff, 'The enforcement of patent rights in the Netherlands', *International Review of Intellectual Property and Competition Law (IIC)* 31 (2000), 706, 709–11.

[218] K. Cremers, M. Ernicke, D. Harhoff, C. Helmers, G. Licht, L. McDonagh, et al. 'Patent litigation in Europe', *ZEW Discussion Paper* No. 13-07 (2013), 1, 29.

the Netherlands and abroad.[219] Cremers et al. note that the popularity of the Dutch litigation system among patentees rose considerably during the mid-to-late 1990s largely for this reason.[220] Nonetheless, two decisions of the Court of Justice of the EU in 2006 placed limits on the issuance of such cross-border injunctions.[221] As a result of the CJEU rulings, today Dutch cross-border injunctions are available only in preliminary relief proceedings and only where the validity of the patent is not in dispute.[222] Moreover, an *ex parte* injunction may not be granted on a cross-border basis.[223]

With respect to post-trial enforcement, following a finding of infringement on the merits a final injunction will generally be granted by the Dutch court against the infringer, and if the infringer fails to abide by the injunction, a further fine can be ordered by the court.[224] In circumstances where an appeal has been launched by a defendant, it is usually the case that the effect of the first-instance decision is suspended. Despite this, a plaintiff can apply for a declaration that the first-instance decision is provisionally enforceable.[225] As a matter of course, the Dutch courts typically grant such

---

219 H. Bertrams, 'The cross-border prohibitory injunction in Dutch patent law', *International Review of Intellectual Property and Competition Law (IIC)* 26 (1995), 618, 618–21.

220 K. Cremers, M. Ernicke, D. Harhoff, C. Helmers, G. Licht, L. McDonagh, et al. 'Patent litigation in Europe', *ZEW Discussion Paper* No. 13-07 (2013), 1, 28.

221 See Case C-539/03 *Roche Nederland BV v Frederick Primus* [2006] ECR I-6569 and Case C-04/93 *Gesellschaft für Antriebstechnik mbH & Co. KG (GAT) v Lamellen und Kupplungsbau Beteiligungs KG (LuK)* [2006] ECR I-6523.

222 W. Hoorneman, 'The Netherlands', in N. Beckett and J. Morton (eds), *CMS International Patent Litigation Guide* (CMS, 2013), 61–6, 65.

223 O. Swens, 'Patent litigation in the Netherlands and recent developments', presentation delivered in Munich (February, 2011), slides 8 and 9, available at www.vondst-law.com/v2/files/Recent%20developments%20in%20Dutch%20patent%20law%20-%20February%202011.pdf.

224 K. Cremers, M. Ernicke, D. Harhoff, C. Helmers, G. Licht, L. McDonagh, et al. 'Patent litigation in Europe', *ZEW Discussion Paper* No. 13-07 (2013), 1, 29, referring to Sec. 3 DPA; Sec. 296 Civil Code and Sec. 611a Rv.

225 W. Hoorneman, 'The Netherlands', in N. Beckett and J. Morton (eds), *CMS International Patent Litigation Guide* (CMS, 2013), 61–6, 65.

a request.[226] Importantly, however, if provisional enforcement takes place at the request of the plaintiff, and subsequently, the case is overturned on appeal, the plaintiff is responsible for any damage caused to the defendant resulting from the provisional enforcement.[227]

The relationship between EPO oppositions and Dutch enforcement
If an EP with a Dutch validation is challenged at the EPO, it is common for any Dutch proceedings concerning the validity of that patent to be stayed pending the EPO opposition decision.[228] Nonetheless, the Dutch courts will normally not stay an infringement action pending the outcome of EPO opposition proceedings.[229] In preliminary injunction proceedings, however, the court will assess 'whether there is a serious, non-negligible chance, that the opposition will succeed and, if so, may deny the injunction'.[230]

Length of proceedings Regarding length of proceedings, it is relevant whether the accelerated or regular proceedings are used.[231] Cremers et al. estimate that in the Dutch accelerated proceedings a decision on the merits is usually reached within 10–11 months of filing, while in regular proceedings a decision on the merits is typically issued within 16–20 months of filing, illustrating the much

---

226 J. Brinkhoff, 'The enforcement of patent rights in the Netherlands', *International Review of Intellectual Property and Competition Law (IIC)* 31 (2000), 706, 721.

227 J. Brinkhoff, 'The enforcement of patent rights in the Netherlands', *International Review of Intellectual Property and Competition Law (IIC)* 31 (2000), 706, 721.

228 S 83(3) Patents Act 1995 (The Netherlands). Like France, although EPs with Dutch validations can be challenged via the EPO opposition procedures, there is no comparative opposition procedure for Dutch national patents (NLs) in the Netherlands.

229 O. Swens, 'Patent litigation in the Netherlands and recent developments', presentation delivered in Munich (February, 2011), slides 7, 8 and 9, available at www.vondst-law.com/v2/files/Recent%20developments%20in%20Dutch%20patent%20law%20-%20February%202011.pdf.

230 W. Hoorneman, 'The Netherlands', in N. Beckett and J. Morton (eds), *CMS International Patent Litigation Guide* (CMS, 2013), 61–6, 65.

231 W. Hoorneman, 'The Netherlands', in N. Beckett and J. Morton (eds), *CMS International Patent Litigation Guide* (CMS, 2013), 61–6, 61–2.

greater pace of the accelerated process.[232] The reason for the greater speed of the accelerated proceedings is straightforward: no filings after the initial exchanges of writs/statements/defences by the parties are allowed. By contrast, no such restrictions apply in the context of the regular proceedings – in fact, as noted above, in regular proceedings an interim order may be issued by the court, requiring the parties to appear to, for example, provide additional information, make oral case pleadings, discuss settlement possibilities, or for other case management purposes.[233]

The award of costs in the Netherlands

For accelerated proceedings on the merits, costs can range from €40,000 to €150,000 per side, while for normal proceedings the costs typically range from €50,000 to €250,000 per side (and potentially can go up to as much as €400,000–600,000 per side if the case is a complex and large-scale one).[234] The average cost of a patent case in the Netherlands is between €60,000 and €200,000 per side, with the majority of the costs accruing as a result of private legal fees.[235]

Like the other European jurisdictions examined earlier, in the Netherlands costs are usually shifted to the loser. Notably, prior to 2007 – when the EU Enforcement Directive was brought into Dutch law – the Dutch courts typically only awarded a small amount of the accrued costs to the winning side.[236] Since 2007, however, the

---

232 O. Swens, 'Patent litigation in the Netherlands and recent developments', presentation delivered in Munich (February, 2011), slides 8 and 9, available at www.vondst-law.com/v2/files/Recent%20developments%20in%20Dutch%20patent%20law%20-%20February%202011.pdf.

233 W. Hoorneman, 'The Netherlands', in N. Beckett and J. Morton (eds), *CMS International Patent Litigation Guide* (CMS, 2013), 61–6, 61–2.

234 W. Hoorneman, 'The Netherlands', in N. Beckett and J. Morton (eds), *CMS International Patent Litigation Guide* (CMS, 2013), 61–6, 61–2. See also G. Corcoran, 'Review of Dutch patents case law', *CIPA Journal* (July 2012), 41, available at www.cipa.org.uk/pages/Dutch-Patents-Case-Law-2012.

235 D. Harhoff, 'Economic cost-benefit analysis of a unified and integrated European patent litigation system', *EU Final Report Tender No. MARKT/2008/06/D* (2009), 1, 31, available at http://ec.europa.eu/internal_market/indprop/docs/patent/studies/litigation_system_en.pdfHarhoff.

236 J. Brinkhoff, 'The enforcement of patent rights in the Netherlands', *International Review of Intellectual Property and Competition Law (IIC)* 31 (2000), 706, 721.

Dutch courts have been willing to award a much higher proportion of costs to the winner.[237] As Hoorneman states: 'The successful party can recover all reasonable and proportionate legal costs (including legal fees and fees of certain experts) and other expenses incurred, but a detailed specification of costs must be provided to the court in good time.'[238]

Exploring the empirical data on patent litigation in the Netherlands

The 2013 Cremers et al. study used data collected for cases filed in 2000–2008 at The Hague. The data were collected by Darts-IP. The data show a total of 326 patent cases at The Hague for this period. The Netherlands has a high rate of infringement – 36% of cases filed as infringement actions resulted in a judgment of infringement.[239] This percentage is even higher than the rate of infringement judgments in Germany (22%), though of course it must be recalled that Germany features vastly more patent cases than the Netherlands. The Cremers data also show that there is a very low rate of settlement of cases in the Netherlands.[240]

In a 2014 paper, Van Zeebroeck and Graham utilized patent litigation data, also gathered from Darts-IP, to examine European patent litigation.[241] In their study, Van Zeebroeck and Graham note the existence of significant differences with respect to the amount

---

[237] K. Cremers, M. Ernicke, D. Harhoff, C. Helmers, G. Licht, L. McDonagh, et al. 'Patent litigation in Europe', *ZEW Discussion Paper* No. 13-07 (2013), 1, 29, referring to § 1019h Rv and *Danisco A/S v Novozymes A/S*, Court of Appeal (The Hague), 26 February 2013, Case no. 200.094.921/01, Dutch version available at www.eplawpatentblog.com/eplaw/2013/03/nl-danisco-v-novozymes-litigation-costs-post-bericap.html.

[238] W. Hoorneman, 'The Netherlands', in N. Beckett and J. Morton (eds), *CMS International Patent Litigation Guide* (CMS, 2013), 61–6, 61–2.

[239] K. Cremers, M. Ernicke, D. Harhoff, C. Helmers, G. Licht, L. McDonagh, et al. 'Patent litigation in Europe', *ZEW Discussion Paper* No. 13-07 (2013), 1, 47.

[240] K. Cremers, M. Ernicke, D. Harhoff, C. Helmers, G. Licht, L. McDonagh, et al. 'Patent litigation in Europe', *ZEW Discussion Paper* No. 13-07 (2013), 1, 47.

[241] N. Van Zeebroeck and S. Graham, 'Comparing patent litigation across Europe: a first look', *Stanford Technology Law Review* 17 (2014), 655, 655–708.

of cases that actually reach a final decision, rather than a settlement, in patent litigation proceedings across jurisdictions. One key point they make about the Netherlands is that there is a much larger relative frequency of final judicial decisions in the Netherlands when compared to the UK, Germany and France, where settlements are more commonplace.[242]

MARKING THE DIFFERENCES BETWEEN THE FOUR JURISDICTIONS: LOOKING AHEAD TO THE UPC

From the analysis undertaken in this chapter, it is clear that there are both substantive and procedural differences between the patent litigation systems of the UK (England and Wales), Germany, France and the Netherlands. These differences are important for assessing the impact the UPC may have on European patent litigation over the coming chapters.

Disclosure and Evidence Gathering

One of the major procedural variances between jurisdictions concerns disclosure and evidence gathering. In the UK, at the PHC, there is very wide disclosure, as well as the use of experiments and expert evidence. In Germany and the Netherlands, disclosure is much more limited. In France, the *saisie* proceedings allow patentees to gather evidence on alleged infringements, even before a full case filing has been initiated.

Judicial Expertise

Regarding the judges, in the UK, Germany and the Netherlands, judges tend to be patent experts. Only in France do judges not tend to be patent experts.

---

242 N. Van Zeebroeck and S. Graham, 'Comparing patent litigation across Europe: a first look', *Stanford Technology Law Review* 17 (2014), 655, 655–708.

Forum Shopping

In the UK (England and Wales), depending on the size and value of the claim, the filing will typically be either at the IPEC or the PHC; in France, patent cases must be taken at the TGI in Paris; and in the Netherlands, first-instance actions must be filed at the patent chamber of the district court in The Hague. Uniquely among the four jurisdictions, litigants in Germany can engage in forum shopping, i.e. they may choose among several regional courts (LG) where to file an infringement claim – for example, Düsseldorf, Mannheim or Munich.

Bifurcation

German bifurcation marks a key variation between the four legal systems (such a system does not exist in the UK, France or the Netherlands). Examining the German experience of bifurcation in detail is of particular importance with respect to the analysis of the UPC undertaken in later chapters because the UPC will feature an option for bifurcation.

One advantage of bifurcation is that from the patentee perspective it can lead to swift and efficient enforcement of a patent at the LG. Another advantage is that the BPatG can train and deploy technical judges who accumulate a large amount of expertise regarding assessing patent validity, something that facilitates coherent claim construction and potentially increases legal certainty regarding the validity of patents.[243]

However, there is one major downside for parties accused of infringement – under the bifurcated system, one of the LG in Germany may grant an injunction to a patentee against a potential infringer with respect to a patent that is later found to be invalid by the EPO or the BPatG. This is the dreaded 'invalid but infringed' scenario investigated by Cremers and colleagues, who state that in the context of infringement cases that involve a parallel revocation claim, in at least 12.3% of all such cases the patents are held to be

---

[243] K. Cremers, F. Gaessler, D. Harhoff and C. Helmers, 'Invalid but infringed? An analysis of Germany's bifurcated patent litigation system', *Max Planck Institute for Innovation & Competition Research Paper* No. 14-14 (2014), 1, 1–3.

infringed at first instance, yet later held invalid, or partially invalid, by the annulment court.[244]

Another potential problem with bifurcation is consistency of patent assessment. Cremers et al. note that in Germany the LG – in infringement cases – and the BPatG – in validity actions – construct the patent's claims independently from one another, something which can result in inconsistent claim constructions. For instance, in infringement cases patent claims may be interpreted broadly, but in validity actions claims tend to be interpreted as narrowly as possible. Cremers et al. state that in Germany this 'creates the problem that an infringement court might issue an injunction against a defendant on the basis of a broad claim construction which would inevitably lead to the invalidation in view of a certain piece of prior art'.[245] Yet, at the BPatG, the patentee typically argues for a narrow interpretation of the patent, which could lead to the patent being upheld.[246] This issue does not, of course, arise when validity and infringement are assessed at the same time by the same court, as happens in the UK, France and the Netherlands.

Cost is another issue of concern. Cremers et al. suggest that within a bifurcated system it may be expensive to make an invalidity counterclaim to an infringement claim, as this must be filed and argued within a separate court system to the infringement claim, further noting that this has the potential to discourage smaller-sized companies with fewer resources from taking such claims.[247] In other words, in a bifurcated system the additional costs involved in maintaining a separate validity challenge to the

---

[244] K. Cremers, F. Gaessler, D. Harhoff and C. Helmers, 'Invalid but infringed? An analysis of Germany's bifurcated patent litigation system', *Max Planck Institute for Innovation & Competition Research Paper* No. 14-14 (2014), 1, 23.

[245] K. Cremers, M. Ernicke, D. Harhoff, C. Helmers, G. Licht, L. McDonagh et al. 'Patent litigation in Europe', *ZEW Discussion Paper* No. 13-07 (2013), 1, 30, noting that a patent claim must be novel 'over the whole breadth of the scope of protection'.

[246] K. Cremers, M. Ernicke, D. Harhoff, C. Helmers, G. Licht, L. McDonagh et al. 'Patent litigation in Europe', *ZEW Discussion Paper* No. 13-07 (2013), 1, 30.

[247] See generally K. Cremers, M. Ernicke, D. Harhoff, C. Helmers, G. Licht, L. McDonagh, et al. 'Patent litigation in Europe', *ZEW Discussion Paper* No. 13-07 (2013), 1.

patent may lead alleged infringers to refrain from taking validity actions. This may help to speed up the enforcement system, but it might also lead to cases of injustice (if an alleged infringer is put off challenging the patent's validity due to cost fears).

Length of Oral Hearing

Notably, the UK features the most lengthy oral hearings, featuring the use of expert evidence and cross-examination, as well as the use of experiment-based evidence. In both Germany and the Netherlands, a paper-based system is used, featuring short oral hearings where 'the courts rely largely on their own technical experience gained in the many patent cases they have handled'.[248] In France, oral hearings are also relatively short when compared to the UK.

Length of Overall Proceedings

Furthermore, given the aim of the UPC to produce a speedier litigation system, it is worth taking into account the overall speed of the current system. Cremers et al. state that the median durations for infringement cases are 9 months in Germany, 10 months in the Netherlands, 11 months in the UK and 20 months in France.[249] Looking ahead to the UPC, it is worth noting that at present the differences in the lag between the filing of a claim and the corresponding judgment provide incentives for the strategic filing of patent actions in faster jurisdictions. For instance, patentees might want to file a case in the speediest jurisdiction – Germany – and then use the threat of an enforceable injunction to obtain a favourable settlement for ongoing litigation in other jurisdictions.

Regarding invalidity, claims for revocation of a patent are decided fastest in the UK (within less than a year), but take considerably longer in Germany (on average, 22 months). Interestingly, Cremers et al. demonstrate that focusing on a single issue does not appear to have any substantial effect on the median

---

[248] Hoffmann-Eitle, *The EU Patents Package Handbook: A Practioner's Guide* (Munich: Hoffmann-Eitle, 2014), 33.

[249] K. Cremers, M. Ernicke, D. Harhoff, C. Helmers, G. Licht, L. McDonagh, et al. 'Patent litigation in Europe', *ZEW Discussion Paper* No. 13-07 (2013), 1, 46.

duration of a case at the PHC; in other words, pure infringement cases in the UK take around the same time as cases involving both infringement and validity.[250] By contrast, in Germany the overall length of proceedings depends to some extent on whether solely an infringement case is filed at the LG or whether the validity of a patent is subsequently challenged at the BPatG. The reasons for this are as follows: (i) the validity action is typically filed several months after the infringement action has been initiated; and (ii) the first-instance validity judgment is commonly handed down at the BPatG with a substantial lag relative to the first-instance infringement judgment at the LG. Cremers et al. state that the total length of an infringement case in Germany, if the alleged infringer challenges validity at the BPatG, takes on average 24 months – far longer than a standalone infringement action (9 months).[251] Thus, with respect to Germany, while bifurcation has the advantage that it allows the infringement courts to focus on a single issue, and thus decide the infringement claim more quickly, the disadvantage is the considerable delay that can arise when both infringement and validity are at issue. The lengthiness of the process provides strong incentives to parties to settle the invalidity challenge out of court (even where there is a strong claim that the patent is invalid).

Regarding the UPC, given the availability of bifurcation it is possible that similar incentives to settle invalidity challenges, even where the alleged infringer thinks the patent is invalid, could emerge within the UPC system. Yet, as explored in detail in Chapter 3, the limits that have been imposed on case length at the UPC, coupled with the crucial fact that bifurcation will be optional at the UPC – not mandatory as it is in Germany – mean that incentives to settle (where there is a strong claim that the patent is invalid) are unlikely to develop into a serious issue at the UPC.

---

[250] K. Cremers, M. Ernicke, D. Harhoff, C. Helmers, G. Licht, L. McDonagh, et al. 'Patent litigation in Europe', *ZEW Discussion Paper* No. 13-07 (2013), 1, 46–7.

[251] The fact that invalidity claims can only be filed at the BPatG after an opposition at the German Patent and Trademark Office (DPMA) or the EPO (or after the period for an opposition has expired) may further delay the decision on validity.

Case Volumes

The volume of court cases differs substantially across jurisdictions. Although Cremers et al. note that comparing case counts across jurisdictions is difficult – given the varying sizes of the economies of the four jurisdictions and the distinction between a bifurcated and a non-bifurcated system – it is clear that a substantially larger number of patent cases is heard by the LG in Germany than the other jurisdictions combined.[252] Reasons for Germany's patent litigation dominance include the fact that (i) obtaining an injunction against a potential infringer in Germany can severely affect that competitor's ability to market products successfully in the EU; and (ii) the German courts have a patentee-friendly reputation, i.e. Germany is seen as the 'go to' jurisdiction to obtain an injunction against an infringer on a speedy, cost-effective basis.

The comparative lack of standalone invalidity challenges in France marks a clear distinction from the German system, where validity actions must be filed separately. Furthermore, in the UK initial validity challenges are common due in large part to the doctrine of 'clearing the way'. However, there is no French equivalent of this doctrine; in fact, with regard to France there is 'no specific advantage to a possible infringer taking the initiative of starting revocation proceedings'.[253]

It is further notable that there are large variances in volumes of cases even within Germany – Cremers et al. show that the LG in Düsseldorf hears more than seven times as many cases as the

---

[252] However, as discussed above, data for case filings in the UK in 2007–2013 point to a substantial increase in the caseload in the UK – see C. Helmers, Y. Lefouili and L. McDonagh, 'Examining Patent Cases at the Patents Court and Intellectual Property Enterprise Court 2007–2013', *A Report Commissioned by the UK Intellectual Property Office* (March 2015), 1, available at www.gov.uk/government/publications/examining-patent-cases-at-the-patents-court-and-ipec-2007-2013.

[253] T. Bouvet, 'France', in M.C. Elmer and C.G. Gramaenopoulos (eds), *Global Patent Litigation* (Arlington, VA: Bloomberg BNA, 2014), 546–89, 589.

regional court in Munich.[254] With regard to the UPC, the dominance of Germany indicates that for the UPC to become the key venue for patent litigation in Europe, it will have to replace Germany as the primary jurisdiction of choice for patent litigants. Furthermore, the existence of forum shopping within Germany, with Düsseldorf the most popular venue, indicates that forum shopping may occur within the UPC. Both of these aspects of European patent litigation are discussed further in the context of the interview data in Chapter 4.

Judicial Outcomes

There are significant differences across jurisdictions with regard to the outcomes of cases that were decided by a first-instance judgment on the merits of the case. In the UK, Cremers et al. note that infringement is the most common initial claim at the PHC, but revocation claims are much more common than in the other three jurisdictions.[255] Revocation is the most common outcome of a judgment at the PHC, even when the original claim is for infringement. Not for nothing has the UK been traditionally viewed as an 'anti-patent' jurisdiction.[256] Yet, as noted earlier, the rate of revocation has begun to decline slightly in recent years, and this may lead to the UK being seen as a less 'anti-patent' jurisdiction in the years to come.

In Germany, Cremers et al. note that infringement is by far the most common initial claim, and a relatively low number of patents are challenged via the separate revocation proceeding – only in around a third of infringement cases does the defendant file a claim for revocation with the BPatG, and only a very low share of patents

---

[254] K. Cremers, M. Ernicke, D. Harhoff, C. Helmers, G. Licht, L. McDonagh, et al. 'Patent litigation in Europe', *ZEW Discussion Paper* No. 13-07 (2013), 1, 1–5.

[255] K. Cremers, M. Ernicke, D. Harhoff, C. Helmers, G. Licht, L. McDonagh, et al. 'Patent litigation in Europe', *ZEW Discussion Paper* No. 13-07 (2013), 1, 1–5.

[256] G. Moss, M. Jones and R. Lundie-Smith, 'Just how "anti-patent" are the UK courts?', *Journal of Intellectual Property Law & Practice* 5 (2010), 148, 148–50.

involved in an infringement suit are actually revoked.[257] Consequently, Germany is viewed as a patent-friendly jurisdiction. In both France and the Netherlands, infringement is by far the most common initial claim and the most common outcome of a judgment. As a result, like Germany, France and the Netherlands are viewed as patent-friendly jurisdictions.[258]

Types of Patents Litigated in the Various Jurisdictions

It is worth taking account of the concentration of cases involving certain technologies in a given jurisdiction. On this, it is clear that cases concerning patents that fall into the areas of machinery and engineering are litigated mostly in Germany; by contrast, the UK courts system deals, proportionately, with the greater share of complex pharmaceutical and chemical patent cases in Europe; while the Paris court is dominated by electronic patents.[259] Further to this, a larger share of EPs is litigated in the UK and the Netherlands than in Germany and France, where national patents are litigated with more frequency than in the UK and the Netherlands.[260]

Injunctions

In Germany, preliminary proceedings are rare due to the speed of the normal infringement proceedings, whereby injunctions can be granted by the LG based solely on an assessment of the infringement claims (with no assessment of validity). For this reason, Germany is the most popular destination for litigants seeking to

---

[257] K. Cremers, M. Ernicke, D. Harhoff, C. Helmers, G. Licht, L. McDonagh, et al. 'Patent litigation in Europe', *ZEW Discussion Paper* No. 13-07 (2013), 1, 47.

[258] T. Bouvet, 'France', in M.C. Elmer and C.G. Gramaenopoulos (eds), *Global Patent Litigation* (Arlington, VA: Bloomberg BNA, 2014), 546–89, 589.

[259] K. Cremers, M. Ernicke, D. Harhoff, C. Helmers, G. Licht, L. McDonagh, et al. 'Patent litigation in Europe', *ZEW Discussion Paper* No. 13-07 (2013), 1, 60.

[260] K. Cremers, M. Ernicke, D. Harhoff, C. Helmers, G. Licht, L. McDonagh, et al. 'Patent litigation in Europe', *ZEW Discussion Paper* No. 13-07 (2013), 1, 5.

obtain injunctions against alleged infringers. Moreover, due to bifurcation, if the LG does not stay the infringement proceedings pending a separate validity action, an injunction may be granted a year or more before the question of validity is considered by the BPatG.

As noted above, in France, preliminary *saisie* proceedings for search and seizure of an alleged infringer's goods are common at the outset of infringement actions. Nevertheless, preliminary injunctions themselves tend to be rarely issued in France. France also takes the longest of the four jurisdictions to reach a first-instance decision on infringement, which has a knock-on effect on enforcement via an injunction.

In the UK (England and Wales) at the IPEC and the PHC, preliminary injunctions are rare, something that might be explained in part by the practice of 'clearing the way' discussed earlier, whereby a competitor, in order to avoid a possible later final injunction, may attempt to 'clear the way' before, for example, releasing a product which could infringe another company's patent.[261] Cross-border injunctions are possible in the UK, but only where patent validity is not in doubt. In the Netherlands, a preliminary injunction to halt infringing activities may be obtained within two weeks of the filing of a case. As noted earlier, a cross-border injunction is only available with respect to preliminary proceedings.

Settlements

Germany features by far the highest proportion of settlements of the four jurisdictions. Cremers et al. show that 46.1% of cases filed as infringement actions in Germany end with a settlement, whereas this is true for only around 33% of the equivalent cases in the UK

[261] In *SmithKline Beecham & Anor v Apotex Europe Ltd & Ors* [2002] EWHC 2556; [2003] EWCA (Civ) 137 Jacob J (as he then was) noted at para. 68: 'Where litigation is bound to ensue if the defendant introduces his product he can avoid all the problems of an interim injunction if he clears the way first. That is what the procedures for revocation and declaration of non-infringement are for.'

and 16.3% in France.[262] Cremers and colleagues state that in Germany there are relatively large incentives for the claimant and defendant to settle the revocation proceedings before a full hearing at the BPatG.[263]

Parallel Litigation across EU Jurisdictions

At present, there is (unnecessary) duplication of litigation concerning the same patent across the four jurisdictions. Cremers et al. state that most EPs that are litigated in a given jurisdiction have also been validated in all four jurisdictions, though fewer are validated in the Netherlands than in the other three.[264] They also note that a relatively high proportion (26%) of cases litigated in the UK are also litigated in one or more of the other jurisdictions; and that for the Netherlands, the equivalent figure is 15%, and for France it is 6%. Meanwhile, only 2% of German cases are litigated in one or more of the other jurisdictions. Overall, looking at pan-jurisdictional litigation, Cremers et al. observe that 'only 8.4% of all litigated EPs are subject to litigation in more than one country', but these patents are likely to be 'important, complex and valuable'.[265]

On this point, Mejer and van Pottelsberghe suggest that there are substantial differences with respect to litigation outcomes concerning the same patent across different European jurisdictions.[266] This is borne out by the Cremers study, something which adds to the

---

[262] See generally K. Cremers, M. Ernicke, D. Harhoff, C. Helmers, G. Licht, L. McDonagh, et al. 'Patent litigation in Europe', *ZEW Discussion Paper* No. 13-07 (2013), 1, 47.

[263] K. Cremers, F. Gaessler, D. Harhoff and C. Helmers, 'Invalid but infringed? An analysis of Germany's bifurcated patent litigation system', *Max Planck Institute for Innovation & Competition Research Paper* No. 14-14 (2014), 1, 23.

[264] K. Cremers, M. Ernicke, D. Harhoff, C. Helmers, G. Licht, L. McDonagh, et al. 'Patent litigation in Europe', *ZEW Discussion Paper* No. 13-07 (2013), 1, 60.

[265] K. Cremers, M. Ernicke, D. Harhoff, C. Helmers, G. Licht, L. McDonagh, et al. 'Patent litigation in Europe', *ZEW Discussion Paper* No. 13-07 (2013), 1, 5.

[266] E. Mejer and B. van Pottelsberghe, 'Economic incongruities in the European patent system', *European Journal of Law and Economics* 34 (2012), 215, 215–17.

argument that parallel litigation creates unnecessary complexities and uncertainties.[267]

This view echoes a point made by Harhoff in a 2009 paper exploring the costs and benefits of the current fragmented patent litigation system in Europe – arguing that the present litigation system leads to costly duplication of cases across Europe.[268] According to Harhoff, one major benefit of the enactment of a new, low-cost, unified patent litigation system would be better access to patent enforcement for companies that cannot currently afford the costs of undertaking patent litigation in multiple jurisdictions.[269]

Court Fees and Litigation Costs

Regarding fees, the most useful comparison can be made between the UK and Germany. As stated earlier, in the UK court fees have traditionally followed a 'fixed' fee model dependent on the number of applications/hearings, while the Germans use a 'value-based' fee system.[270] German court fees often exceed €10,000, and can even sometimes fall into the range of €100,000–200,000 in high-value cases.[271] Moreover, the UK has recently switched to a value-based model of 5% of case value up to a ceiling of £10,000 for cases valued at £200,000 or more. The existence of this (prior) divergence between the two systems is of interest given the fact that the UPC

---

[267] K. Cremers, M. Ernicke, D. Harhoff, C. Helmers, G. Licht, L. McDonagh, et al. 'Patent litigation in Europe', *ZEW Discussion Paper* No. 13-07 (2013), 1, 60.

[268] D. Harhoff, 'Economic cost-benefit analysis of a unified and integrated European patent litigation system', *EU Final Report Tender No. MARKT/2008/06/D* (2009), available at http://ec.europa.eu/internal_market/indprop/docs/patent/studies/litigation_system_en.pdf.

[269] See generally K. Cremers, M. Ernicke, D. Harhoff, C. Helmers, G. Licht, L. McDonagh, et al. 'Patent litigation in Europe', *ZEW Discussion Paper* No. 13-07 (2013), 1.

[270] S. Cohen, 'Selected IP jurisdictions: Germany' (2007), 1, 4, available at www.taylorwessing.com/uploads/tx_siruplawyermanagement/Handbook_of_European_IP_-_Simon_Cohen.en.pdf. The chapter is also published in A. Jolly and J. Philpott (eds), *The Handbook of European Intellectual Property Management* (London: Kogan Page, 2007).

[271] Bardehle Pagenberg, *Patent Infringement Proceedings* (2013), 1, 12, available at www.bardehle.com/fileadmin/contentdocuments/broschures/Patent_Infringement_Proceedings.pdf.

will feature a mixture of fixed and value-based fees. Comparisons between the two systems with respect to the UPC are made in the context of the empirical research in Chapter 4.

With respect to overall costs, the UK is by far the most costly jurisdiction to litigate in, with costs typically reaching £1–1.5 million per side (potentially reaching £2–3 million per side in complex cases).[272] In Germany, the private legal costs of patent litigation usually range between €40,000 and €100,000 per side, though they can go higher in lengthy and complex proceedings.[273] In France, one estimate states that the private costs range from €50,000 to around €200,000 per side,[274] figures backed up by another estimate giving a costs range of around €40,000–150,000 per party (though the costs can potentially be higher in technical cases).[275] In the Netherlands, there is an average range of around €60,000–200,000 per side, but costs can go significantly higher than this, especially in non-accelerated proceedings.[276]

Reducing the costs of litigation is one of the key aims of the UPC. One reason for this is to allow a greater spread of companies to enforce their patents. Rodwell et al. state that at present SMEs often do not file actions even where infringement has taken place as they fear the costs of litigation.[277]

---

[272] L. McDonagh and C. Helmers, 'Patent litigation in England and Wales and the issue-based approach to costs', *Civil Justice Quarterly* 32 (2013), 369, 384.

[273] G. Schoenen, M. Deck and M. Eck, 'Germany', in N. Beckett and J. Morton (eds), *CMS International Patent Litigation Guide* (CMS, 2013), 45–50, 47; and Bardehle Pagenberg, *Patent Infringement Proceedings* (2013), 1, 12, available at www.bardehle.com/fileadmin/contentdocuments/broschures/Patent_Infringement_Proceedings.pdf.

[274] B. van Pottelsberghe, *Lost Property: The European patent system and why it doesn't work* (Brussels: Bruegel Blueprint Series, 2009), available at http://bruegel.org/wp-content/uploads/imported/publications/patents_BP_050609.pdf.

[275] J.-G. Moninand and S. Vilfeu, 'France', in N. Beckett and J. Morton (eds), *CMS International Patent Litigation Guide* (CMS, 2013), 39–44, 41.

[276] D. Harhoff, 'Economic cost-benefit analysis of a unified and integrated European patent litigation system', *EU Final Report Tender No. MARKT/2008/06/D* (2009), 31, available at http://ec.europa.eu/internal_market/indprop/docs/patent/studies/litigation_system_en.pdfHarhoff.

[277] S. Rodwell, P. van Eeckhout, A. Reid and J. Walendowski, *Effects of counterfeiting on EU SMEs and a review of various public and private IPR*

SUMMARY: WHAT ARE THE KEY CHALLENGES THE UPC NEEDS TO ADDRESS?

As explored over the course of this chapter, the current fragmented system brings up a number of challenges. With respect to the existence of parallel litigation (and divergent case outcomes) across multiple European jurisdictions, can the UPC's centralized procedures harmonize the legal procedures concerning patent enforcement across the various European patent territories, and at the same time offer greater procedural and legal clarity? Can the UPC also increase the speed of decision making, removing the time-lag between jurisdictions that currently exists? Will the UPC help to lower the costs of patent litigation, something particularly important to SMEs? All of these key questions are considered in Chapters 3 and 4, which explore the UPC and UP reforms and, in particular, address the issues most relevant to users of the system in the legal and business communities.

---

enforcement initiatives and resources, Final Report to the Enterprise and Industry Directorate-General Directorate B1 – Development of industrial policy (2007) (Framework Contract B3/ENTR/04/093-FC-Lot 6).

3. Analysing the reforms: the Unified Patent Court (UPC) and the European Patent with Unitary Effect (UP)

THE EU PATENT REFORM PACKAGE

The previous chapter established the extent of the fragmentation of the current patent litigation system in Europe, including the issues of inconsistency of decision making across jurisdictions and the costs of parallel litigation.[1] It almost goes without saying that 'a more efficient and less expensive litigation system is desirable'.[2] For this reason, unifying the patent system has for decades been a goal of the European Union;[3] yet progress towards this goal was slow until finally, on 19 February 2013, 25 members of the European Union signed an intergovernmental agreement ('the Agreement') to create a Unified Patent Court (UPC) – a new specialist patents court common to participating states.[4] The UPC

[1] K. Cremers, M. Ernicke, D. Harhoff, C. Helmers, G. Licht, L. McDonagh, et al. 'Patent litigation in Europe', *ZEW Discussion Paper* No. 13-07 (2013), 1, 1–5.

[2] EPO Economic and Scientific Advisory Board, *Recommendations for Improving the Patent System* (2012), 1, 4, available at http://documents.epo.org/projects/babylon/eponot.nsf/0/835DA6DA218CB760C1257B2C004E809E/$FILE/ESAB_statement_en.pdf4=.

[3] J. Pila, 'The European patent: an old and vexing problem', *International & Comparative Law Quarterly* 62 (2013), 917, 917–21. See also B. van Pottelsberghe, *Lost Property: The European patent system and why it doesn't work* (Bruegel Blueprint Series, 2009), available at http://bruegel.org/wp-content/uploads/imported/publications/patents_BP_050609.pdf.

[4] Agreement on a Unified Patent Court (UPC Agreement), OJ C 175/01 (2013), available at http://eur-lex.europa.eu/LexUriServ/LexUriServ.do?uri=OJ:C:2013:175:0001:0040:EN:PDF.

Agreement is part of a package of measures designed to establish and enforce unitary patent protection within Europe.[5] The aim of the establishment of the UPC is to offer a more streamlined, less costly and easy-to-use system with the ambition of unifying the European patent system as much as possible.[6]

In addition to the UPC Agreement, the new reform measures also include two EU regulations which establish the European Patent with Unitary effect – a.k.a. the Unitary Patent (UP) – and the associated translation arrangements.[7] As explored over the course of this chapter, the application and grant process for the UP will be the same as for the regular European Patents (EPs) – the option for unitary protection across participating EU member states comes post-grant.

Overall, while the package is not without its critics, the reforms provide individuals and businesses with the opportunity to protect their inventions across participating states under a single patent (UP), and to have disputes (on infringement or validity) settled under a court system common to the participating states (the

---

[5] Regulation (EU) No. 1257/2012 of the European Parliament and of the Council of 17 December 2012 implementing enhanced cooperation in the area of the creation of unitary patent protection (UP Regulation), OJ L 361/1 (2012) and Council Regulation (EU) No. 1260/2012 of 17 December 2012 implementing enhanced cooperation in the area of the creation of unitary patent protection with regard to the applicable translation arrangements (Translation Regulation), OJ L 361/89 (2012) – both documents available at: http://ec.europa.eu/internal_market/indprop/patent/documents/index_en.htm. For a further explanation of the changes, see the EPO website – www.epo.org/law-practice/unitary.html. See also R. Romandini and A. Klicznik, 'The territoriality principle and transnational use of patented inventions: the wider reach of a unitary patent and the role of the CJEU', *International Review of Intellectual Property and Competition Law* 44 (2013), 524; A. West, S. Kusumakar and T. Powell, 'Unitary patents and the Unified Patent Court', *Computer and Telecommunications Law Review* 19 (2013), 105; and M. Brandi-Dohrn, 'Some critical observations on competence and procedure of the Unified Patent Court', *International Review of Intellectual Property and Competition Law* 43 (2012), 372.

[6] EPO Economic and Scientific Advisory Board, *Recommendations for Improving the Patent system* (2012), 1, 1–5, available at http://documents.epo.org/projects/babylon/eponot.nsf/0/835DA6DA218CB760C1257B2C004E809E/$FILE/ESAB_statement_en.pdf.

[7] UP Regulation and Translation Regulation.

UPC).[8] Importantly, the UPC will not only hear disputes regarding the validity and infringement of the new UPs but also existing and prospective EPs (subject to the transition period discussed later on in this chapter).[9]

The Legal Sources of the Unified Patent Court and the UPC

Legally, the existence of the Unitary Patent is enabled by a long-standing option under the EPC, allowing the validation of patents on a supra-national basis.[10] Specifically, the UP and UPC are governed by the following sources of law:

- Regulation 1257/2012, passed on 17 December 2012, creating the European patent with unitary effect (UP).
- Regulation 1260/2012, passed on 17 December 2012, governing the translations arrangements for the UP.
- The International Treaty of the Unified Patent Court, signed on 19 February 2013. This international treaty creates and governs the operations of the UPC, which has the same legal personality as a national court, in accordance with Article 1(2) of the UPC Agreement.[11]

The EU regulations were passed into law via the system of enhanced cooperation introduced by the Lisbon Treaty.[12] Enhanced cooperation allows a sub-group of EU MS to proceed with a new form of regulation without every EU MS being subject to it, though

---

[8] R. Hilty, 'The unitary patent package: twelve reasons for concern', *CIPA Journal* 10 (2012), 553.

[9] T. Cook, 'The progress to date on the Unitary European Patent and the Unified Patent Court for Europe', *Journal of Intellectual Property Rights* 18 (2013), 584.

[10] Articles 2 and 142 EPC.

[11] D.P. Sant and C. de Coster, 'The unitary patent and the European Patent Court', *Bioscience Law Review* 12 (2012), 27, available at www.taylorwessing.com/fileadmin/files/docs/unitary_patent_court.pdf.

[12] Treaty of Lisbon amending the Treaty on European Union and the Treaty establishing the European Community, signed at Lisbon, 13 December 2007, entered into force on 1 December 2009, OJ C 306 (2007) – http://eur-lex.europa.eu/legal-content/EN/TXT/?uri=celex:12007L/TXT.

any EU MS that chooses not to participate at the initiation of the new system is free to join at a later date.

The EU regulations are technically already in force.[13] However, in reality they will apply only once the UPC Agreement is ratified by the requisite 3 + 10 countries, i.e. Germany, France and the UK + 10 more Signatory States. As of January 2016, this ratification has yet to take place. With the expectation that ratification will be completed in late 2016, what is required at this stage – and what the remainder of this chapter provides – is a thorough assessment of the UPC and the UP.

THE UNIFIED PATENT COURT

Overview

The Unified Patent Court (UPC) is a new specialist patents court common to participating EU Signatory States (SS) to the UPC Agreement (all EU MS except Spain, Poland and Croatia).[14] The UPC offers a more streamlined, centralized system of patent adjudication than the current fragmented system, giving patent litigants the opportunity of resolving disputes (concerning infringement or validity) via the centralized procedures of the UPC.

Structurally, the UPC will be comprised of a Court of First Instance (CFI), consisting of central divisions and local and/or regional divisions, hosted by Signatory States or groups of Signatory States, and a Court of Appeal in Luxembourg. The seat of the primary central division will be in Paris, with specialist technology divisions to be set up in London and Munich according to subject matter: the London central division will deal with the chemical and pharmaceutical fields, including life sciences; while the Munich central division will deal with engineering patents. In addition to validity challenges, the central divisions will also deal with infringement actions in their respective technological fields where these are transferred from the UPC local or regional divisions; and

[13] Article 18(2) UP Regulation and Article 7(2) Translation Regulation.

[14] UPC Agreement. See also joined cases C-274/11 and C-295/11, *Spain and Italy v Commission*, Judgment of 16 April 2013, OJ C175/1 (2013), available at http://curia.europa.eu/juris/liste.jsf?num=C-274/11.

they will also hear infringement cases from countries where there is no UPC local or regional division. The UPC will also have new mediation and arbitration facilities in Portugal and Slovenia.

The UPC is intended to be self-financing, generating sufficient revenue to pay for the associated administration costs.[15] In accordance with Article 36(3) of the UPC Agreement, the UPC fees will be based on a hybrid system – there will be both a fixed fee and a value-based fee set above a pre-defined ceiling. The precise fee levels were agreed by the Preparatory Committee of the UPC in early 2016 after lengthy negotiations.[16]

International Jurisdiction

With respect to the UPC's international jurisdiction, the Brussels I Regulation, which governs international jurisdiction for EU MS courts, is highly relevant.[17] Moreover, the Regulation has recently been amended to take account of the UPC.[18] The aim of the Brussels I Regulation is to prevent parallel litigation proceedings

[15] Article 36(1) UPC Agreement.

[16] See details of the UPC court fees at http://www.unified-patent-court.org/news/upc-court-fees-and-recoverable-costs.

[17] Regulation No. 1215/2012 of 12 December 2012 on jurisdiction and the recognition and enforcement of judgments in civil and commercial matters (recast) (hereafter known as Brussels I Regulation recast), OJ L 351 (2012) – available at http://eur-lex.europa.eu/LexUriServ/LexUriServ.do?uri=OJ:L:2012:351:0001:0032:en:PDF which recast Council Regulation (EC) No. 44/2001 of 22 December 2000 on jurisdiction and the recognition and enforcement of judgments in civil and commercial matters (Brussels I), OJ L 12 (2001) and the original Brussels Convention on Jurisdiction and the Enforcement of Judgments in Civil and Commercial Matters of 27 September 1968 (Brussels Convention), OJ L 304 (1978). Meanwhile, the Convention of Sept 16 1988 on jurisdiction and the enforcement of judgments in civil and commercial matters (hereinafter 'Lugano Convention'), OJ L 319 (1988) covers non-EU MS such as Iceland, Liechtenstein, Norway and Switzerland, and is also relevant to Denmark, where it preceded the application of the Brussels I Regulation. If a defendant is domiciled within a Brussels I Regulation MS, i.e. the vast majority of EU MS, then its provisions will apply; if however, the defendant is domiciled within a MS of the Lugano Convention – including Denmark – then its provisions apply (Article 54b Lugano Convention and Article 68(2) Brussels I Regulation recast).

[18] Brussels I Regulation recast. See also Article 31 UPC Agreement and the Lugano Convention.

occurring before different EU MS courts; in line with this, the standard rule under the Regulation is that jurisdiction is exercised by the MS in which the defendant is domiciled, as determined by reference to its statute, place of administration or place of business.[19] Nationality is not relevant.

Nevertheless, there are exceptions under the Regulation that allow a defendant to be sued in jurisdictions other than the place of domicile. For instance, in accordance with Article 7(2) of the Brussels I Regulation (as amended), legal action may be taken against a tortious infringer – such as a patent infringer – in the MS where the act of infringement is about to occur, is occurring or has already occurred. In practice, this means that the patentee often has a choice of jurisdiction, i.e. either the place where the infringer is domiciled or the place of infringement. Similarly, in a case where there is more than one infringer, under Article 8(1) of the Brussels I Regulation (as amended), legal action can be taken against all defendants in an MS where one of the defendants is domiciled, so long as the 'claims are so closely connected that it is expedient to hear and determine them together to avoid the risk of irreconcilable judgments resulting from separate proceedings'.[20]

If the infringing party does not have its place of domicile within an EU MS (or a Lugano MS) but is instead located within, for example, the USA or Japan, under Article 6(1) of the Brussels I Regulation recast, the jurisdiction of the legal action does not depend on the terms of the Regulation, but on the national laws of the relevant member state.

The Substantive Patent Law of the UPC

In light of the sources of law discussed above – primarily the UPC Agreement – it is worth taking a closer look at the specific law to be applied by the UPC. Articles 25–30 of the UPC Agreement set forth the conditions for a new substantive patent law which shall apply to 'patents', i.e. UPs and EPs (and related SPCs) that fall within the jurisdiction of the UPC.[21] The new substantive law will

---

[19] Article 4(1) Brussels I Regulation recast.
[20] Article 8(1) Brussels I Regulation recast.
[21] See also Articles 3b and 32(1) UPC Agreement.

also need to be interpreted by national courts in some circumstances, though the precise boundaries of when this will happen have yet to be decided.[22] The reason for this uncertainty is that Articles 25–30 of the UPC Agreement lack the language found in Articles 24 and 56 of the UPC Agreement which limits the impact of these provisions in the context of the UPC. If the Preparatory Committee is correct, the intention behind the UPC Agreement was not to harmonize the substantive patent law of Signatory States, and, consequently, national courts should continue to apply their own national laws to EPs and related SPCs (something that will be of particular importance during the transition period discussed later on in this chapter).[23] This may mean in certain circumstances that activities that would be construed as infringing by the UPC under Articles 25–30 would not be construed in that way by a national court applying its own national laws on infringement.[24] Also of importance are the rules found in Article 8 Regulation 864/2007 concerning the law applicable to non-contractual obligations (Rome II).[25] Under these rules, national law may apply to fill gaps left by the various agreements – EU, UPC Agreement, EPC, etc. – with regard to the traditional EPs (with the national law of the territory where protection is sought applying) and with the UPs (with the national law of the territory where the acts of infringement take

---

[22] National courts will necessarily have a role in determining this – see UPC Preparatory Committee's Interpretative Note on the consequences of the application of Article 83 UPC Agreement, 29 January 2014, available at www.unified-patent-court.org/news/71-interpretative-note-consequences-of-the-application-of-article-83-upca.

[23] UPC Preparatory Committee's Interpretative Note on the consequences of the application of Article 83 UPC Agreement, 29 January 2014, available at www.unified-patent-court.org/news/71-interpretative-note-consequences-of-the-application-of-article-83-upca.

[24] Hoffmann-Eitle, *The EU Patents Package Handbook: A Practioner's Guide* (Munich: Hoffmann-Eitle, 2014), 37. See also B. Schröer, 'Einheitspatentgericht: Überlegungen zum Forum-Shopping im Rahmen der alternativen Zuständigkeit nach Article 83 Abs. 1 EPGÜ', *Gewerblicher Rechtsschutz und Urheberrecht international (GRUR Int.)* 1 (2013), 1102.

[25] Regulation 864/2007 of the European Parliament and of the Council of 11 July 2007 on the law applicable to non-contractual obligations (Rome II), OJ L 199/40 (2007).

place applying).[26] Moreover, there may be further complications if the infringing acts have taken place in a number of different countries.[27]

While some of its elements are not yet settled, it is clear that the new substantive patent law is to be modelled on the Community Patent Convention (a convention which never actually entered into force but which has been influential on much subsequent national patent law within the EU).[28] The new substantive law will be primarily relevant in the context of infringement (direct and indirect) as well as defences to infringement. In addition to the new substantive law, general principles of civil law will also have to be observed.

With respect to the new substantive patent law, the scope of patent protection will be determined by its claims, as envisaged by EPC Article 69. Regarding direct infringement under Article 25 of the UPC Agreement, an issue that the UPC will have to deal with is maintaining consistency across all UPC divisions. Consider one of the key directly infringing acts: 'making'. Although this category of making is an act common to the laws of EPC MS, its interpretation can vary within each jurisdiction. For example, within the UK and German jurisdictions, a current variance exists concerning how to define 'making' in the context of repairs and replacement parts. In both the UK and Germany, the courts look at the 'relation of the replacement part to the inventive idea'; however, inconsistency can nonetheless arise because the German courts additionally look at the question of whether the relevant trade circle would – regardless of patent law – consider the part to be a 'replacement part'.[29] Similarly, with respect to the 'offering' for sale/supply of a patented

---

[26] Hoffmann-Eitle, *The EU Patents Package Handbook: A Practioner's Guide* (Munich: Hoffmann-Eitle, 2014), 112–15.

[27] Hoffmann-Eitle, *The EU Patents Package Handbook: A Practioner's Guide* (Munich: Hoffmann-Eitle, 2014), 115.

[28] Convention for the European patent for the common market (Community Patent Convention) 76/76/EEC, OJ L 17 (1976), available at http://eur-lex.europa.eu/legal-content/EN/TXT/?uri=CELEX:41975A3490.

[29] *Bundesgerichtshof* (BGH) decision of 17 July 2012, as reported by *International Review of Intellectual Property and Competition Law (IIC)* 44 (2013), 351, *Pallet Container II* (X ZR 97/11); also noted by Hoffmann-Eitle, *The EU Patents Package Handbook: A Practioner's Guide* (Munich: Hoffmann-Eitle, 2014), 124.

product under Article 25 of the UPC Agreement, judicial divergences may appear. At present in Germany, for instance, 'offering' is considered to be an infringing act in and of itself – with an offer potentially encompassing a written/oral approach or even an internet advertisement – regardless of when the supply is due to take place;[30] but in the UK an offer is not infringing if it is made clear that the actual supply of the patented product to, for example, the buyer will only take place once the patent has expired and not before.[31] Moreover, there are other potential divergences between the UK and Germany in the context of direct infringement – such as 'using', 'storing' and 'placing on the market'.[32] Similarly, regarding defences – such as invalidity,[33] prior use,[34] research use and the Bolar Exemption,[35] exhaustion[36] and competition law-related defences[37] – it will be vital for national variations in judicial reasoning to be smoothed over by the UPC. Indeed, regarding the 'Bolar Exemption' for clinical trials, it is important to recall that this was framed by an EU Directive which gave EU MS a certain margin to interpret the exemption.[38] As a result, some EU MS interpreted the exemption more broadly than others, expanding it to include not only trials/studies relating to the abbreviated procedure for obtaining marketing authorization for a generic drug, but also trials/studies relating to new and innovative drugs. Under the UPC

---

[30] *Bundesgerichtshof* (BGH) decision of 5 December 2006, as reported by *Gewerblicher Rechtsschutz und Urheberrecht international (GRUR Int.)* (2007), 221, *Simvastatin*; also noted by Hoffmann-Eitle, *The EU Patents Package Handbook: A Practioner's Guide* (Munich: Hoffmann-Eitle, 2014), 125.

[31] *Gerber Garment Technology v Lectra Systems* [1995] RPC 383.

[32] For a full account of these, see Hoffmann-Eitle, *The EU Patents Package Handbook: A Practioner's Guide* (Munich: Hoffmann-Eitle, 2014), 125–6.

[33] Article 32(1) UPC Agreement.

[34] Article 28 UPC Agreement.

[35] Article 28(b) and (d) UPC Agreement.

[36] Article 6 UP Regulation.

[37] Article 15 UP Regulation.

[38] Article 10(6) of Directive 2001/83/EC of 6 November 2001 on the Community code relating to medicinal products for human use (as amended), OJ L 311 (2001) – http://ec.europa.eu/health/files/eudralex/vol-1/dir_2001_83_consol_2012/dir_2001_83_cons_2012_en.pdf.

Agreement, the Bolar Exemption will apply only to generic drugs, resulting in a change to the scope of the law in some MS.[39]

Finally, with respect to UPs as 'objects' of property under national law, they are to be treated as if they were national patents of the territory where unitary protection applies and where the patent applicant had his/her/its principal residence/place of business when the application was filed.[40] If at time of filing the applicant had no principal residence/place of business within the EU, the national law of the EPO, i.e. Germany, will apply. Thus, German law will come to be of importance for determining issues related to UP ownership and transactions where the applicant is a non-EU inventor/company.

The UPC's Relationship with the CJEU

The CJEU is a supra-national court and the final arbiter of all EU law matters.[41] Once up and running, the UPC will be the final arbiter of substantive patent matters such as validity and infringement in the context of UPs, and, where relevant, EPs. The relationship between the two courts is therefore of great significance. In this regard, it is worth recalling that even though the EPC is not an EU treaty – and the EPO is not an EU body – the EU and its Court of Justice (CJEU) have for more than a decade played a prominent role within the European patent system as a result of the EU Biotechnology Directive and the EU provisions regarding Supplementary Protection Certificates (which are discussed in detail later).[42] Nonetheless, the CJEU's role in patenting is quite limited, and it is not foreseen that the CJEU will have an oversight role with

---

[39] Hoffmann-Eitle, *The EU Patents Package Handbook: A Practioner's Guide* (Munich: Hoffmann-Eitle, 2014), 38.

[40] Article 7 UP Regulation.

[41] R. Romandini and A. Klicznik, 'The territoriality principle and transnational use of patented inventions: the wider reach of a unitary patent and the role of the CJEU', *International Review of Intellectual Property and Competition Law* 44 (2013), 524, 524–7.

[42] Directive 98/44/EC of the European Parliament and of the Council of 6 July 1998 on the legal protection of biotechnological inventions, OJ L 213 (1998). For analysis of the conflicts that can arise from the CJEU's role, see G. Gaskell, S. Stares and A. Pottage, 'How Europe's ethical divide looms over biotech law and patents', *Nature Biotechnology* 30 (2012), 392.

respect to the primary matters within the UPC's remit – validity and infringement of EPs and UPs.[43]

However, it is further worth noting that, unlike the CJEU, the UPC has been constructed with the legal status of a national court; and in line with this, under Article 21 of the UPC Agreement a referral can be made by the UPC to the CJEU in much the same way as an EU MS national court would make such a referral.[44] Specifically, a matter may be referred by the UPC to the CJEU where there is an issue covered by EU law, such as in the following circumstances:

- where there is an issue of EU patent law governed by Directive 98/44/EC (biotechnological inventions)[45] and/or Regulation 2100/94 (plant variety rights)[46]
- where there is an issue governed by Enforcement Directive 2004/48/EC
- where there is an issue covered by Regulation 469/2009 (SPCs for medicinal products)
- where there is an issue covered by one of the other EU Directives explicitly mentioned in the UPC Agreement under Article 27; that is, Directive 2001/82/EC (veterinary medicinal products);[47] Directive 2001/83/EC (medical products for human use), Directive 2009/24/EC (computer programs),[48]

---

43 Hoffmann-Eitle, *The EU Patents Package Handbook: A Practioner's Guide* (Munich: Hoffmann-Eitle, 2014), 46.

44 See also Article 1(2) UPC Agreement and Article 267 Consolidated version of the Treaty on the Functioning of the European Union (TFEU), C 326/01 (2012), available at http://eur-lex.europa.eu/legal-content/EN/TXT/?uri=OJ:C:2012:326:TOC.

45 Directive 98/44/EC of the European Parliament and of the Council of 6 July 1998 on the legal protection of biotechnological inventions, OJ L 213/13 (1998).

46 Council Regulation (EC) No. 2100/94 of 27 July 1994 on Community plant variety rights OJ L 227 (1994). See also Council Regulation (EC) No. 873/2004 of 29 April 2004 amending Regulation (EC) No. 2100/94 on Community plant variety rights, OJ L 162 (2004).

47 Directive 2001/82/EC of the European Parliament and of the Council of 6 November 2001 on the Community code relating to veterinary medicinal products, OJ L 118 (2001).

48 Directive 2009/24/EC of the European Parliament and of the Council of 23 April 2009 on the legal protection of computer programs, OJ L 111 (2009).

Directive 98/44/EC (biotechnological inventions) and Regulation 2100/94 (plant variety rights)
- where there is a question of how to interpret Regulation 1257/2012 (UP Regulation).

Thus, the CJEU will undoubtedly have some judicial input within the UPC system, though every effort has seemingly been made by the planners to keep this role to a minimum with regard to substantive patent matters.[49] The experience of the CJEU's expansive interventions in the areas of trade mark law and copyright law within the EU may have had an influence in this respect.[50]

Standing and Legal Representation before the UPC

With respect to standing before the UPC, the usual legal requirement that a party is a natural or legal person applies. Regarding infringement actions, under Article 47(1) the patent proprietor has the right to bring a case before the UPC. An exclusive licensee to the patent may also bring a case (unless the licence stipulates otherwise) but must inform the patent owner that he/she/it intends to do so;[51] however, a non-exclusive licensee will not have this right unless it is specifically granted to the licensee in the terms of the licence. Where an infringement claim is brought by a licensee, if the patent's validity is then disputed, for example via a revocation counterclaim, the patentee must join and take part in the proceedings; or, alternatively, a separate revocation claim must be brought against the patentee.[52]

Any legally qualified person qualified to practice law in a national SS may represent a party before the UPC at the Court of

---

[49] R. Romandini and A. Klicznik, 'The territoriality principle and transnational use of patented inventions: the wider reach of a unitary patent and the role of the CJEU', *International Review of Intellectual Property and Competition Law (IIC)* 44 (2013), 524, 524–9.

[50] See J. Griffiths, 'Constitutionalising or harmonising: the Court of Justice, the right to property and European copyright law', *European Law Review* 38 (2013), 65; and L. McDonagh, 'From brand performance to consumer performativity: assessing European trade mark law after the rise of anthropological marketing', *Journal of Law & Society* 42 (2015), 611.

[51] Article 47 UPC Agreement.

[52] Article 47(2–5) UPC Agreement.

First Instance, regardless of whether it is a local, regional or central division, or at the Court of Appeal. In addition, appropriately qualified patent attorneys, such as those possessing the European Patent Litigation Certificate, may also represent their clients before the UPC.[53]

Focusing on the Structure of the UPC across the Local, Regional and Central Divisions

As outlined earlier, the UPC will feature an institutional architecture comprising a Court of First Instance (CFI), consisting of three central divisions as well as a number of local and/or regional divisions hosted by SS, or groups of SS; and a Court of Appeal.[54] In addition to the courts, the UPC will also have new mediation and arbitration facilities in Portugal and Slovenia, and a facility to train judges in Hungary.[55]

There is no hierarchy as such between the UPC CFI central and local/regional divisions, but the divisions do have different competences, as detailed below.[56] As noted earlier, the seat of the primary central division will be in Paris, with specialist technology divisions in London and Munich.[57] The precise technological division between the UPC central divisions will be based on the WIPO International Patent Classification (IPC) of the patent. In line with the IPC, the London central division will deal with validity actions in the chemical and pharmaceutical fields, including life sciences (corresponding to WIPO IPC classifications A and C); the Munich central division, meanwhile, will deal with patents in the engineering field (corresponding to WIPO IPC classification F). The Paris central division will deal with all other patents. As explored in further detail later on in this chapter, the central divisions will also deal with infringement actions transferred from local or regional divisions as well as those from countries where there is no local or regional division.

---

53 Article 48(2) UPC Agreement.
54 Articles 6(1) and 7(1–2) UPC Agreement.
55 Articles 19 and 35(1) UPC Agreement.
56 Article 33 UPC Agreement.
57 Article 7(2) UPC Agreement.

The UPC will also feature a Registry and a number of committees – Advisory, Budgetary and Administrative.[58] The Statute of the Unified Patent Court ('UPC Statute') envisages the setting up of a UPC 'Presidium' made up of the various presidents of the CFI and Court of Appeal along with additional judges from the courts and Registrar.[59]

So far, Austria, Belgium, Denmark, Finland, Ireland, Italy, the Netherlands and the UK have confirmed they will set up one local division each. Germany – as the largest patent jurisdiction – will set up four local divisions; indeed, it has been suggested that the German local divisions are likely to prove popular given the experience of German judges – who will form a majority on the panels – and the perception that they are patentee-friendly.[60]

In accordance with Article 7(5) of the UPC Agreement, a regional division may be set up by a number of different UPC SS. Such divisions might make sense for territories that share borders as well as similar legal systems such as the Scandinavian and Baltic regions. However, under Article 33(2) of the UPC Agreement in the case of an infringement action filed at a regional division, if the allegedly infringing acts have taken place within the territories covered by three or more regional divisions, the relevant regional division must refer the case to the central division if so requested by the defendant (a requirement that does not apply to the local divisions). This may make it less attractive for patentees to file an infringement case before a regional division, something which may have a knock-on effect on the willingness of UPC SS to form such divisions.[61] Indeed, only one UPC regional division has been confirmed so far: a Nordic–Baltic UPC regional division, serving Sweden, Lithuania, Latvia and Estonia (with an English-language court based in Stockholm). The absence, thus far, of 'three or more' UPC regional divisions means that Article 33(2) is unlikely to kick

---

[58] Articles 10, 12 and 13 UPC Agreement.

[59] Annex I UPC Agreement.

[60] Hoffmann-Eitle, *The EU Patents Package Handbook: A Practioner's Guide* (Munich: Hoffmann-Eitle, 2014), 34.

[61] Hoffmann-Eitle, *The EU Patents Package Handbook: A Practioner's Guide* (Munich: Hoffmann-Eitle, 2014), 93.

in, in the near future.[62] So far, no local or regional divisions are planned for Romania, Bulgaria, Greece, Cyprus, the Czech Republic, the Slovak Republic, Slovenia or Hungary, which means that when infringement takes place within these territories, infringement cases may be filed at the relevant UPC central division.

Assessing the Competence of the UPC

Under Article 32 of the UPC Agreement, the UPC has exclusive competence with respect to litigation relating to the infringement and validity of UPs as well as – upon expiry of the transitional regime (discussed further below) – EPs.[63] This includes actions relating to:

- claims of patent infringement and related defences
- claims for the revocation of patents and counterclaims for revocation
- claims for declarations of non-infringement
- claims for provisional and protective measures and injunctions.

With respect to claims for infringement, Articles 25 and 26 of the UPC Agreement define the infringing acts in the context of direct and indirect infringement.[64] Article 27 of the UPC Agreement lists the exemptions from patent infringement, including acts done privately and for non-commercial purposes; acts done for experimental purposes; and acts done in the context of certain tests and

---

[62] A. Johnson, 'Latest on local and regional divisions', *Bristows* (2015), available at www.bristows.com/articles/latest-on-local-and-regional-divisions-upc.

[63] Articles 3 and 32 UPC Agreement. The UPC may hear litigation matters cited in Article 32 UPC Agreement such as validity and infringement; meanwhile, national courts retain the competence regarding litigation matters not mentioned in Article 32, such as entitlement actions.

[64] Under Article 25 UPC Agreement, acts constituting infringement of a product include making, offering, placing the product on the market, using the product, importing or storing the product; acts constituting infringement of a process include using the process or offering the process for use. Under Article 26 UPC Agreement, infringement includes providing the means relating to the essential element of the invention.

trials for medicinal products. Notably, Article 32 of the UPC Agreement does not cover the majority of licensing agreements, or disputes over ownership, inventorship or entitlement to the patent, meaning that these remain within the competence of national courts. However, in the context of an infringement claim related defences, such as counter-claims concerning licences, are allowed, something that is particularly relevant to licences of right and 'fair and reasonable' (FRAND) cases where alleged infringers claim they are entitled to a patent licence on FRAND terms.[65]

Concerning the crucial issue of validity under Articles 32(d) and 32(e), a revocation action may be filed at one of the UPC central divisions (i.e. at either Paris, Munich or London, depending on the patent's IPC). The effect of a successful UPC revocation action is the invalidation of the patent across all SS. It is, therefore, a novel and highly powerful tool for competitors seeking to invalidate their competitors' patents across almost the entire EU; at present, such actions must be commenced at the various national levels (while lengthy opposition proceedings may be pending at the EPO).

With regard to claims for declarations of non-infringement, these are covered by Article 32(b) of the UPC Agreement.[66] Such an action is typically filed by a party seeking to establish that the party's actions have not infringed the relevant patent(s). Under the UPC Rules of Procedure, a party does not need to wait until he/she/it has been accused of infringement to file a claim for a declaration of non-infringement.[67] Action can be taken as long as the claimant has contacted the relevant patentee/exclusive licensee, providing all relevant details, as well as a request for the patentee/exclusive licensee to acknowledge that the patent does not infringe; and following this, that the patentee/exclusive licensee has failed to give written acknowledgement within one month.[68] These provisions will enable competing companies to 'clear the way' before they invest in costly R & D and/or marketing of goods. Under

65 Article 32(1)(h) UPC Agreement gives the UPC exclusive jurisdiction for disputes on the level of the licence fees for 'licences of right' under Article 8 UP Regulation.

66 See also Rules 61–74 UPC Rules of Procedure – www.unified-patent-court.org/images/documents/UPC-Rules-of-Procedure.pdf.

67 Rules 61–74 UPC Rules of Procedure.

68 Rule 61(1)(a–b) UPC Rules of Procedure.

Article 33(4) of the UPC Agreement, an action seeking a declaration of non-infringement must be commenced at the UPC central division; however, under Article 33(6) if a patentee/exclusive licensee commences a patent infringement action at one of the local or regional divisions within three months of the UPC central division filing, the UPC central division action will be stayed pending the outcome of the local/regional decision.

Concerning actions for provisional and protective measures and injunctions, Articles 32(c) and 62 of the UPC Agreement are highly relevant. Provisional injunctions may be granted by the UPC to prevent an imminent act of infringement or to stop an ongoing one.[69] The seizure of allegedly infringing goods – to prevent them being placed on the market – is also permitted.[70] In order to obtain one of these provisional remedies, a claimant patentee/exclusive licensee must provide reasonable evidence of actual or imminent infringement of one or more of its patents. Once a verdict of infringement has been handed down by the UPC, a permanent injunction may be granted. With regard to damages/compensation under Article 32(f) of the UPC Agreement, the key provisions are found in Article 68 of the same document – in addition to the injunctive relief, damages may be granted by the UPC.[71] Under the UPC Rules of Procedure, interim damages may be granted.[72] In the context of settlement negotiations between parties concerning the level of damages, it is worth noting the time limit: an application to the UPC for a determination of damages must be filed within one year of the final decision on the merits.[73] Regarding use of the invention prior to a patent grant under Article 32(g) of the UPC Agreement, only a claim of compensation may be brought. On this it is worth noting, however, that the issue of a prior use right is more commonly a defensive claim than an offensive one.[74]

Article 8 of the UP Regulation and Article 32(1)(h) of the UPC Agreement cover actions for compensation for patent licences

---

69 Article 62(1) UPC Agreement.

70 Article 62(3) UPC Agreement.

71 See also Rule 10(d) UPC Rules of Procedure.

72 Rule 119 UPC Rules of Procedure.

73 Rule 126 UPC Rules of Procedure.

74 Hoffmann-Eitle, *The EU Patents Package Handbook: A Practioner's Guide* (Munich: Hoffmann-Eitle, 2014), 89.

where a statement offering licences to all willing parties (in return for compensation) is filed with the EP. In this context, the UPC may decide on royalty disputes that occur.[75]

With respect to the breakdown between the various UPC divisions, Articles 32–33 of the UPC Agreement state that with regard to first-instance proceedings at the local or regional divisions, the following types of claims can be filed:

- actions for patent infringement and related defences
- actions for provisional and protective measures and injunctions
- actions for damages or compensation derived from provisional protection
- actions relating to prior use
- counterclaims for revocation in pending infringement cases.

The choice of local or regional divisions is framed by the questions of:

- where the infringement has occurred or may occur
- or, alternatively, where the defendant has a residence or place of business.

Meanwhile, with respect to the UPC central divisions, Articles 32–33 of the UPC Agreement state that the following claims can be filed centrally:

- actions for declarations of non-infringement
- actions for revocation of patent(s)
- all actions related to Signatory States without a local division or regional division.

Thus, if the defendant has no residence/place of business within the contracting Signatory States of the UPC, the competent court will be the local or regional division where the (alleged) infringement

[75] W. Pors, 'Property and contractual aspects of unitary patents and of patents in the UPC system', *EPLAW Patent Blog* (2014), 1, 2, available at www.eplawpatentblog.com/2014/December/Wouter%20Pors%20Property%20and%20Contractual.pdf.

has occurred. Alternatively, in such circumstances the action may be filed at the central division; and actions may also be filed at the central division if there is no local or regional division covering the territory of the infringement. This means that in some cases patentees will have the opportunity to bypass the local/regional divisions entirely, and proceed immediately to the relevant central division. Despite this, given the remit of the UPC local/regional divisions to zero-in on infringement issues, it seems likely that these divisions of the UPC will handle the majority of infringement actions.

Nonetheless, it is worth noting that in accordance with Article 33(2) of the UPC Agreement, if the case is already pending at one division, any other legal dispute which occurs between the same parties, concerning the same patent, must be filed at the same division. For example, it is not possible to file a claim for non-infringement or for revocation of a patent at the UPC central division if an action for infringement between the same parties concerning the same patent(s) has already been brought before one of the UPC local or regional divisions. In such circumstances, under Article 33(4) of the UPC Agreement a claim for non-infringement or for revocation of a patent can only be filed at the same local or regional division as the ongoing/pending infringement action. In addition, under the UPC Rules of Procedure a legal party who considers that there is a looming possibility that an application seeking provisional measures could be taken against him (as a defendant at the UPC) may file a protective letter, in the language of the patent, with the UPC Registry.[76] Moreover, under Article 33(6) of the UPC Agreement an action for a declaration of non-infringement that is pending at the central division will be stayed if an infringement action involving the same parties concerning the same patent is filed at a local/regional division within three months.

A defendant may seek to challenge the UPC's competence and jurisdiction in order to try to prevent the UPC case from proceeding. Under the UPC Rules of Procedure, any objection to the UPC's international jurisdiction, its internal competence or the particular

[76] Rule 207 UPC Rules of Procedure.

division where suit is filed must be submitted within one month of the claim being served on the defendant.[77]

Filing a UPC Action and the Issue of Bifurcation of Proceedings

A patent infringement action may be filed at the UPC local/regional division where the infringement has occurred, or where the defendant is domiciled; and as noted earlier in this chapter, in certain circumstances an infringement case can be filed at the technically competent section of the UPC central division in Paris, London or Munich.[78]

Due to the limits on the written, interim and oral stages of proceedings, the expected time frame of a UPC action, from case filing until a first-instance decision is rendered, is approximately 12 months.[79] In other words, the UPC has been set up so that it can reach decisions concerning infringement quickly – for instance, it is envisaged that the UPC's first-instance ruling on the merits will be handed down in written form within six weeks of the oral hearing.[80] In some cases, the UPC may, in fact, give a decision on the merits of the case immediately after the hearing's conclusion, and then give its reasons subsequently.[81]

Meanwhile, a standalone patent revocation action may be filed at the technically competent section of the UPC central division in Paris, London or Munich; notably, however, if revocation is filed as a counterclaim to an initial infringement claim, it may be filed at the UPC local/regional division where the infringement action was

---

[77] Rule 19 UPC Rules of Procedure.

[78] See Article 32(1)(a) UPC Agreement in conjunction with Article 33(1) UPC Agreement. See also generally K. Cremers, M. Ernicke, D. Harhoff, C. Helmers, G. Licht, L. McDonagh, et al. 'Patent litigation in Europe', *ZEW Discussion Paper* No. 13-07 (2013), 1.

[79] Rule 10 UPC Rules of Procedure. See also K. Mooney, 'The new European Unified Patent Court and the unitary patent', presentation given at the UCL Institute of Brand and Innovation Law, George Washington University's Faculty of Law, GSMA, ITU and ETSI conference 'Patents in Telecoms' (2015), available at www.ucl.ac.uk/laws/patents-in-telecoms-2015/docs/02_judges_0915_mooney.pdf.

[80] Rule 118(6) UPC Rules of Procedure.

[81] Rule 118(7) UPC Rules of Procedure.

commenced and/or is pending.[82] In this scenario – where a counterclaim for revocation has been filed at the UPC local/regional division – the local/regional division court panel has three possible options: first, it may decide to proceed with both the action for infringement and the revocation counterclaim, issuing rulings on both issues; second, it may refer the counterclaim for revocation to the UPC central division – and either suspend or proceed with the action for infringement; or third, with the agreement of the parties, it may refer the case to the central division.[83]

Regarding the first option – where the local/regional division decides to go ahead and hear arguments concerning both infringement and validity – a technically qualified judge will be allocated to the panel by the CFI president (at the request of the judge-rapporteur).[84]

The second option is the one that has caused the most controversy in discussions over the working of the UPC – the reason being that it gives the local/regional division court panel the option to bifurcate the proceedings into (i) an infringement case, to be heard and decided at the UPC local/regional level, and (ii) a revocation case, to be heard and decided at the UPC central division. Some patent litigants are likely to be wary of bifurcation; after all, the system is utilized by very few European jurisdictions, and of those that are major patent jurisdictions, only Germany uses it.[85] Yet, on the other hand, due to the fact that Germany is the most prominent jurisdiction, many patent litigants will have some experience of the system. Moreover, bifurcated patent proceedings are utilized in some major patent jurisdictions outside the EU, including China and South Korea, so parties with experience of using the litigation systems in these territories may find bifurcation less intimidating. Finally, it is worth emphasizing that in Germany bifurcation is *mandatory*; within the UPC, by contrast, bifurcation

---

82 See Articles 32(1)(d–e) and 33(3) UPC Agreement. See also generally K. Cremers, M. Ernicke, D. Harhoff, C. Helmers, G. Licht, L. McDonagh, et al. 'Patent litigation in Europe', *ZEW Discussion Paper* No. 13-07 (2013), 1.

83 See Article 33(3) UPC Agreement.

84 Rule 37(3) UPC Rules of Procedure. Of course, if a technically qualified judge has already been allocated to the panel under Rule 33 UPC Rules of Procedure, there is no need to do this.

85 In Europe, bifurcation occurs in Austria, Germany and Hungary. Worldwide, other countries that bifurcate include China and South Korea.

will be *optional*, and for this reason is unlikely to occur as often as it does in Germany.[86]

The Procedural Stages of a UPC Action

Under Article 52(1) of the UPC Agreement, a case at the UPC will typically involve three procedural stages – written, interim and oral. This is a 'front-loaded' process, with the plaintiff/claimant expected to have a well set-out case ready from the first filing.[87]

Under the UPC Rules of Procedure, the written stage is to be comprised of four filings: (i) a statement of claim; (ii) a statement of defence; (iii) a reply to the statement of defence; and (iv) a rejoinder to the reply.[88] A counterclaim for revocation of the patent may be filed as part of the statement of defence.[89] The written stage is expected to last approximately six months.

Working through the processes of the interim procedure – lasting approximately three months – enables the judge-rapporteur (the reporting judge) to prepare for the oral procedure. During this interim period, the judge-rapporteur may require the parties to clarify specific issues/points/questions, produce evidence and file specific documents relating to the upcoming oral hearing.[90] Under Rule 101 of the UPC Rules of Procedure, this stage may also involve one or more interim conferences; such a conference should usually take place via telephone or video technology, but as an alternative it can take place in court, publicly, with the parties appearing in person, in circumstances where there is agreement between the parties and the judge-rapporteur about this (confidentiality is at the discretion of the court).[91]

Regarding the oral procedure, this primarily consists of an oral hearing which is envisaged to be completed within one day (general

[86] Article 37(4) UPC Rules of Procedure.
[87] Hoffmann-Eitle, *The EU Patents Package Handbook: A Practioner's Guide* (Munich: Hoffmann-Eitle, 2014), 33.
[88] Rule 12(1) UPC Rules of Procedure.
[89] Rule 12(2) UPC Rules of Procedure.
[90] Rule 101 UPC Rules of Procedure.
[91] Rule 105 UPC Rules of Procedure.

rule).[92] To help keep this one-day limit in place, in advance of the oral hearing the presiding judge has the power to set relevant time limits with respect to the length of the parties' oral submissions. The oral hearing will be recorded for posterity (via audio or video equipment).[93]

It is during the interim stage that decisions and orders will be made with respect to whether – and to what extent – witnesses and (scientific) experts ought to be heard during the oral hearing.[94] Then, during the oral hearing, acting under the presiding judge – along with the judges of the panel and the representatives of each party – questions will be asked of the ordered witnesses and experts.[95] In contrast with the UK, the use of witness testimony and cross-examination of experts will be severely limited in oral hearings at the UPC. In this sense, the procedures are closer to those of the German and Dutch jurisdictions.

At the UPC, there is no general wide rule of disclosure comparable with that found in the UK – on this, the UPC procedures more closely mirror those of the German, French and Dutch courts. Thus, in the context of the UPC the acceptable evidence is to be located in the submissions made by each party, and gathered via the making of requests for information, as well as via inspections and the provision of documents (somewhat akin to the French *saisie* procedures), as well as via the use of comparative experiments and the gathering of sworn evidentiary statements/affidavits.[96] It seems likely, however, that the *saisie*-style procedures at the UPC will be more burdensome for patentees to avail of than currently is the case in France.[97]

Overall, it is notable that the UPC Rules of Procedure leave the judges 'considerable discretion' with respect to the conduct of proceedings.[98] As discussed further in Chapter 4, this means that

---

[92] Rule 113 UPC Rules of Procedure.

[93] Rule 115 UPC Rules of Procedure.

[94] Rule 112(2)(b) UPC Rules of Procedure.

[95] Rule 112(3–5) UPC Rules of Procedure.

[96] Article 53(1) UPC Agreement and Rules 192–198 UPC Rules of Procedure.

[97] A.-L. Bouzanquet, A. Bowler and A. Johnson, 'The role of the saisie in the UPC', *Bristows* (2013) – www.bristowsupc.com/commentary/saisie-upc/.

[98] Hoffmann-Eitle, *The EU Patents Package Handbook: A Practioner's Guide* (Munich: Hoffmann-Eitle, 2014), 33.

the make-up of the judicial panels, as well as their individual levels of expertise and experience, will be crucial for ensuring consistency of decision making within the UPC. In terms of the nationalities and experience of judges, it is quite possible that experienced judges from, for example, Germany, the UK, France or the Netherlands will seek to draw from the case law of their home jurisdictions; on the other hand, for judges coming from territories that do not have a long history of patent litigation or much current case law, a different challenge will arise – that of inexperience. Maintaining judicial consistency will be particularly crucial with respect to infringement, since while there is a body of EPO jurisprudence on validity questions that the UPC judges can follow, there is no equivalent centralized body of jurisprudence concerning infringement (which, under the EPC, has remained within the remit of national courts).

Appeals to the UPC Court of Appeal (Luxembourg)

With respect to appeals, an appeal against a decision of the Court of First Instance – whether from a local, regional or central division – must be filed within a two month time limit post-notification of the UPC CFI decision.[99] As outlined in Article 73(3), appeals are available both on points of law and with respect to factual and evidentiary matters. Nonetheless, an appellant may only be allowed to introduce new facts/evidence if, as stated in Article 73(4), the appellant could not have been reasonably expected to have submitted the relevant 'new' facts/evidence at the time of the CFI proceedings.

Supplementary Protection Certificates in the context of the UP and the UPC

Supplementary Protection Certificates (SPCs) were introduced under the auspices of EU law in order to compensate patentees where they had experienced the loss of an effective patent term due to a delay in obtaining the crucial EU marketing authorization for a pharmaceutical product, without which a product cannot be put on

---

[99] Article 73(1) UPC Agreement.

the EU market.[100] The EU SPC system allows for the national patent offices of EU MS to grant SPCs for both national patents and for EPs validated within that MS. With respect to the UPC, of relevance is an SPC that is based on either an existing or a prospective EP; and second, an SPC that is based on a prospective UP.

Regarding an SPC which refers to an underlying EP, once the UPC is up and running the SPC – like the underlying EP – will come within the UPC's jurisdiction (though as noted below, the opt-out possibility is relevant during the transition period).[101]

For UPs, any associated SPCs will come under the remit of the UPC. However, due to the terms of the EU regulation, it appears that despite their unitary nature, SPCs for UPs will have to be granted at a national level.[102] At some point, the EPC might be amended to allow the EPO to grant SPCs, but for now that is not on the cards.

Opt-Out of EPs and Related SPCs from the UPC's Jurisdiction

As noted earlier, in accordance with Article 83 of the UPC Agreement, all existing EPs and prospective EPs that are applied for within the transitional period can be opted out of the UPC via application to the UPC Registry.[103] The EP opt-out will be applicable to all national parts of the EP in all relevant UPC Agreement Signatory States.[104] The opt-out will be registered only if there is no existing/pending UPC action, and is expected to last for the lifetime of the patent.[105]

---

[100] Regulation 469/2009 concerning the supplementary protection certificate for medicinal products, OJ L 152 (2009) and Regulation 1610/1996 concerning the creation of a supplementary protection certificate for plant protection products, OJ L 198/30 (1996).

[101] P. England, 'In? Out? What's it all about? Patent opt-out and withdrawal in the UPC', *Journal of Intellectual Property Law & Practice* 9 (2014), 10, 10–12.

[102] L. Reynolds, 'SPCs and the UPC: current status', *Bristows* (2015), available at www.bristowsupc.com/commentary/spcs-and-the-upc/.

[103] Article 83(3) UPC Agreement.

[104] Rule 5(1–13) UPC Rules of Procedure.

[105] Rule 5(5) UPC Rules of Procedure.

To ensure patentees can avoid the UPC's jurisdiction from day one – should they choose to – opt-outs may be accepted by the EPO before the UPC Agreement is ratified and enters into force; these opt-out notices will then be registered with the UPC Registry immediately post-ratification, when the UPC is up and running.[106]

The opt-out of an EP/SPC may be withdrawn at any time – even after the transition period ends – an act which would re-establish the UPC's jurisdiction regarding that EP/SPC.[107] Nevertheless, the withdrawal of the UPC opt-out will not be allowed if there is an existing/pending action at a national court.[108] Thinking about this in terms of eventual patent term, in practice this means that if an SPC for an 'opted out' EP is applied for in, for example, 2020, it would still be litigated in the national system until its expiry, which may not come until 2045. This neatly illustrates how long the new system may take before it fully unifies the system of European patent litigation.[109] It is not envisaged that patentees will be able to opt out, opt back in and then opt out a second time.[110] Despite initial proposals, there will not be a fee to opt out an EP from the UPC's jurisdiction (the possible impact of the initial proposed opt-out fee is discussed in detail in light of the empirical data in Chapter 4).[111]

It is important to take note of the effect of the UPC opt-out on the substantive law to be applied by the relevant national court: even if an EP/SPC is opted out of the UPC, the substantive law to be applied by the national court is intended to be the same as would have been applied by the UPC, i.e. decisions at the national level

---

106 Rule 5(9) UPC Rules of Procedure.

107 Rule 5(6) UPC Rules of Procedure.

108 Article 87(4) UPC Agreement.

109 P. England, 'In? Out? What's it all about? Patent opt-out and withdrawal in the UPC', *Journal of Intellectual Property Law & Practice* 9 (2014), 10–17.

110 Hoffmann-Eitle, *The EU Patents Package Handbook: A Practioner's Guide* (Munich: Hoffmann-Eitle, 2014), 80.

111 A. Johnson, 'Opt-out fee for future Unified Patent Court is (unsurprisingly) much too high', *Kluwer Patent Blog* (2015), available at www.kluwerpatentblog.com/2015/05/15/opt-out-fee-for-future-unified-patent-court-is-unsurprisingly-much-too-high/.

will be made based on the new substantive law, not on the prior national jurisprudence concerning infringement.[112]

Restraining Infringement: The Powers of the UPC

Under the UPC Agreement, the UPC has the power to enjoin an infringer from direct infringement (Article 25) as well as from indirect infringement (Article 26). With respect to direct infringement, the infringer can be enjoined from making, offering, using and/or placing on the market a product covered by the respective patent-in-suit, or from importing or storing the patented product for any of these purposes.[113] If the infringed patent covers a process, rather than a product, the UPC can enjoin the infringer from using the patented process, as well as from offering the patented process (if the infringer knows or ought to have known that use of the process is prohibited); in addition, the infringer can be enjoined from offering, using, importing and/or placing on the market products directly obtained via the patented process. With regard to indirect infringement, the UPC has the power to enjoin the indirect infringer from supplying, or offering to supply, any means relating to an essential element of the patented invention (if the means are suitable and intended to operate, put into effect or work the invention).[114]

Effectively, the UPC will provide patentees with the ability to obtain an injunction against an infringer that is enforceable in all 25 Signatory States of the UPC. This will no doubt prove to be a potent remedy. Conversely, it will be possible for competitors to seek to revoke a patentee's patent centrally, with the effect of that single judgment being that the patent is no longer valid within all 25 Signatory States. Both of these options have received much academic and practitioner discussion recently, and they are analysed in detail in the next chapter.

---

112 Articles 25–30 UPC Agreement.
113 Article 25 UPC Agreement.
114 Article 26 UPC Agreement.

The UPC Judiciary

The make-up of the UPC judiciary is likely to prove to be one of the key factors that will determine the potential success of the court system. The existence of multi-judge panels will be the norm within the UPC, though in some circumstances a case may be decided by a single judge.[115]

Under Article 18(3) of the UPC Agreement, the president of the CFI will allot judges from an agreed 'pool of judges' to the various CFI divisions based on a number of key criteria. In accordance with Articles 15(1) and 18(1–2) of the UPC Agreement, the UPC judicial panels are required to be multi-national and to consist of judges who are both legally and technically qualified, as well as being competent and experienced in the area of patent litigation.[116] With respect to CFI courts, the judicial panels of both the local and regional divisions will be formed of three legally qualified judges; meanwhile, at the three outposts of the CFI central division – Paris, London and Munich – there will also be three-person judicial panels, comprised of two legally qualified judges and a single technical judge. Additionally, the chairman of a judicial panel must always be a judge who is legally qualified.[117]

For second-instance decisions (Court of Appeal), the panels will comprise of a total of five persons – three legally qualified judges (all from different Signatory States) and two technically qualified judges, who will come from the UPC pool of judges.[118] The Court of Appeal's panels will be chaired by a legally qualified judge. If a Court of Appeal case is deemed to be of 'exceptional importance', it may be heard by the 'full court', i.e. all judges of the Court of Appeal.[119] Exceptional importance is not defined in the UPC

---

[115] Article 8(7) UPC Agreement and Articles 19(3) and 21(3) Statute of the Unified Patent Court ('UPC Statute'), available at http://documents.epo.org/projects/babylon/eponet.nsf/0/A1080B83447CB9DDC1257B36005AAAB8/$File/upc_agreement_en.pdf.

[116] See also Articles 8(8) and 9(3) UPC Agreement.

[117] Articles 8(8) and 9(1) UPC Agreement.

[118] Article 9(1) UPC Agreement.

[119] Article 21(2) UPC Statute and Article 35(3) UPC Agreement.

Agreement or the UPC Statute, so it is a potential source of ambiguity and will need to be interpreted by the courts.[120]

With respect to the local and regional divisions, each judicial panel will feature at least one judge from the UPC pool of judges who is not a national of the UPC Signatory State where the court is located. In fact, there are circumstances where a local division may feature only one national judge.[121] The full Article 8 criteria are as follows:

- For local divisions in UPC member states that have fewer than 50 patent litigation cases per year, there will be one national judge + two judges from the UPC pool.
- For local divisions in UPC member states that have more than 50 patent litigation cases per year, there will be two national judges + one judge from the UPC pool.
- For all regional divisions, there will be two national judges (from the Signatory States comprising the regional division) + one judge from the UPC pool.

The panel itself may decide, or a litigating party may request, that an additional technically qualified judge be allocated from the UPC pool of judges to join a local/regional division judicial panel.[122] Judges will spend a period of one year on a particular division panel, as determined by the presiding judge.[123] Consequently, litigating parties are likely to have 'at least some predictability in advance with regard to the question of which panel or which judge will hear the case'.[124] With respect to litigant choice of venue, this predictability may contribute to the 'forum shopping' issue, discussed further in the context of the empirical data in Chapter 4.

In light of the above rules, and due to the fact that the overwhelming proportion of European patent litigation takes place in Germany, there is no doubt that two out of the three judges on

---

[120] Hoffmann-Eitle, *The EU Patents Package Handbook: A Practioner's Guide* (Munich: Hoffmann-Eitle, 2014), 98.

[121] Article 8 UPC Agreement.

[122] Article 8(5) UPC Agreement.

[123] Rule 345(1–3) UPC Rules of Procedure.

[124] Hoffmann-Eitle, *The EU Patents Package Handbook: A Practioner's Guide* (Munich: Hoffmann-Eitle, 2014), 97.

the four planned UPC local division panels in Germany will be German. This will also be the case, for example, at the UK's local division, as it is a jurisdiction which, although it has much less patent litigation than Germany, nonetheless has well over 50 patent cases filed each year at the Patents Court and IPEC.[125] This will not be the case for countries with less popular patent courts: Ireland, for example, is likely to have only one national judge on its local division panel, as it does not feature more than 50 patent cases filed per year.[126]

For central divisions, the make-up of the three-person judicial panels, comprised of two legally qualified judges and a single technical judge, will not be dependent on the location of the host country – these judges will be drawn from the general UPC pool of judges.[127]

All 'legally qualified' judges must be of sufficient qualification to be appointed as a judge in one of the UPC MS, and all 'technically qualified' judges must have both a university degree and sufficient technological and litigation expertise.[128] Since the positions were first advertised, many applications to be appointed to the UPC pool of judges have been received by the UPC Advisory Committee – they are at time of writing being processed before appointments are made.[129]

Judges will be trained at the UPC Centre in Budapest, Hungary. Each judge must have a strong working ability to deal with (at least) one of the EPO's official languages, i.e. English, German or French.[130] A judge's term will be six years, though reappointments are a possibility.[131] Furthermore, UPC judges will be allowed to act

---

125 C. Helmers, Y. Lefouili and L. McDonagh, 'Examining patent cases at the Patents Court and Intellectual Property Enterprise Court 2007–2013', *A Report Commissioned by the UK Intellectual Property Office* (March 2015), available at www.gov.uk/government/publications/examining-patent-cases-at-the-patents-court-and-ipec-2007-2013.

126 A. Casey, 'Unified Patent Court (UPC) and Ireland' (2015), available at http://frkelly.com/unified-patent-court-upc-ireland.

127 Articles 8(6), 18(3) and Article 32(1)(i) UPC Agreement.

128 Article 15(2–3) UPC Agreement.

129 Articles 16(1–2) and 18 UPC Agreement.

130 Article 2(2) UPC Statute.

131 Article 4(1) UPC Statute.

as judges in their respective national jurisdictions concurrent with their UPC role.[132]

Language of Proceedings

At UPC local divisions, the language of proceedings will be the official language of the relevant UPC MS where the division is located.[133] This will generally be the case for the regional divisions as well, though, as an alternative, the language of proceedings at a regional division may be one of the official languages of any of the UPC MS that share that particular regional division.

Furthermore, there are a number of other possibilities regarding the language of proceedings: (i) local or regional divisions may designate one of the EPO official languages – English, German or French – as the language of proceedings;[134] (ii) the UPC judicial panel in agreement with the case parties may also decide, for example, on the basis of fairness and convenience that the language of the patent-in-suit ought to be the language of proceedings (the case parties may also request the case to be referred to the relevant central division if there is no agreement with the judicial panel on this point);[135] and (iii) if only one of the case parties requests a language change, the President of the Court of First Instance, taking into account all the relevant circumstances, issues of fairness and having heard the views of the other party to the case and the judicial panel, may make the decision that the language of the patent ought to be used as the language of proceedings.[136]

The language situation is much more straightforward at the UPC central division; regardless of whether the case is heard in Paris, Munich or London, the language of the patent will be the language of proceedings.[137] Since most EPO-granted patents are in English,

---

[132] Article 17(3–4) UPC Agreement. In addition, patent attorneys will be allowed to act as technically qualified part-time UPC judges, where appropriate.

[133] Article 49(1) UPC Agreement.

[134] Article 49(2) UPC Agreement.

[135] Article 49(3–4) UPC Agreement.

[136] Article 49(5) UPC Agreement.

[137] Article 49(6) UPC Agreement.

this means that English will be the most commonly used language at the central division.[138]

At the Court of Appeal, the language of proceedings will be the same as the language used in the Court of First Instance – whether the local/regional division or the central division – unless the case parties are in agreement that the language of proceedings at the Court of Appeal ought to be the language of the patent.[139]

Jurisdiction and the Transition Period

With respect to the UPC's jurisdiction, there will be a transition period of 7 years (potentially extendable to up to 14 years) whereby national courts will share jurisdiction with the UPC over EPs/SPCs.[140] Furthermore, during the transition period patentees who currently hold EPs or who apply to obtain EPs during this time will be able to opt out of the UPC system, and instead continue to use the current system of national litigation of EP validations, for example, EP (UK), EP (DE).[141] As discussed later on in this chapter, and in Chapter 4, while the provision of a transitional period is understandable given the fundamental nature of the reforms, the result will be that the coming into being of the UPC will initially result in an even more fragmented litigation system for EPs than exists at the present time, with the additional layer of UPC litigation coming on top of the current national systems. It will also result, at least for the transitional period, in some ungainly legal complexities, including the issue of the choice of venue under the Brussels I Regulation discussed earlier in this chapter, and the substantive law to be applied by national courts for EPs that have been opted out of the UPC.

---

[138] A. Johnson, 'Latest on local and regional divisions', *Bristows* (2015), available at www.bristows.com/articles/latest-on-local-and-regional-divisions-upc.

[139] Article 50 UPC Agreement.

[140] Article 83(1) UPC Agreement.

[141] Article 83(3) UPC Agreement.

THE EUROPEAN PATENT WITH UNITARY EFFECT (UNITARY PATENT)

Currently, there is co-existence between (i) national patents, granted by national patent offices within Europe (e.g. GBs, DEs, NLs and FRs) and (ii) European patents (EPs) granted by the EPO with one or more national variation(s). It is important to emphasize that the European patent with unitary effect (unitary patent, or UP) will not replace, but will instead complement, the current system of patenting in Europe; in other words, the primary benefit of the UP will be that it provides an additional option for protection, and one that is broader in scope than any of the existing options.[142]

What this means is that businesses and inventors will soon face a choice between three different ways of protecting their patents: (i) the national route (e.g. GB, DE, FR, NL); (ii) the traditional EPO-granted European Patent (EP) validated in individual territories; or (iii) the new EPO-granted European Patent with unitary effect (UP).[143] Crucially, as explored earlier on in this chapter, the choice that patentees make, with respect to whether to protect their inventions via national patents, EPs or UPs, will affect the potential litigation venues – something particularly important during the UPC transition period.

The way the new UP option will work is as follows: once a patentee's application is granted by the EPO, the patentee may choose to obtain a UP rather than the traditional EP. Thus, in order to get unitary protection, a prospective patentee must apply to the EPO in the usual way, and then, within one month of grant, request that the patent be registered as a UP.[144]

During the transitional period, the patentee will, along with the UP request, need to provide a translation of the patent, something discussed further on in this chapter. From the date the relevant Regulation becomes 'live', i.e. when the UPC Agreement has been

---

[142] Articles 3 and 5 UP Regulation. See also generally J. Pila and C. Wadlow (eds), *The Unitary EU Patent System* (Oxford: Hart, 2015).

[143] A. Kaisi, 'Finally a single European right for the EU? An analysis of the substantive provisions of the European patent with unitary effect', *European Intellectual Property Review* 36 (2014), 170.

[144] Article 9(1)(g) UP Regulation.

ratified and is in full force, any new EPO-granted patent may be registered as a UP.[145]

Choosing UP protection will eliminate the need to obtain separate validations from each MS where protection is sought – something which of course removes the need to pay separate translation/validation fees to the various MS national patent offices.[146]

Addressing the UP's Territorial Scope

The issue of the coverage of the UP is framed by the fact that the establishment of the UP falls within an area of European Union policy – in fact, because the new UP is an EP with unitary effect across many jurisdictions, a state must be a member of both the EPC and the EU in order to join up with the EU Enhanced Cooperation procedure and ratify the UPC Agreement. Due to the consequences of Opinion 1/09, the UPC is considered to be a court 'common to' the EU MS – and only EU MS may join the new system.[147] Therefore, signatories to the EPC that are not EU MS – including, for example, Switzerland, Turkey and Iceland – will not be part of the new system.[148] This also means that if the UK pulls out of the EU following the referendum on membership in June 2016, it will no longer be able to participate.

The UP will facilitate patent protection over 25 out of 28 EU member states on the basis of a single application to the EPO – Spain and Croatia are definitively outside the UP's coverage at present; while Poland initially participated in the UP Enhanced Cooperation procedure but has since decided not to become an SS of the UPC Agreement, which has had a knock-on effect on the UP's coverage in Poland; and Italy, once a hold-out country, formally joined the UP in late 2015.[149]

---

145 Hoffmann-Eitle, *The EU Patents Package Handbook: A Practioner's Guide* (Munich: Hoffmann-Eitle, 2014), 21.

146 The loss of revenue that will potentially be suffered by national patent offices will be set off via a system of revenue-sharing of UP fees between the EPO and the various national patent offices.

147 CJEU, Opinion 1/09, 8 March 2011, para. 82, available at http://ec.europa.eu/dgs/legal_service/arrets/09a001_en.pdf.

148 CJEU, Opinion 1/09, 8 March 2011, para. 82, available at http://ec.europa.eu/dgs/legal_service/arrets/09a001_en.pdf.

149 Http://europa.eu/rapid/press-release_MEX-15-5748_en.htm.

Importantly, however, in practice the UP's territorial scope is to some extent dependent on the ratification of the UPC Agreement: once the minimum 13 (3 + 10) SS ratify the UPC Agreement, UPs may be registered at the EPO. However, since the system will come into force on the first day of the fourth month following the requisite 13th ratification, the initial territorial scope of the UP may be limited to those SS that have already ratified.[150] Post-grant, there are two key dates for UP validation: (i) the date of application for registration as such at the EPO and (ii) the date of the UP registration itself. The UP will be valid in all Signatory States (i) that have joined the EU Enhanced Cooperation procedure at the time of application for UP registration; and (ii) where the UPC Agreement is in force on the date of registration.[151]

This is of concern in the sense that it is quite possible that there will be some lag between the initial ratifying Signatory States – such as Austria, the first to ratify, as well as the UK, Germany and France – and the later ratifying Signatory States, such as Ireland, which for constitutional reasons will have to hold a referendum (not yet scheduled) in order to ratify the UPC Agreement. This is potentially significant because it is understood that the territorial scope of a UP 'will not subsequently be extended' when the UPC Agreement is ratified by later Signatory States.[152] For this reason, patentees may seek to delay the granting of forthcoming patents by the EPO until full 25 UPC Agreement Signatory State ratification.

To avoid this scenario, and to decrease unnecessary complexity within the system, it is hoped that the requisite 13th ratification happens concurrently with all other MS ratifications, or as soon as possible thereafter. Also worth bearing in mind is the fact that even after the UPC Agreement is ratified by the requisite 13 Signatory States, for states that ratify at a later date, the UPC Agreement will only come into force on the first day of the fourth month after ratification. One final note is worth reiterating: for EPO-granted

---

150 Articles 84, 85 and 89 UPC Agreement.

151 Articles 2(a) and 18(2) UP Regulation.

152 Hoffmann-Eitle, *The EU Patents Package Handbook: A Practioner's Guide* (Munich: Hoffmann-Eitle, 2014), 22.

patents that are intended to cover EPC jurisdictions such as Spain or Switzerland, national validation will still be required even where unitary protection has been obtained for the participating EU member states.

Unitary effect

Once registered, a UP will have unitary effect in all participating EU member states from the date of publication of the grant in the European Patent Bulletin.[153] In contrast to EPO-granted EPs – which are subject to national laws concerning infringement in the member states of the EPC where they are validated – the UP will be subject to the same legal conditions in all UPC Signatory States – at the various local, regional and central divisions.[154] The issues of validity and infringement of UPs will be subject to the UPC's exclusive jurisdiction and will be considered under the UPC's substantive law, as discussed earlier on in this chapter. When a UP lapses, or is revoked, limited or transferred, this will have unitary effect in all Signatory States where it is valid.[155] Notably, however, due to the fact that licensing is not entirely within the UPC's exclusive jurisdiction, patent licences concerning UPs may be limited to certain territories.[156] Oppositions to UPs will occur in exactly the same way as current oppositions to EPs – they must be filed with the EPO.[157]

Translations

A central aim of the UP's existence is to eliminate the need for multiple post-grant patent validations/translations in Europe. The current cost to validate and translate an EP across all EU territories is very high, especially when compared to the equivalent costs in other large markets such as the USA.[158] The various procedural fees for applying for, and receiving, an EP from the EPO total €4045

---

[153] Article 4(1) UP Regulation.

[154] Article 2(2) EPC and Article 64(1) EPC.

[155] Article 3(2) UP Regulation.

[156] Hoffmann-Eitle, *The EU Patents Package Handbook: A Practioner's Guide* (Munich: Hoffmann-Eitle, 2014), 23.

[157] Articles 99–105b EPC.

[158] EU Commission Staff Working Paper (Impact Assessment) SEC(2011) 482/2 (2011), 1 – http://ec.europa.eu/internal_market/indprop/docs/patent/20110413-impact-assessment_en.pdf.

(online filing).[159] Once granted, the cost of validating an EP in 27 EU MS (not including Croatia) is estimated at €28,074, giving an overall cost total of €32,119, largely due to the translation costs.[160] The UP option eliminates these additional post-grant costs.

However, during the UP transition period, expected to be 6 or 12 years,[161] a post-grant full patent translation – which in the UP/UPC context will not have legal standing, but will be informational in nature – will still be required for UPs.[162] During the UP transition period, if the language of application/grant is German or French, a patent translation into English will be required; if the application/granted patent is in English, a translation into any EU official language will suffice (including, interestingly, a language of a non-Signatory State, such as Spanish or Polish). At present, around 75% of EPs are in the English language, so it is likely this high proportion will continue, and may even increase, during the transition period. By applying for a patent to be granted in English, the patentee could choose to then nominate one of the non-Signatory State languages – Spanish or Polish – and, thus, can use the translation to validate the patent as an EP within that territory. On the other hand, given the strength of German patent litigation, and the fact that this is expected to continue at Germany's four UPC local divisions, it may make sense for patentees who have filed in English to provide the additional translation in German.

Even after the transition period, translations may occasionally be required. With regard to litigation, it must be noted that during proceedings a court or an alleged infringer can request a translation of the patent.[163] Moreover, a translation of the UP may be required

---

[159] EU Commission Staff Working Paper (Impact Assessment) SEC(2011) 482/2 (2011), 1, 16.

[160] EU Commission Staff Working Paper (Impact Assessment) SEC(2011) 482/2 (2011), 1, 16.

[161] The transition period is expected to last until patent machine translations can be produced to a sufficiently high quality, something the EPO and Google are currently working on.

[162] Articles 6(1), 6(3) and 6(5) Translation Regulation.

[163] Article 4 Translation Regulation.

when enforcing the patent in circumstances where the UPC proceedings 'are conducted in a language other than the language of the granted patent and the submitted translation'.[164]

Leaving aside litigation-required translations, during the transition period the total cost of the UP is estimated to be €6425 (covering the EPO procedural cost and the cost of one translation); whereas it will be €4045 after the transition period (covering solely the EPO's procedural costs). Furthermore, for EU-based natural persons (individual inventors), SMEs, non-profit organizations, universities and public research facilities, there will be a compensation/reimbursement scheme where applications are filed in an EU official language that is not English, German or French.[165] Thus, there is no question that by largely eliminating the need for translations the UP will in fact be much cheaper to obtain than the traditional EP validated in every EU territory.

Yet, it is worth bearing in mind that only around 2% of all EPs are validated in every EU MS (about 1,000 out of the approximately 50,000 annually validated EPs); meanwhile, 8% of EPs are validated in 13 EU MS (around 4,000), with 50% validated only in Germany, the UK and France (approximately 25,000).[166] Since most patents are validated only in these three major territories, any analysis of the potential cost savings of the UP with respect to translations – as well as with regard to renewal fees (discussed further later on) – must take this into account. Moreover, it has been suggested that the translation costs for obtaining a UP would be more expensive than obtaining an EP with national validations in Germany, France and the UK, because post-London Agreement, translations are not required for these territories.[167]

UP renewal fees

On the subject of fees, the EPO Economic and Scientific Advisory Board report, *Recommendations for improving the patent system*,

---

[164] Hoffmann-Eitle, *The EU Patents Package Handbook: A Practioner's Guide* (Munich: Hoffmann-Eitle, 2014), 24 and 56.

[165] Article 5 Translation Regulation.

[166] EU Commission Staff Working Paper (Impact Assessment) SEC(2011) 482/2 (2011), 14.

[167] Hoffmann-Eitle, *The EU Patents Package Handbook: A Practioner's Guide* (Munich: Hoffmann-Eitle, 2014), 26.

holds considerable interest.[168] The EPO report states that with respect to patent fees the existence of 'harmonised fee policies at European level could help to avoid low-quality applications, reduce complexity and discourage certain patent filing practices', while it also warns that any reforms to the current system 'should have a clear rationale and beware of unintended consequences'.[169]

There is little doubt that the pricing of the renewal fee and associated fees will be crucial for the UP.[170] At present, the vast majority of EPs are validated in the UK, Germany and France, followed by Italy and Spain. Only 20–30% of EPs are validated in the Netherlands, Belgium and Sweden, and validations are even rarer in other countries.[171] Given the fact that Spain, Poland – and, initially, Croatia – will not participate in the new system, further validations must be sought in these countries (though, as noted earlier on in this chapter, if the language of patent prosecution at the EPO is English, it is acceptable for the additional required translation to be in e.g. Spanish or Polish.

Clearly, inventors and other prospective patentees will need to consider whether they need the wider protection offered by the UP. If the costs of the renewal fees – currently expected to be levelled at the equivalent of the 'top four' EPC MS fees – outweigh the benefits of obtaining wider protection, then the traditional EP with a limited number of validations may be a better option (see also the London Agreement).[172]

---

[168] EPO Economic and Scientific Advisory Board, *Recommendations for Improving the Patent System* (2012), 1, available at http://documents.epo.org/projects/babylon/eponot.nsf/0/835DA6DA218CB760C1257B2C004E809E/$FILE/ESAB_statement_en.pdf.

[169] EPO Economic and Scientific Advisory Board, *Recommendations for Improving the Patent System* (2012), 1, available at http://documents.epo.org/projects/babylon/eponot.nsf/0/835DA6DA218CB760C1257B2C004E809E/$FILE/ESAB_statement_en.pdf.

[170] Article 12(1) UP Regulation.

[171] Hoffmann-Eitle, *The EU Patents Package Handbook: A Practioner's Guide* (Munich: Hoffmann-Eitle, 2014), 26.

[172] EPO, 'Business-friendly fee pattern adopted for the unitary patent' (2015), available at www.epo.org/news-issues/news/2015/20150624.html.

Property Considerations: Governing Law for Unitary Patents and Patentees from States that are not Part of the UPC Agreement

When considered from the point of view of property rights – which are highly relevant to assignments, licensing, securitization, etc. – a UP will be under the jurisdiction not of the UPC and its substantive law, but instead under the national laws of the Signatory States.[173] For patentees holding UPs who are based, in some form or other, within a UPC MS, there is a system of 'conflict of laws' – rules which set the applicable national law, and in most cases this will be where the applicant has his/her/its main place of business or residence at the patent application filing date.[174] However, it is clear that for a large amount of UPs – any patent where the applicant/patentee is resident outside the UPC SS, such as the USA, China, Japan, South Korea – these are likely to be considered as objects of property under German law, because these patents will be viewed as legally granted within the territory of Germany at the EPO.[175]

However, there is one type of licence that will certainly be considered by the UPC: the 'licence of right' facilitated by the EPO and usually agreed on FRAND terms.[176] Particularly important in this regard is the concept of 'appropriate compensation' – an EU law concept that may lead the UPC to refer questions to the CJEU.[177]

National patents and utility models

National patents will largely be unaffected by the coming into force of the new UP system.[178] However, most EPC MS have enacted

---

[173] Recital 6 and Articles 3(2) and 7(1) UP Regulation.

[174] Hoffmann-Eitle, *The EU Patents Package Handbook: A Practioner's Guide* (Munich: Hoffmann-Eitle, 2014), 24.

[175] Hoffmann-Eitle, *The EU Patents Package Handbook: A Practioner's Guide* (Munich: Hoffmann-Eitle, 2014), 224. See also Hogan Lovells, 'Property in unitary patents' (2015), available at www.theunitarypatent.com/property-in-unitary-patents-.

[176] Article 32(1)(h) UPC Agreement and Article 8 UP Regulation.

[177] Bird & Bird, 'Property and contractual aspects of unitary patents and of patents in the UPC system' (2014), available at www.twobirds.com/en/news/articles/2014/netherlands/property-and-contractual-aspects-of-unitary-patents-and-of-patents-in-the-upc-system.

[178] Recital 26 UP Regulation.

prohibitions against 'double protection' of patents at the EPC and national levels.[179] This means that once the UP is available, it won't always be possible to enforce a national patent once an UP based on the same invention has been applied for/granted. In Germany, where utility models are available, the UP will not change anything – a national Germany utility model capable of immediate enforcement, and which uses the priority date of a national or EPO application, may still be granted and litigated before the national courts in accordance with current processes and procedures. In fact, there will be the possibility to enforce the utility model at the national level in Germany and, subsequently, the EP or UP before the UPC, covering all UPC Signatory States.[180]

SUMMARY OF THE KEY ASPECTS OF THE UPC AND THE UP

- The UPC will have the exclusive jurisdiction to hear substantive patent matters – primarily infringement and validity issues – concerning UPs; and, during the transition period (of at least seven years), the UPC will share jurisdiction with national courts over all EPs except those that are opted out of its jurisdiction during the transition period. Following the end of the transition period, the UPC will have exclusive jurisdiction to hear substantive patent matters with regard to all UPs and EPs (except those EPs that have already been opted out).
- Key remedies available at the UPC will be the pan-25 EU MS injunction in the case of patent infringement and the pan-25 EU MS revocation in the case of patent invalidity. Both of these are novel within the EU, and are likely to prove to be powerful weapons in the field of patent litigation.
- UPC central divisions will be based in Paris, London and Munich. Local divisions in Germany will be based in the

[179] Article 139(3) EPC.

[180] A. Tombling and A. Fleuchaus, 'Creative filing strategies for the unitary patent' (2014), available at www.fleuchaus.de/wp-content/uploads/2015/06/MIP-Patentstrategies-UPC.pdf.

traditionally strong patent jurisdictions of Düsseldorf, Mannheim and Munich as well as Hamburg. The local divisions in the UK, France and the Netherlands will be located in London, Paris and The Hague, respectively. Furthermore, Sweden, Estonia, Latvia and Lithuania are planning to form a regional division, using English as the common language of proceedings, while other local divisions will be formed, including in Ireland.

- Due to bifurcation, local/regional divisions will hear first-instance infringement cases; meanwhile, the central divisions will hear patent revocation actions. However, central divisions may also hear patent infringement actions (and their respective counterclaims for revocation) where these are: (i) referred by local/regional divisions; or (ii) heard at the central division because there is no local/regional division in the territory of infringement. Forum shopping will thus likely be available to litigants at the UPC.
- Regarding second-instance decisions, the Court of Appeal of the UPC (situated in Luxembourg) will render final decisions on patent infringement actions and revocation actions, respectively.
- The CJEU will deal only with referrals from the UPC on the interpretation of EU law.
- The application process for a UP will be the same as for an EP – the option for unitary protection comes post-grant.
- Initially, a UP will offer unitary protection in all SS of the UPC (i) that have joined the EU Enhanced Cooperation procedure at the time of application for UP registration; and (ii) where the UPC Agreement is in force on the date of registration.[181] When full ratification of the UPC has occurred, a newly granted UP will cover 25 EU MS (potentially rising to 26 if and when Poland signs up to the UPC Agreement, and 28 if both Spain and Croatia join up in the future). So, full EU territorial scope for the UP is a possibility in the future – however, due to EU law the UP cannot be

181 Articles 2(a) and 18(2) UP Regulation.

extended to cover non-EU MS that are parties to the EPC such as Switzerland, Iceland and Turkey.

- The UP will fall under the exclusive jurisdiction of the UPC, but most UP property considerations remain within the remit of national courts, with German law being of significance for non-EU-based patentees.
- The UP will be much cheaper to obtain than the EP validations required to cover the equivalent 25 EU MS due to the UP translation provisions. As noted in later chapters, however, the overall cost savings must be considered in light of the UP renewal fees, as well as from the patentee point of view – do patentees actually need/desire wider protection?

4. Exploring perspectives of the Unified Patent Court and the Unitary Patent within the business and legal communities

OVERVIEW OF THE STUDY

During early January 2014, I was commissioned by the UK IPO to undertake an empirical, qualitative study of the UPC from the perspectives of those in the legal and business communities who will use the new system. The principal objective of the study was to identify and analyse what the key aspects of the UPC and the UP are for those who will use the new system. The aim was not to limit the study to UK participants but to include participants from within and outside the EU.

EMPIRICAL RESEARCH METHODOLOGY

I worked with the IPO to ensure that the overall research methodology – and particularly the list of interview questions and the representative sample of interviewees – was appropriate and tailored to meet the primary aim of the project, i.e. establishing what the most significant issues are for potential users of the new system.

In this respect, I first examined the available literature on (i) the current state of patent litigation in Europe and (ii) the UPC/UPC reforms in order to discover what questions needed to be asked about the key patent issues in Europe. In this regard, the research presented in Chapters 2 and 3 of this book corresponds to this aspect of the study: in Chapter 2 I examined the current state of European patent litigation, and in Chapter 3 I explored the nature and characteristics of the UPC and the UP.

Having outlined these aspects of the European patent system, I created (i) an initial representative sample to cover the projected 25–30 interviews and (ii) a list of provisional interview questions which drew on the insights gathered from the literature review. The representative sample and provisional interview questions were created with the intention of running four initial pilot interviews to gauge the responses of interviewees to the questions. During and immediately after the pilot, the questions were reviewed and re-designed, incorporating suggestions made by the pilot interviewees, before the remaining interviews took place. Once the core set of questions had been finalized (following the four pilot interviews), the remaining interview candidates were invited to take part, and the remaining interviews took place from February to March 2014.

Developing the Interview Questions

Regarding the subjects of discussion in the interviews, the research undertaken in Chapters 2 and 3 of this book highlighted a number of significant insights that informed the writing of the specific interview questions shown in the Annex. Of particular importance in this respect were the following points:

- The vast majority of patent litigation in Europe occurs in Germany, a jurisdiction which is known for speedy, bifurcated infringement proceedings – something which often results in a high rate of patent infringement and a high rate of settlement; the UK meanwhile is a jurisdiction with a high proportion of pharma and chemical patent litigation, and with a high rate of patent revocation; proceedings are also speedy in the Netherlands and take the longest in France.
- The private litigation costs of patent litigation are very high in the UK, which features wide disclosure, use of expert and experimental evidence, and long oral hearings; private costs are much lower in Germany, France and the Netherlands, all of which use a paper-based system, with very short oral hearings and more limited required disclosure.

- Value-based court fees have been used for a long time in Germany and have recently been introduced in the UK.
- While only relevant for a minority of litigated patents, parallel litigation does take place across EU jurisdictions and often results in different outcomes. This creates a problem of legal uncertainty, as well as competition issues.
- The UPC will have the exclusive jurisdiction to hear substantive patent matters – primarily concerning infringement and validity – concerning UPs; and, during the transition period (of at least seven years), the UPC will share jurisdiction with national courts over all EPs except those EPs that are opted out of its jurisdiction during the transition period. Following the end of the transition period, the UPC will have exclusive jurisdiction to hear substantive patent matters with regard to both UPs and EPs (except those EPs that have already been opted out). Key remedies available at the UPC will be the pan-25 EU MS injunction in the case of patent infringement and the pan-25 EU MS revocation in the case of patent invalidity.
- UPC central divisions will be based in Paris, London and Munich. Local divisions in Germany will be based in the traditionally strong patent jurisdictions of Düsseldorf, Mannheim, Munich as well as Hamburg. The local divisions in the UK, France and the Netherlands will be located in London, Paris and The Hague, respectively. Furthermore, Sweden, Estonia, Latvia and Lithuania are planning to form a regional division, using English as the common language of proceedings, while other local divisions will be formed, including in Ireland.
- Due to bifurcation, local/regional divisions will hear first-instance infringement cases; meanwhile, the central divisions will hear patent revocation actions. However, central divisions may also hear patent infringement actions (and their respective counterclaims for revocation) where these are: (i) referred by local/regional divisions; or (ii) heard at the central division because there is no local/regional division in the territory of infringement. Forum shopping will thus likely be available to litigants at the UPC.

- Regarding second-instance decisions, the Court of Appeal of the UPC (situated in Luxembourg) will render final decisions on patent infringement actions and revocation actions, respectively.
- The CJEU will deal only with referrals from the UPC on the interpretation of EU law.
- The application process for a UP will be the same as for an EP – the option for unitary protection comes post-grant.
- Initially, a UP will offer unitary protection in all SS of the UPC (i) that have joined the EU Enhanced Cooperation procedure at the time of application for UP registration; and (ii) where the UPC Agreement is in force on the date of registration.[1] When full ratification of the UPC has occurred, a newly granted UP will cover 25 EU MS (potentially rising to 26 if and when Poland signs up to the UPC Agreement, and 28 if both Spain and Croatia join up in the future). So, full EU territorial scope for the UP is a possibility in the future – however, due to EU law the UP cannot be extended to cover non-EU MS that are parties to the EPC such as Switzerland, Iceland and Turkey.
- The UP will fall under the exclusive jurisdiction of the UPC, but most UP property considerations remain within the remit of national courts, with German law being of significance for non-EU-based patentees.
- The UP will be much cheaper to obtain than the EP validations required to cover the equivalent 25 EU MS, due to the UP translation provisions. However, the overall cost savings must be considered in light of the UP renewal fees, as well as from the patentee point of view – do patentees actually need/desire wider protection?

With respect to qualitative IP research more generally, Greenhalgh et al. collected survey data on a small sample of patenting and non-patenting companies (active between 2002 and 2009) to analyse the IP litigation activity of micro firms and SMEs, with a

---

1 Articles 2(a) and 18(2) UP Regulation.

particular focus on IP disputes that did not make it to court.[2] Greenhalgh et al. found that approximately 40% of patent-holding firms were involved in some kind of IP dispute during the five years prior to the survey. The study highlights the challenges that SMEs face in conducting IP litigation – noting, in particular, the fact that IP litigation is typically viewed by SMEs as being too costly and time-consuming for them to realistically engage in, even in situations where they think infringement of their rights has occurred. In addition to the points highlighted above, this insight informed the question design for the SME interviews undertaken during the development of this book project.

Overall, therefore, regarding the approach taken in drawing up the questionnaire for the interviews, the process was informed by insights drawn from the above research and literature review, and several recent academic publications on the subject of the UPC/UP reforms.[3]

As shown in part I of the Annex, the provisional list of questions was drawn up to include general questions covering interviewee attitudes towards the UPC/UP (including hopes and fears), and specific questions on the opt-out option, the various UPC/UP fees, the UPC locations and several business sector-specific issues.

Creating the Representative Sample

I drew up a purposive qualitative case study sample featuring direct and indirect potential users of the UP/UPC.[4] The sample included a total of 28 interviewees from the following categories:

---

2 C. Greenhalgh, J. Philips, R. Pitkethly, M. Rogers and J. Tomalin, *Intellectual Property Enforcement in Smaller UK Firms: A Report for the Strategy Advisory Board for Intellectual Property Policy* (SABIP, 2010), 1, 69–70.

3 See e.g. A. Kaisi, 'Finally a single European right for the EU? An analysis of the substantive provisions of the European patent with unitary effect', *European Intellectual Property Review* 36 (2014), 170; J. Pila, 'The European patent: an old and vexing problem', *International & Comparative Law Quarterly* 62 (2013), 917; and A. West, S. Kusumakar and T. Powell, 'Unitary patents and the Unified Patent Court', *Computer and Telecommunications Law Review* 19 (2013), 105.

4 For discussion of the way 'samples' and 'fields' are constructed in relation to empirical research, see S. Dalsgaard, 'The field as a temporal entity

(i) representatives of large businesses based in the UK (in-house counsel and IP experts);
(ii) representatives of large businesses based in the EU (in-house counsel and IP experts);
(iii) representatives of SMEs in the UK;
(iv) patent attorneys in the UK and elsewhere in the major EU jurisdictions (e.g. Germany);[5]
(v) solicitors/attorneys/lawyers in the UK and elsewhere in the major EU jurisdictions (e.g. Germany);[6]
(vi) representative bodies.

Thus, the interviewee sample included representatives – such as in-house counsel/patent attorneys/IP experts – of large businesses based in the EU, with a particular emphasis on UK-based companies. This sample included a broad spectrum of large companies in the various sectors that reflect the three UPC central divisions in London (Pharma/Chemicals), Munich (Engineering) and Paris (everything else, including Information and Communications Technology (ICT) and Electronics). For simplification purposes, and to enhance anonymity, the analysis provided over the course of this chapter uses the category of the 'ICT sector' (ICT) to include both ICT companies and companies that manufacture consumer electronics, while the 'Engineering sector' (ENG) includes a broad range of companies involved in large-scale manufacturing, such as automotive and defence companies. Where the term 'Pharma/Chemicals sector' is used, it encompasses pharmaceutical and chemicals companies (though, at other times, where necessary, these sectors are analysed separately). I took care to ensure that a balanced number of representatives from all three of these broad sectors were invited to participate. Finally, it is important to note that for the

---

and the challenges of the contemporary', *Social Anthropology* 20 (2013), 213. Regarding analysis of what the appropriate length and breadth of empirical research projects is, see G. Marcus, 'How short can fieldwork be?', *Social Anthropology* 15 (2007), 353.

5 It was initially intended that the project would include French lawyers, but unfortunately this proved impossible within the time frame of the project. Despite the efforts of the author and the IPO (six email invitations were issued), no French invitees from the legal community accepted the invitation to participate.

6 As note 5.

purposes of clarity, and to enhance anonymity, the various in-house counsel/patent attorneys/IP experts working at each company are referred to in the analysis below as 'in-house counsel'.

Regarding SMEs, there are significant challenges to obtaining a representative sample of SME interviewees, given the size and diversity of the SME sector; moreover, its patentee members tend to be less visible than their larger peers. Indeed, early responses from interviewees during the pilot stage of the data-gathering process underlined this challenge: unlike larger businesses, SMEs often do not have an in-house dedicated team of IP experts/counsel, and for this reason SMEs tend to follow closely the advice of their patent attorneys in legal matters. In light of this, the SME perspective is represented in this report via two methods – first, through examination of the interview data gathered from solicitors and patent attorneys with direct experience of advising SMEs; and second, via analysis of the interview data gathered from interviews undertaken with in-house IP experts operating at one Pharma SME and one ICT SME.

Ultimately, with regard to the business community a total of 15 interviews took place featuring a total of 17 respondents (two interviews were dual interviews). Of the 15, seven interviews (featuring nine participants) took place with in-house representatives of the ICT sector (including one ICT SME); five interviews took place with in-house representatives of the Pharma/Chemicals sector (including one Pharma SME);[7] and three interviews took place with experienced in-house counsel at engineering firms. These in-house interviewees include a number of qualified lawyers and patent attorneys, several of whom have experience of representative organizations.

The reason for the slight over-emphasis of the ICT sector in terms of the number of interviewees is that, on average, invitees from this sector responded more positively and much more quickly

[7] It is worth noting that one of these 'Pharma' multi-national companies was a large 'diversified' company which also had business in areas other than Pharma, including in the Engineering sector. However, the greater emphasis during the interview was on the Pharma side of the business, than on other areas, which is why it is put into this category.

to the invitations than invitees in other sectors.[8] This may well indicate that patent experts in the ICT sector are particularly engaged with the UPC/UP discussions. Moreover, during the initial pilot and early interviews, several interviewees suggested other potential participants who might be interested in the study – three of the eventual ICT interviewees were initially contacted via this 'snowball' method, as was one Pharma interviewee.

With respect to the legal community, a total of 11 interviews took place, featuring 11 individual participants – three of whom have experience of working in representative organizations. Of the 11, six interviews took place with UK solicitors who have experience of patent litigation (including two who have experience of SME patent litigation). Meanwhile, two interviews took place with UK patent attorneys – one who has experience working with larger businesses in private practice and one whose main experience comes from advising SMEs. Finally, one interview took place with an experienced German lawyer and two interviews took place with experienced German patent attorneys.

Ultimately, a total of 26 interviews (featuring a total of 28 interviewees) took place – 15 from the business community and 11 from the legal community. The interviewees agreed to participate voluntarily under the condition of anonymity. They gave up their time generously, for which I am most grateful. All data is held and used anonymously in accordance with the Data Protection Act 1998.

The Conduct of the Interviews: January–March 2014

As noted earlier in this chapter, during early-to-mid January 2014 I worked with the IPO to identify the specific questions that the project ought to ask.[9] Following the creation of the list of provisional questions, four pilot interviews took place during late January 2014. The first two involved a UK patent attorney and an ICT

---

8 Overall, an equal number – approximately nine to ten – invitations were sent out to representatives from each sector – 'Pharma/Chemicals', 'Engineering' and 'ICT'.

9 This list of provisional interview questions is shown in part I of the Annex.

in-house counsel. The main feedback comments from these interviews were as follows:

- Both interviewees noted that the questions covered most of the key issues, but they argued that there were too many questions in the list; they felt that although the right questions were asked, the interview did not flow as easily as it could have. For this reason, they felt the list needed to be simplified and framed around six to seven core questions.
- One of the interviewees made the suggestion that two additional questions be added – one on the possible interplay between UPC revocation actions and EPO oppositions in light of the EPO backlog; and one on the issue of whether patentees would consider a return to the national patenting systems once the UPC transitional period ends and they can no longer opt out of the UPC system.

In light of this feedback, the author designed two new questions covering these issues and added them to the provisional list of questions – as shown in part I of the Annex. Following this, the final two pilot interviews were carried out – both of these interviews featured in-house ICT counsel. These final pilot interviews followed the initial provisional list of questions (with the addition of the two new questions) with the intention of gauging responses/interview flow in order to restructure the list of questions post-pilot. Then, following the final two pilot interviews, I re-oriented and to some extent simplified the interview questions in order to create the final list of questions – shown in part II of the Annex. The remaining 22 out of the overall total of 26 interviews took place using this final list of questions.[10] In total, 23 out of 26 interviews were carried out over the phone, two were carried out face-to-face and one interview was carried out in a truncated form via email in line with the participant's wishes after he had been forced

[10] However, it is notable that the first eight interviews did not feature Question 7 – which asked interviewees about their sources of information on the UPC – as this question was only added following a suggestion by the IPO after the first eight interviews took place.

to withdraw from a phone interview at the last minute due to work constraints.[11]

Empirical Data Analysis

By asking a set of seven to eight core questions to each interviewee (as detailed in the Annex), I sought to discover what stakeholders consider to be the most important issues with respect to the UPC and the UP. The key issues explored below include the costs of using the UPC and the UP, the opt-out decision, various business sector-specific concerns, as well as the changes the new system will bring to the legal community.

Assessing the costs of the UPC and the UP

All interviewees, whether from the business field or from the legal community, stated that they were concerned about some or all of the costs of using the new system, namely the (then proposed) UPC opt-out fee, the fees for using the UPC, and the UP renewal fees. These issues were of particular concern for businesses at the time of interview since the levels of these fees had not yet been finalized, which meant that businesses were unable to properly weigh up the costs/benefits of using the new system.[12] The views the interviewees expressed in the study regarding the fees ended up feeding back into the preparations for the organization of the court, something I discuss further in the following chapter.

The opt-out fee The (then proposed) UPC opt-out fee was noted as a major concern for patentees: the interviewees stated universally that a relatively high opt-out fee would dissuade businesses from opting out their entire portfolio from the courts system. For this reason, several interviewees argued that this fee should be set at a relatively low, administrative level. Nonetheless, interviewees from the ICT sector noted that these small administrative fees would

[11] Not all questions were asked/answered during this truncated interview, due to the participant's time constraints. Where a question was not asked/answered, this is noted in the Annex.

[12] J. Nurton, 'Patent practitioners call for UPC cost clarity', *Managing Intellectual Property* (2014), available at http://.managingip.com/Article/3320776/Patent-practitioners-call-for-UPC-cost-clarity.html.

soon add up for companies seeking to opt out large portfolios. In this respect, one interviewee solicitor argued that 'bulk opt-outs should get a discount on the opt-out fees'.

Court fee levels at the UPC Generally, the UPC fees issue was stated by stakeholders to be a less important one than the issue of the UP renewal fees. Indeed, as detailed in the Annex, around half of the interviewees stated that they do not see the UPC fees issue as a major concern. The reason for this comparative lack of concern about court fees, in comparison with the UP renewal fees discussed further on, is that while renewal fees have to be paid for every patent, court fees only come into play for litigated patents – and the vast majority of patents are never litigated. Moreover, in the UK (at time of interview) the PHC fees were dwarfed by the private legal costs of undertaking litigation at the court, which typically amount to more than £1 million for each side.[13] Interestingly, as noted in Chapter 2, the UK has now switched to a system of value-based fees, something I reflect on in the analysis below and in the final concluding chapter of this book.

That being said, even though the UPC fees issue was generally seen by interviewees as less important than the UP renewal fees issue, several interviewees made important observations concerning the UPC fees. In particular, it was noted that in Germany the costs of the court fees in patent cases can often rival the private legal costs – court fee figures of between €100,000 and €200,000 per case were regularly cited by interviewees based on their prior experience of the German system. Given the fact that there are great disparities in court fees between different European jurisdictions – and in particular between the traditional fixed UK fees (now changed) and the value-based fees found in Germany – there was understandably a great deal of scepticism amongst some stakeholders about basing the UPC fees on a combination of the current court fee levels in, for example, 3–4 EU MS.

For this reason, just over a quarter of all interviewees argued that the UPC fees should be set at a level significantly lower than the current German fees – and not at a combined DE + UK + NL level.

---

[13] L. McDonagh and C. Helmers, 'Patent litigation in England and Wales and the issue-based approach to costs', *Civil Justice Quarterly* 32 (2013), 369.

In terms of specifics, one solicitor interviewee argued that the initial filing fee 'should be less than £10,000' and that the overall court fees ought to amount to 'much less than the €200,000 level that commonly results in Germany'.

Other stakeholders were more sanguine on the fees issue. A small minority of interviewees stated that they would be willing to accept UPC fees approximating the fees of litigating in 1–2, or even 3–4, jurisdictions. For instance, one Germany-based lawyer stated that a fee level at the 1–2 MS level would be ideal because at present most patentee companies do not litigate in more than 1–2 jurisdictions. Furthermore, one in-house ICT counsel even stated that high upfront filing fees are 'something they favour' because such fees 'act as a deterrent to the filing of frivolous lawsuits'.

Value-based fees The proposed fee system for the UPC will feature a mixture of fixed and value-based fees, with the value-based fees coming into play once a certain value threshold is met. Some potential users of the UPC voiced scepticism about the use of a value-based fees system. For example, one experienced solicitor argued that using a German-style value-based fee system within the UPC would not provide litigants with a reliable costs gauge 'given that in Germany damages can be claimed which go beyond this "value"'. Instead, he argued that it would be better to establish an instalment-based, incremental fee system, based on how much the parties use the court, for example the number of hearing days or applications.

By contrast, a German lawyer I spoke to argued that the value-based system 'works very well' in the vast majority of cases in Germany where 'it is used in order to cap costs'. He noted that in the majority of cases 'parties tend to come to agreement' with respect to what level the value should be set at. Similarly, a Germany-based patent attorney (PA) remarked: 'The value-based fees system in Germany works well because it is transparent and it caps the court fees and lawyers' fees – especially for the defendant who knows his liability for these fees.'

This comment highlights an important feature of the value-based system in Germany – it caps not only the court fees but also the recoverable private legal costs. This second element – the limit on recovery of private legal costs – provides an incentive to each side to keep their own costs low. At time of interview it was not yet known whether the UPC system would include a cap on recoverable costs, but this possibility was of interest to participants, and the final UPC fees schedule, discussed further in the next chapter, does indeed include a ceiling on recoverable costs.

One in-house ICT counsel consulted with his colleagues based in Germany about their experiences of the value-based fee system there, and he then related their comments to me as part of the interview process. With regard to positive comments, he stated that the value-based system 'acts as a disincentive' to the kind of 'patent trolling' behaviour commonly found in the USA, because 'taking a speculative case against a big player can mean high costs reimbursement'. He noted that another positive of the value-based system is that at the end of the case there is no argument between parties about the amount of costs. He remarked: 'By contrast, it is not uncommon for parties in the UK to spend as much money arguing about the costs award as they spend on the case itself.'

With respect to negative comments about the value-based system, the same interviewee argued that the German system does not provide SMEs with adequate incentives to make counterclaims for invalidity in the context of infringement actions, something which in his opinion ultimately favours larger companies. One final thing he commented on relates to case-counting, which works very differently in the UK and Germany.[14] He remarked:

> If 3 parties attack the same patent, these count as three separate cases, even if they are heard jointly … So the loser may have to pay three times. In the context of the UPC this is an important consideration in either multi-party or multi-patent cases, and the Rules of Procedure need to get this right to ensure overall fees remain within reasonable levels.

Will the UPC help to lower the costs of patent litigation in Europe?

With respect to the idea that the UPC will reduce the overall costs of patent litigation in Europe, the interviewees expressed scepticism that this will in fact be the result. Indeed, one in-house Pharma counsel stated confidently that the costs of litigating at the UPC

---

[14] K. Cremers, M. Ernicke, D. Harhoff, C. Helmers, G. Licht, L. McDonagh, et al. 'Patent litigation in Europe', *ZEW Discussion Paper* No. 13-07 (2013), 1.

will not, in fact, turn out to be lower than the costs of litigating within the current national systems. He argued that the coming into force of the new system 'will effectively move cases from Germany, where most patent litigation happens, to the UPC';[15] moreover, since, in his view, litigation at the UPC is likely to prove to be more expensive than the current costs of German patent litigation, the overall costs of patent litigation in Europe are likely to go up. In a similar vein, one in-house ICT counsel remarked that 'realistically the costs of the new system will inevitably be higher than they are now'.

Nonetheless, a Germany-based lawyer put forward a dissenting view, arguing that the UPC will, in fact, reduce the costs of litigation in Europe. Crucially, however, she argued that this will only be the case if the UPC litigation costs do not go beyond the current costs of litigating in 1–2 MS, noting that at present most litigated patents are not litigated beyond two European jurisdictions. Similarly, a German-based PA stated that the UPC fees 'will be lower than the current German fees' – though, conversely, he remarked that the private legal costs of litigating at the UPC will probably 'be closer to the UK level' than the lower level currently found in Germany.

In light of this, and the comments made above concerning the value-based system, it is reasonable to summarize the UPC costs issue as follows: the expectation amongst stakeholders at time of interview was that the UPC fees would be higher than the traditional non-value-based UK fees (which ended in 2015), but they expressed hope that the fees would not be as high as the current German fees. With respect to private legal costs, some interviewees expressed the fear that the private legal costs of taking a UPC case will end up being closer to the high UK level than the comparatively lower German level, given the fact that the UPC has a much wider jurisdictional remit than the individual national courts, something that may require a lot of legal resources to be expounded by

---

15 K. Cremers, M. Ernicke, D. Harhoff, C. Helmers, G. Licht, L. McDonagh, et al. 'Patent litigation in Europe', *ZEW Discussion Paper* No. 13-07 (2013), 1, 5, noting that most patent litigation in Europe takes place in Germany at present; moreover, only a relatively small proportion of EPs are litigated in more than one jurisdiction. It is likely, therefore, that the UPC will take many cases that would otherwise be heard in Germany.

each side. On the other hand, the absence of lengthy, UK-style oral hearings is likely to keep costs down. Given that it has now been confirmed that the UPC will, as some interviewees hoped, feature a ceiling on recoverable private legal costs (depending on case value), this may give both sides an incentive to keep their own costs down.[16]

The overall worst case UPC costs scenario for stakeholders would be one featuring court fees at the German level, or higher, and private legal costs close to the UK level, or higher. However, given the absence of lengthy oral hearings at the UPC it seems unlikely – though not impossible – that the private legal costs will reach UK levels. Moreover, as I discuss in the next chapter, the benefits of one-stop enforcement (such as the availability of 25 EU MS injunctions) also need to be taken into account when the costs are considered, as these benefits may make litigation at the UPC worthwhile, even if the litigation costs end up being higher than stakeholders hope.

UP renewal fee levels The crucial importance of the renewal fees issue was emphasized by all interviewees. For instance, one Germany-based PA I spoke to remarked that the key issue for the future success of the UP 'is this renewal fees issue'. In fact, he argued that 'this is currently being underestimated in terms of its importance' by policy-makers.

It is clear from the interview responses, as further detailed in the Annex, that at time of interview the majority of stakeholders felt that in order to encourage utilization of the UP the level of the renewal fees ought to be set around the 3 MS level (UK + DE + FR). They argued any fee level that goes significantly beyond this runs the risk of creating a serious disincentive to utilization of the UP. Indeed, one interviewee argued that the 'ideal fee' would be at the 2 MS level – and specifically a UK + DE fee – stating that 'only that would be a genuine incentive'. He argued that a 3 MS fee would merely be 'neutral' since this represents the costs of patenting for most companies in the present system. On the other hand, one in-house ICT counsel stated that her company 'would like to

16 Details of the final fees schedule are available here – www.unified-patent-court.org/sites/default/files/agreed_and_final_r370_subject_to_legal_scrubbing_to_secretariat.pdf.

see a higher renewal fee because higher fees discourage spurious patenting'. Notably, this was a uniquely held view amongst the interviewees.

With respect to specific figures for renewal fees, one experienced Germany-based PA gave some relevant estimates. As an example, he focused on the sixth year of renewal fees for the UK + DE + FR, which he said amounts to a total of approximately €350, further noting that with the addition of NL + SWE this total would increase to €520. Regarding the proposed UP renewal fee level, he remarked: 'I've heard some speculation that the equivalent UP renewal fee will be close to €600.'

In his opinion, this €600 fee would be 'far too high' as it goes beyond even the renewal fees of 4–5 MS. For him, the ideal fee would lie between 3 and 4 MS, i.e. not more than €400.

Similarly, one in-house Chemicals counsel stated that if the renewal fee is set at a level above 3–4 MS this will result in there being 'very few UP cases in the system' – something that will not bode well for establishing a strong body of UPC jurisprudence. For him, the crucial issue that policy-makers 'must take into account' is that 'the increased protection is not really worth paying extra for'. Similarly, a German-based PA warned that the UP will probably be seriously under-utilized unless the fee levels are set 'well below the 6 MS fees that have been discussed'.

Indeed, with the exception of the Pharma sector – where the in-house interviewees acknowledged that patenting in all, or a great many, EU MS is relatively common – most interviewees from the ICT and ENG sectors stated that their companies tend to patent in no more than 3–4 MS. In this respect, the representatives from ICT and ENG companies said that their companies typically validate in a selection of the UK, Germany, France, the Netherlands, Sweden, Italy and Spain – with the UK and Germany being relative constants. Nonetheless, exceptions to this do exist: one in-house ENG counsel said that her company tends to patent in only 1–2 MS (UK + DE); meanwhile, another interviewee – also an in-house ENG counsel – stated that her company typically seeks to patent in 7–15 MS, with the larger number of validations coming into play in the case of a highly valuable patent. In addition, the in-house Chemicals counsel I interviewed noted that his company commonly tends to patent in 8 MS.

Therefore, looking at all of the various sectors it is clear that only the Pharma sector would find a renewal fee set far above the 3 MS level – such as at the 6–8 MS level – to be advantageous, since this would still be a significant cost saving on validating in all the MS separately. Nonetheless, despite this apparent benefit to the Pharma sector, one German-based lawyer I spoke to argued that for Pharma the costs of renewing the patent are not actually the ultimate 'deal-breaker' with respect to prospective use of the UP and the UPC; instead, the interviewee argued that Pharma companies are actually willing to pay whatever the necessary fees are in order to secure EU-wide protection, regardless of the cost, because for Pharma these fees amount to a small cost in the grand scheme of things. The interviewee went on to say that the key factor for Pharma with respect to use of the UP is likely to be the UPC's success (or not) in generating a consistent body of case law across the system – only that would persuade the Pharma sector to adopt the UP wholesale. The impact of the fact that the UP renewal fee has, post-interviews, now been set at the 4 MS level is discussed in the next chapter.

Pruning of the Patent Portfolio

Several interviewees noted that many companies, particularly those who patent in only 3–4 MS, tend to 'prune' their patent validations selectively towards the end of patent life, i.e. they may choose to drop the validations in the more expensive jurisdictions and simply keep up protection in the cheapest 1–2 MS.

Crucially, with the UP this type of selective pruning will not be possible – a company will either renew the UP entirely or not at all. Thus, keeping a patent 'alive' in the final few years of its life is likely to be more expensive with a UP than with an EP validated in 1–2 jurisdictions (after a couple of the initial 3–4 jurisdictions have been dropped). On this point, an experienced PA I spoke to argued that even if the UP renewal fee is set at the 3 MS level this will not actually provide much of an incentive to use the UP because of the loss of the ability to prune selectively.

Nonetheless, as shown in the Annex, while pruning was cited as an important consideration by the majority of interviewees, a substantial minority did not cite it as significant. This indicates that the pruning issue, while a legitimate concern, may not in itself be a 'deal-breaker' regarding use of the UP.

The UP versus the EP

One further point is of interest – a small number of interviewees argued that the UP offers little cost benefit over the EP in light of the 'London Agreement', which reduces EP translation costs.[17] In line with this, an experienced Germany-based PA remarked that the supposed advantages of the UP are currently being exaggerated by its proponents, noting that the current EP 'remains quite attractive because of the London Agreement'. Moreover, a small number of interviewees further stated that any possible benefits of the UP over the EP will be tempered by the fact that although the UP offers wider protection, not all EU MS are taking part in the new system, which leaves the EU patent system still partially fragmented.

KEY CONCERNS FOR USERS OF THE UPC

The interview participants cited a number of major concerns about the UPC – namely, the quality and composition of the UPC judicial panels, the use of bifurcation in the context of the issuance of injunctions at the UPC, patent troll litigation and forum shopping.

Judicial Composition and Quality

It is crucial that potential users of the court perceive the UPC as being a venue for high-quality, consistent decision-making. Many interviewees stated, in fact, that this would actually prove to be the most important factor in their determination of whether or not to use the UPC – more important even than the cost factor. Indeed, all interviewees said that the UPC policy-makers must take the issues of judicial composition and quality very seriously, and that the necessary funds and structures ought to be put in place to ensure proper judicial training.

In this vein, one experienced solicitor I interviewed stated that the training of judges 'will prove to be vital', especially for

---

[17] www.epo.org/law-practice/legal-texts/london-agreement/key-points.html.

jurisdictions where there is little or no established history of patent litigation. On this point, one in-house Chemicals counsel argued on a positive note that there is sufficient EU-wide expertise – especially in the major patent litigation states of the UK, Germany and France – available to train the judges. On this issue, a useful point was made by one interviewee – a German-based PA – who suggested that analysis of how exactly experts from more than 30 EPC MS have been integrated into the EPO Technical Boards could prove to be a useful model for training judges across the UPC Signatory States.

With respect to how the three-person judicial panels are likely to work in practice, one solicitor interviewee stated that the single experienced visiting judge would probably come to be dominated by the two local judges, stating that 'this inevitably tends to happen within judicial panels'. Meanwhile, some interviewees noted that fears over composition and quality at the local/regional levels could be allayed by establishing strong central divisions and a solid Court of Appeal, so that the jurisprudence of the UPC filters down to the lower divisions, thereby ensuring consistency across the entire UPC system.

Bifurcation and injunctions

Businesses – and ICT companies in particular – expressed a great deal of worry about how bifurcation will operate at the UPC. Interestingly, in the legal community few interviewees expressed concern over bifurcation – it was described by more than one legal interviewee as an 'overblown' issue.

The interviewees who expressed concern about bifurcation were particularly worried that there will be an 'injunction gap' between the infringement hearing and the validity hearing, i.e. that a decision to grant an injunction could be issued by a lower court before the patent is officially declared valid by the upper court.[18]

On this issue, several ICT interviewees argued that UPC judges ought to be provided with clear guidelines governing when bifurcation should occur, so that businesses can be reasonably certain,

---

[18] K. Cremers, F. Gaessler, D. Harhoff and C. Helmers, 'Invalid but infringed? An analysis of Germany's bifurcated patent litigation system', *Max Planck Institute for Innovation & Competition Research Paper* No. 14-14 (2014), 1.

prior to the opt-out decision, about how bifurcation will actually work in practice. Indeed, universally within the ICT sector the interviewees stated that the (then) current draft guidelines were insufficient. However, one experienced solicitor remarked that 'it is probable that there won't be guidelines and that courts will just have discretion regarding when to bifurcate'. Despite this, he argued that the bifurcation 'problem' has been 'overstated' because 'bifurcation is unlikely to happen very often', and that even where it does happen 'section 220(2) is crucial because it allows appeals on procedural matters'.[19]

In a similar vein, one in-house Chemicals counsel was more relaxed about the bifurcation and injunction gap issues, noting that the UPC will not feature German-style mandatory bifurcation; instead, it will feature what he described as 'bifurcation-lite', whereby the judges will have discretion concerning whether or not to bifurcate. He also expressed the view that even where bifurcation does occur in the new system, it is likely the UPC will be much quicker than the German courts currently are at deciding bifurcated validity/infringement decisions. This will (hopefully) prevent the dreaded 'invalid, but infringed' scenario from occurring.

Looking at the issue of injunctions more generally, the interview data indicate that the UPC's ability to issue pan-25 EU MS injunctions ought to be viewed very much as a double-edged sword: those who tend to act as claimants in litigation want the ability to seek pan-25 EU MS injunctions against their competitors via the UPC, while those who act primarily as defendants fear the consequences of those same injunctions.

Interestingly, a relatively large number of interviewees from the Pharma sector stated that they had either a positive or neutral view of the availability of pan-25 EU MS injunctions at the UPC. By contrast, in the ICT sector the opposite view was prevalent; for instance, one in-house ICT counsel remarked that because her company tends to act primarily as a defendant in litigation, it is currently very concerned about the interplay between bifurcation and the issuing of injunctions at the UPC. Like many other interviewees, she said that her company is taking a cautious 'wait and see' approach towards the UPC on this issue.

---

19 UPC Rules of Procedure.

Patent Troll Litigation and Forum Shopping

The uncertainty inherent in any new court system is of itself likely to attract NPEs, or patent trolls, to the UPC. On this point, one experienced solicitor remarked that 'patent trolls may like the new system because they like uncertainty'. With this in mind, many interviewees argued that the Rules of Procedure for the UPC ought be clarified and finalized as soon as possible to help businesses plan for the new system (something that occurred, post-interviews, in late 2015, as noted in the next chapter).

It is also important to note that fears concerning a possible growth in patent troll litigation at the UPC are closely related to the above issues of bifurcation and injunctions, since exploitation of the 'injunction threat' is a common tactic in patent troll litigation.[20] A number of interviewees argued that the patent troll issue has exploded in the USA in recent years largely because it is possible to obtain a pan-US injunction from a single regional court. In this vein, one in-house ICT counsel stated that 'there's a big problem with trolls in the USA and the new UPC system must avoid this problem'. Indeed, the same interviewee stated that if the ICT sector 'sees trolls getting injunctions across all UPC Signatory States' then the sector will quickly lose faith in the UPC. The positive corollary to this point is that if fears over bifurcation and injunctions can be allayed – ideally, by the setting up of a high quality judicial system across the UPC – the risk of patent troll litigation can probably be minimized.

However, another concern – and one that is closely related to the patent trolls issue – is the question of whether forum shopping will occur within the UPC system. On this point, one experienced solicitor said confidently that 'there will be competition' between the various local/regional courts under the new UPC system. Nonetheless, he argued that this may not prove to be as problematic as some fear, noting that to some extent competition already exists under the current EPC system – for example, there is competition between the UK courts and the German courts (as well as between the various German courts). Indeed, one Germany-based PA

[20] L. McDonagh and C. Helmers, 'Patent litigation in England and Wales and the issue-based approach to costs', *Civil Justice Quarterly* 32 (2013), 369.

remarked that Germany is a useful comparator since 'there are three major patent courts' in Germany and although 'forum shopping does occur' within the German system, it does not create major problems. In fact, he argued that the existence of forum shopping at the UPC will 'increase competition, which in turn will increase the quality of the court system, as in Germany'.

For others, however, the possibility that forum shopping may occur within the local/regional divisions of the new system raised a lot of concerns. For instance, one in-house ICT counsel remarked that 'litigation is about playing games' and that 'you pick the most difficult forum for your opponent'. In this respect, he stated that the ability to engage in forum shopping 'is an advantage for patentees, and a disadvantage for potential infringers'. Continuing in this vein, one in-house Pharma counsel stated that his big fear is that the various regional courts will decide 'to compete with each other for business' by becoming very 'patentee friendly', i.e. there could be a 'race to the bottom' in terms of the quality of judicial decision making. In that context, a patent troll could identify the most 'patentee-friendly' local or regional court, and then seek to obtain a pan-25 EU MS injunction from that court. A small number of interviewees even drew parallels with the 'US Eastern District of Texas' – a court which is often said to be notoriously 'patent troll friendly'.[21] Interviewees noted that preventing this patent troll/forum shopping fear from becoming a reality will likely require maintaining close interplay between the local/regional courts and the central divisions, and Court of Appeal.

One final point must be made about the risks of patent troll litigation at the UPC. Notably, the rise of this form of litigation in the USA is often linked to the absence of the 'loser pays' costs system in that jurisdiction.[22] On this point, one solicitor interviewee argued that with respect to the UPC the NPE/patent troll issue has 'probably been overstated' because, unlike in the USA, any potential 'troll litigants' at the UPC 'will be forced to pay their own

---

[21] L. McDonagh and C. Helmers, 'Patent litigation in England and Wales and the issue-based approach to costs', *Civil Justice Quarterly* 32 (2013), 369.

[22] C. Helmers, B. Love and L. McDonagh, 'Is there a patent troll problem in the UK?', *Fordham Intellectual Property, Media and Entertainment Law Journal* 24 (2014), 509, 509–15, available at http://papers.ssrn.com/sol3/papers.cfm?abstract_id=2331543.

costs' – something which at present appears to discourage patent troll litigation in the UK.[23] Therefore, while the possibility of obtaining a pan-25 MS injunction at the UPC is likely to attract patent troll litigants – and some forum shopping does seem inevitable – the presence of the 'loser pays' costs system at the UPC is likely to alleviate the patent troll risk to some extent at least.

Revocation of Patents

The interview data demonstrate that the 'revocation risk' works differently from sector to sector: generally, concern about this risk is much more apparent in the Pharma sector than in ICT.[24] The reason for this is that in the ICT sector companies tend to hold numerous patents of mid-range value, and as a result the revocation of a small number of patents is unlikely to have a drastic impact on the value of the company's overall portfolio. By contrast, one solicitor interviewee noted that the 'central revocation possibility is the key worry' for his Pharma clients; indeed, one in-house Pharma counsel remarked that being exposed to 'one-stop revocation' could prove very risky for Pharma companies because 'if a key, valuable Pharma patent is revoked this can affect the company's share price considerably'. He went on to explain that in the Pharma field 'a lot of key drugs are based on one big innovation' per product, i.e. a key single patent or a few key patents, further noting that 'one bad revocation decision' could have a huge impact on a company's revenues.

There is little doubt, therefore, that establishing a high quality body of revocation jurisprudence at the UPC is of the utmost importance. On this point, it is worth recalling that currently within Europe the UK is seen as the jurisdiction that undertakes the most

---

[23] C. Helmers, B. Love and L. McDonagh, 'Is there a patent troll problem in the UK?', *Fordham Intellectual Property, Media and Entertainment Law Journal* 24 (2014), 509, 509–15, available at http://papers.ssrn.com/sol3/papers.cfm?abstract_id=2331543.

[24] None of the interviewees from the ENG sector highlighted revocation as a concern.

stringent validity analysis.[25] However, the UPC will not feature the in-depth oral hearings commonly found at the UK's PHC, and will instead operate a 'paper-based' system, featuring relatively short hearings, more akin to the litigation systems of Germany and the Netherlands. Given that there has been, traditionally, a substantially higher rate of patent revocation in the UK than in either Germany or the Netherlands,[26] there may be a correlation between the rate of revocation and the type of hearing featured at the court (lengthy and in-depth vs. short and paper-based). For this reason, it is possible that the UPC will be viewed as a more 'patentee-friendly' court than the UK's PHC. Indeed, one interviewee stated that the UPC 'will, on balance, favour rights-holders/patentees' more than potential infringers/competitors.

Could Speedy UPC Revocations Help Clear the EPO Oppositions Backlog?

As noted in the Annex, around half of all interviewees stated that the availability of UPC revocation actions will likely help to ease the EPO oppositions backlog. Indeed, one experienced UK PA stated that in order to be successful the new UPC system must 'crack the backlog problem'. However, around a quarter of all interviewees said that they were not confident that the UPC will actually help to alleviate the backlog. One major reason for this scepticism is that taking a UPC revocation action is likely to prove to be much more expensive than the current cost of opposing a patent at the EPO – something that is likely to mean that many businesses will continue to prefer the EPO route. In this vein, while one experienced solicitor acknowledged that some oppositions may effectively 'move to the UPC', he argued 'crucially, there will be no easing of the backlog' because 'clients will keep opposing despite the UPC option'. In fact, one in-house ICT counsel remarked: 'The issue is that it will be possible to do both – to file an opposition in

25 K. Cremers, M. Ernicke, D. Harhoff, C. Helmers, G. Licht, L. McDonagh, et al. 'Patent litigation in Europe', *ZEW Discussion Paper* No. 13-07 (2013), 1, 46–51.

26 K. Cremers, M. Ernicke, D. Harhoff, C. Helmers, G. Licht, L. McDonagh, et al. 'Patent litigation in Europe', *ZEW Discussion Paper* No. 13-07 (2013), 1, 46–51.

the EPO and an invalidity action before the UPC. Opponents are likely to do both especially in important cases.'

In light of the above, it is clear that the impact of the UPC in this area will to some extent be tempered by the fact that businesses are likely to choose to use both systems in parallel. Nonetheless, even if opponents do challenge the patent at both venues, provided that the UPC proves itself able to resolve invalidity actions in a speedy fashion, there could well be a net overall reduction in the EPO backlog over the coming years.

A Return to the National Patent Systems?

One solicitor interviewee argued that some companies could return to the national patent systems if the UPC develops in a 'problematic' way, though he noted that 'within different sectors different factors are at play'. For instance, he said that in the context of the Pharma industry use of 25–28 national systems within the EU 'may be impractical and too expensive' since Pharma companies tend to patent in virtually all jurisdictions using the EPO route. However, he argued that for those companies that currently only patent in 1–2 jurisdictions there may be a temptation to return to the national systems. If this were to happen, he further noted that the UK IPO would see an increase in patent applications. In other words, he argued that the coming into force of the UPC 'may have the opposite effect than is intended' – that rather than unifying the practice of patenting in Europe, patentees may instead turn away from the EPO and return to the national systems. On this point, a highly experienced solicitor I interviewed argued that the UPC/UP system really 'has to be got right' because 'if the goal is to create greater unity' within the European patent system, getting the new system 'wrong' – by failing to provide a high quality litigation service at a reasonable cost – would have a 'devastating' impact on efforts to achieve this goal of unity.

Regarding the likelihood of companies actually returning to the national systems, an experienced Germany-based PA remarked: 'At the moment the pessimistic users are considering doing this, and it might already have started.'

Indeed, one in-house ENG counsel confirmed that her company had already decided to return to patenting solely in the national systems of the UK and Germany. She stated that the key issue for her company in this respect is that in their industry technological innovations tend to have a commercial life of 5–7 years, which means that as a company they need to obtain patents quickly. She noted that if her company files an application at the EPO, the delays 'mean that we often don't get a patent until 5–7 years down the line'. Thus, her company's decision to 'go national' was taken largely because of problems with the existing EPC system – though the interviewee also stated that she is not confident that the UPC/UP system will improve things. Overall, therefore, while it seems that a large-scale return to the national system is unlikely, largely due to the costs issue, some companies will surely keep this option open.

It must also be stated that despite the existence of some pessimism, many interviewees expressed great hope that the UPC would prove to be a success. Indeed, several interviewees stated that a possible return to the national systems is being contemplated 'only as a last resort'.

THE OPT-OUT

As noted in Chapter 3, there is an option for an opt-out of EPs from the UPC's jurisdiction during the transition period of 7 or 14 years. If opted out, an EP will only be litigated at the national level.

The Unfamiliar UPC: How to Adapt to the New System?

A point that emerges strongly from the interview data is that businesses – in every sector – are generally wary of the new system. Even though the current fragmented system has its problems, businesses and lawyers are at least familiar with it at the procedural and substantive levels. It is known, for instance, that if a company wishes to challenge the validity of a competitor's patent, filing a UK revocation action is a strong statement of intent. On the other hand, if a company wants to obtain an injunction against a competitor for allegedly infringing a patent, taking a case at one of the German regional courts represents the best option. In line with this, one solicitor interviewee argued that under the current fragmented system businesses already possess an adequate EU-wide ability to 'interfere with competitors' wherever the actions of their competitors are infringing.

By contrast, the new system is unfamiliar and it also lacks certainty with respect to its procedures and jurisprudence. For this reason, one solicitor interviewee stated that his clients are taking a cautious view of the UPC. He remarked that 'most would like to opt out and if it is easy to do so they will'. Nonetheless, for most businesses the final decision on whether to opt out had not been made at time of interview; indeed, 13 out of 15 in-house counsel I spoke to stated that their companies had not yet made their decision regarding the opt-out. These interviewees emphasized that no decision in this regard could be made until all the details regarding how the UPC will actually work in practice were finalized (something that did not occur until the post-interview period, in late 2015).

Nevertheless, even though in most cases final decisions had not yet been made, all the in-house counsel I interviewed stated that their companies were seriously considering opting out at least some of their patents. However, several interviewees noted that the (then proposed) opt-out fee would mean that companies would likely not be able to opt out everything in their portfolios. The impact of the fact that there will not be an opt-out fee after all is considered further in the next chapter. Interestingly, the interview data given in the Annex show that while all interviewees were preparing to opt out some or all patents, just over half were planning to keep at least some patents within the UPC's jurisdiction – for example, the 'strongest', the 'least valuable' or a 'broad spectrum across the value range'.

With respect to the patentees who were considering opting out only their most valuable patents (MVPs), one in-house Chemicals counsel stated that his company would probably opt out their 'crown jewel patents'. Nonetheless, he asserted confidently that 'more than 90% of our portfolio will be in'. Regarding the making of this determination, he remarked: 'It's a question of the advantage of being able to get an injunction versus the risk of having a valuable single patent revoked.'

The importance of this consideration was confirmed by an in-house Pharma counsel, who stated that Pharma companies would probably opt out their MVPs due to the pan-25 EU MS revocation risk at the UPC. However, he said that his company would probably decide to keep within the UPC the patents they hold over consumer/household products because these patents are less valuable.

Meanwhile, all the interviewees from the legal community stated that they expect their clients to opt out at least some patents, though none said that they expect their clients to opt out everything. For instance, one German-based lawyer I interviewed stated that she is advising her clients to 'opt out their most valuable patents and test the system with their mid-range value patents'. By contrast, a small number of interviewees stated that it is not a question of whether or not to opt out a company's MVPs; rather, it is a question of whether or not to keep within the UPC the strongest patents in the company's portfolio. Indeed, one experienced Germany-based PA remarked: 'I advise my clients to opt in strong patents.'

How will an Opted-out Patent be Perceived by Competitors?

As noted above, one German PA I interviewed stated that he was advising his clients to keep 'strong' patents within the UPC (to avail of one-stop enforcement), and to opt out 'weak' patents (to avoid the one-stop revocation risk). This raises the very interesting question of how patents opted out of the UPC will be perceived. On this very point, one interviewee – an experienced solicitor – stated that some of her clients fear 'that an opted-out patent will be perceived as weak, and thus might be attacked by competitors' (via litigation undertaken in one or more EPC jurisdictions). This is an important insight into the way the UPC/UP reforms are likely to alter the European patent litigation paradigm; indeed, the coming into force of the UPC could create a two-tier patent litigation system, with patents that are perceived as being of 'high quality' dealt with at the UPC, and patents that are perceived as being of 'low quality' dealt with by national courts.

Do EU and Non-EU Businesses View the New System Differently?

One additional point needs to be made regarding the opt-out decision: it appears that there is a difference in attitudes to the new system between EU and non-EU businesses. Several interviewees from the legal community stated that their non-EU clients are taking a more positive view of the UP/UPC system than their EU clients are. One interviewee stated that the reason non-EU companies tend to be upbeat about the UP/UPC is that they see the EU as a unitary market, and thus they want unitary protection; EU companies, on the other hand, tend to be more invested in, and more familiar with, the national systems, and thus are more resistant to change.

BUSINESS SECTOR ISSUES

As noted in Chapter 3, the central divisions of the UPC are divided between Pharma/Chemicals (London), Engineering/Mechanical (Munich) and everything else, including ICT (Paris). It is worth considering whether the impact of the reforms will affect some sectors more than others, and whether it will affect the various sectors in different ways.

Which Sector will Benefit the Most from the New System?

Since Pharma companies tend to patent in all EU MS, there does appear be at least one major long-term benefit of the UP for the sector – a 'cost and simplification' benefit. Conversely, this benefit will not be felt so keenly in the ICT sector, because ICT companies tend not to seek EU-wide patent protection; indeed, they often seek protection in only 2–4 EU MS. Similarly, interviewees from the ENG sector noted that their companies rarely obtained patent validations in more than 3–4 MS, and sometimes only in 1–2 MS. As such, like ICT companies, ENG companies are unlikely to benefit greatly from the wider protection offered by the UP. Nonetheless, a German-based PA argued that the ICT and ENG sectors are still likely to benefit from the UP in the sense that the UP will 'allow more efficient patenting'.

There may also be a benefit for the Chemicals sector since Chemicals companies tend to patent in up to 8 MS (meaning that in some cases it would still be worthwhile to get the UP even if the renewal fees were set above the 3 MS level). On this point, one interviewee remarked: 'For Chemicals the price is key – the costs must not outweigh the benefits.'

Overall, therefore, for Pharma companies – and, to a lesser extent, for Chemicals companies – utilization of the UP will greatly simplify the process, and cut down on the costs, of obtaining wider patent protection in Europe. However, as noted above, there is also a major disadvantage for the Pharma sector which tempers this – namely, the potential for a highly valuable single Pharma patent to be revoked across 25 EU MS.

Despite the revocation risk, Pharma is likely to benefit from the ability to enforce the UP centrally at the UPC. For instance, one German-based lawyer stated that Pharma will benefit from the ability to get a 25 EU MS-wide injunction. Conversely, as noted above, the great fear in the ICT sector relates to the 'injunction risk' (and the related concern that there will be a growth in patent troll litigation at the UPC). Indeed, one interviewee noted that Pharma may benefit more than ICT precisely because 'there is less risk of troll litigation in Pharma' than in the ICT sector. Nonetheless, the same interviewee argued that overall the UPC is likely to benefit all patentees, including those in ICT and ENG.

So while it can be observed that the UPC 'revocation risk' is a major fear for the Pharma sector, a clear benefit can be seen for Pharma with respect to obtaining wider protection, more efficiently, for lower costs via the UP. To some extent, this appears to be the view in the Chemicals sector as well, though the renewal and litigation costs remain a major concern. For the ICT sector, the wider protection offered by the UP is viewed positively, though the interviewees stressed that the wider protection is not worth paying more than a 3 MS renewal fee for. More importantly perhaps, the ICT sector appears to be very wary of the combination of the 'bifurcation/injunction risk' and the 'patent troll risk'. Companies in the Engineering sector, meanwhile, appear to be fairly ambivalent towards both the UPC and the UP, and they are undertaking a major review of the costs involved before committing to either.

SMEs in the New System

With respect to SMEs, three key concerns came up in the interviews – cost, the revocation risk, and the injunction risk. Regarding the costs of the UPC, the in-house ICT SME counsel stated that 'the costs associated will be fundamental in deciding whether it is worth going down this route'. This was also noted by a UK PA I interviewed who remarked: 'The main issue for the SMEs is cost.'

As part of the discussion of the value-based system, a total of seven interviewees – two in-house counsel (one Pharma SME and one Pharma) and five lawyers – noted that some form of value-based system could benefit SMEs. For instance, a German-based lawyer I interviewed argued that the value-based fee system could help to encourage SMEs to use the system – provided that the parties can agree to set the fees at a low value.[27] Similarly, an experienced solicitor remarked that the value-based fee system will give SMEs 'the option of using the court at a reasonable cost'. This was echoed by an experienced patent attorney I interviewed who stated that the value-based fee could prove to be beneficial to SMEs if in practice it works to 'cap' fees for low-value cases. On this point, it must also be noted that if the value of the case does not reach the value-fees threshold, only fixed fees will be payable – something that may give SMEs the option of litigation for lower value cases (provided that the SME can afford the fixed fees).

On this point, one PA I interviewed stated that the idea of a 'small-claims track' (SCT) for the UPC, similar to the one that has been successfully brought into the UK Intellectual Property and Enterprise Court (IPEC) – though the IPEC SCT does not apply to patent cases – ought to be explored by the planners/organizers of the new system.

However, the in-house Pharma SME counsel I interviewed expressed scepticism about the usefulness of the value-based fee in this regard. She said that SMEs tend to be risk-averse and litigation-averse, noting that 'SMEs tend not to go to court at a multi-jurisdictional level unless the case is of high value, so a value-based fee may not benefit SMEs that much'. She further remarked that Pharma SMEs 'tend not to go to court at all for low value claims'. Indeed, while she acknowledged that some SMEs would be open to the idea of a UPC SCT for SMEs, she nonetheless stated that she did not think that her firm would necessarily choose to avail of it, given that they seek to avoid litigation wherever possible.

---

[27] A similar point is made in Bardehle Pagenberg, 'Unitary patent and Unified Patent Court' (2013), 1, 19, www.bardehle.com/fileadmin/content documents/broschures/Unitary-Patent_Unified-Patent-Court.pdf.

With respect to the UP, the level of the renewal fees is of significant concern to SMEs in the UK and elsewhere in Europe.[28] One UK PA I interviewed remarked: 'Most SMEs are looking to protect their inventions in a small number of member states … the UP is likely to be more expensive than the current system for SMEs.'

With respect to specific fee levels, the in-house Pharma SME counsel stated that setting the renewal fee at the 3 MS level 'would create a very powerful incentive for SMEs to use the UP'. Similarly, a UK PA I interviewed also argued that a 3 MS fee would certainly provide an incentive to SMEs; but he warned that any fee over the 3–5 level would actually create a serious disincentive to use the system. Indeed, from the above analysis it appears that the absence of either a fee set at the 3 MS level – or, alternatively, a reduced fee system for SMEs – there is likely to be a serious lack of incentives for SMEs to obtain UPs, something that is further noted in the next chapter.

Regarding the revocation risk, the in-house Pharma SME counsel I interviewed remarked that 'there is a strong culture of risk aversion amongst SMEs … and the possibility of a patent being revoked is worrying'. She stated that if an SME were to have a patent revoked within the UPC system, 'this could be fatal' to the company's finances. As a result, she argued that Pharma SMEs ought to seriously consider opting out their MVPs. Similarly, the in-house ICT SME counsel remarked that 'it will be necessary to assess the strength of the patent concerned to ascertain its suitability for use in a potential bifurcated process'. He argued that unless 'there is clear guidance provided to Courts and judges that will deliver consistency, it is likely that my company's strategy will be to wait and see before risking valuable company intellectual property to courts and proceedings where the outcome is uncertain or of variable quality'. In particular, he said that in the absence of clarity regarding how procedures of the UPC will work – and with fears over the quality of decisions – 'risking "crown jewel" patents to the system may be hard to justify'. On a more positive note, while he

---

[28] On the issue of SMEs and renewal fees, the PA firm EIP recently published a paper noting that generally SMEs validate and renew patents in fewer MS than larger companies – EIP, 'Europe's unitary patent system: a horse designed by committee' (2014), 1, 1–13.

noted that there would inevitably be a period of uncertainty at the beginning, he remarked that 'with upfront guidance and directions, this period hopefully will be kept to a minimum, and users will be able to get involved with the system earlier and with confidence as to the quality of the decisions'.

With respect to the interplay between EPO oppositions and UPC revocations, the in-house Pharma SME counsel stated that for SMEs 'it is not necessarily a good thing that revocation can happen more quickly at the UPC than at the current EPO hearings'. The reason for this is that for an SME – especially if it is seeking investment – having a patent application listed as 'pending opposition' is generally seen in a more positive light than having applied in earnest for a patent which was then speedily revoked.

Regarding injunctions, one solicitor interviewee stated that 'SMEs are very concerned about the possibility of pan-EU injunctions'. He noted that while the impact of such an injunction would merely reduce revenues at a large multinational company, and perhaps affect the company's share price, the impact of a pan-EU injunction 'would be absolutely devastating for an SME'. This point was echoed by an experienced in-house ENG counsel, who stated that 'a pan-EU injunction would be fatal to most SMEs – they could not survive it'. Conversely, while the in-house Pharma SME counsel acknowledged this risk, she nevertheless argued that SMEs do, in fact, want the ability to obtain such pan-25 EU MS injunctions against competitors/potential infringers.

SMEs, therefore, share many of the primary concerns of the larger companies regarding the UPC. However, the major difference for SMEs viz. larger companies is the *scale* of the risk involved. The revocation risk is substantial for SMEs because the loss of a single patent across 25 EU MS could prove to be fatal to a company's prospects. Similarly, if a European SME is hit with a pan-25 EU MS injunction preventing one of its products being sold in the EU, this too could be a fatal blow, as an SME is less likely to have a strong foothold in other large markets such as the USA and Asia – something that would cushion the revocation blow for larger companies. Nonetheless, SMEs do see potential positives in the new system – particularly with respect to the ability to centrally enforce their own patents at the UPC.

Are Stakeholders in the Various Sectors Well Informed on the UPC/UP?

At the time of interview, it was notable that stakeholders – with no apparent difference between sectors – appeared to be well informed about the UPC/UP. Indeed, most interviewees noted that they had read at least some official UPC documents online, including the various drafts of the UPC Rules of Procedure. Furthermore, several interviewees stated that the UK IPO had presented them with additional information.

Location of the Central Divisions

With respect to the London-based UPC Central Division, all the in-house Pharma counsel stated that this is a positive of the new system. Moreover, one experienced solicitor argued that the existence of the UPC division would benefit the Pharma sector since 'there's a great deal of expertise in London'. He stated that 'London is a centre of excellence' in the Pharma patent field and that the location 'is likely to be influential' in this positive way 'even if the panels don't feature a majority of English judges'.

Conversely, the non-Pharma interviewees stated that they have some minor concerns about the locations of the other courts. For instance, one in-house ENG counsel stated that she 'is a little concerned' that the Munich Central Division 'might bifurcate more than the other divisions'. Similarly, some interviewees from the ICT sector expressed concern about how the Paris Central Division will operate. Nonetheless, a large proportion of interviewees stated that they did not think that the location of the court will prove to be of great importance, given that the judicial panels will consist of judges from a variety of different countries and legal/technical backgrounds.

WHAT WILL THE IMPACT OF THE REFORMS BE ON THE LEGAL COMMUNITY?

One solicitor interviewee remarked that 'the UPC will bring big changes to the law profession', noting that 'most major industries are global, and multi-national litigation has become the norm'. He argued that all law firms 'will have to engage with the UPC' and that 'the British and the German firms will probably come to dominate' at the expense of firms in other territories – including even in France – since English is likely to become the dominant language of litigation at the UPC. This point was also made by a Germany-based lawyer I spoke with, who noted that 'there won't be a great change for a German lawyer other than English becoming the main language of patent litigation, as clients will likely expect their lawyers to plead in English'. She noted that this will be a major challenge for the older generation of German lawyers, who may be unwilling to spend time mastering the English language.

With respect to patent attorneys, an experienced Germany-based PA stated that the PA's job would not change much. However, he noted that 'for advocates, litigators and judges there will be a great deal of change' as the new system will establish, for the first time, EU-wide competition in litigation. He further remarked: 'Since the EPC came into force there has been EU-wide competition for PAs, but the litigators are not used to it, and it will come as a bit of a shock to the system.'

Continuing with the idea of competition in the litigation field, another German-based PA I interviewed stated that large law firms would probably benefit from the UPC reforms more than smaller ones, noting that the tight time schedule envisaged by the UPC will require a great deal of resources, and especially manpower, to be expounded, noting that 'only large firms will have these resources'.

Two solicitor interviewees noted that members of the UK IP Bar could struggle to adapt to the UPC. They argued that solicitors 'are probably better placed' to work within the UPC system than barristers because the UPC will operate 'a continental-style, paper-based system', featuring short hearings rather than the in-depth hearings that frequently take place at the PHC.

Both of the UK PAs I interviewed stated that their jobs would probably become more complex, and that costs for PA firms would inevitably rise. For instance, one PA interviewee argued that the new UPC system would increase costs for PA firms, and that firms may have to absorb some of these costs (though he acknowledged that some would inevitably be passed on to clients). Moreover, he remarked that for PAs the amount of work 'is likely to increase' since a 25-MS UP will mean 'there are many more countries to monitor', further noting that 'examining diligent use within all of these member states will be a huge challenge'. The same interviewee stated that for some PAs there may be a big change in terms of representing their clients in court – though he acknowledged that the rules for when and how patent attorneys (as opposed to solicitors/barristers) may represent their clients before the UPC had yet to be finalized.[29] Indeed, a further two non-PA interviewees remarked that it would be important that PAs have the right to represent their clients at UPC hearings, stating that this would be of great benefit to their profession.

SUMMARY OF KEY ISSUES FOR USERS OF THE NEW SYSTEM

From the above, it is clear that the issues of (i) judicial composition/quality and (ii) the costs of litigating at the UPC and obtaining and renewing UPs are paramount. Also of great concern are the risks of the new system – pan-25 EU MS injunctions, pan-25 EU MS revocations, patent troll litigation and forum shopping. The issue of how SMEs may fare at the UPC is an additional worry. In Chapter 5, I outline and assess these issues further and highlight the progress that has been made since 2014 in setting up the UPC and the UP.

---

[29] www.unified-patent-court.org/images/documents/Draft-EPLC-2015-07-01-final-clear.pdf.

5. Conclusion

THE UPC OUT OF THE SHADOWS: LOOKING AHEAD TO 2017

This concluding chapter presents a number of observations about the key elements of the Unified Patent Court and the Unitary Patent, referring to the empirical data examined in Chapter 4 and also looking at how the issues raised by interviewees in 2014 have been dealt with since then, with a view to the UPC's launch in 2017.

UPC Observations

Judicial composition and quality at the UPC

The issues of judicial composition and quality are crucially important for three major reasons: first, there are substantial concerns amongst potential litigants over bifurcation and the granting of injunctions – concerns that are felt particularly keenly by companies in the ICT sector (though much less by those in the Pharma sector); second, the possibility that a valuable single patent could be revoked across 25 EU MS is a major concern, especially for Pharma companies (though this concern is felt much less by companies in the ICT and ENG sectors); third, forum shopping is likely to occur, to some extent at least, within the UPC – and companies in all sectors have concerns about the maintenance of common standards across the UPC, especially with respect to local divisions operating in jurisdictions that do not have an established history of patent litigation.

The interview data show that those in the business and legal communities are unlikely to support the UPC unless the judges make consistent, balanced decisions. Indeed, 'the technical capability of judges' and 'the quality and predictability of decision making' are the most important considerations for potential users of the UPC.[1] Put simply, concerns about bifurcation, injunctions, revocations and forum shopping can only be alleviated by effective judicial decision making. The process of sorting out applications and making judicial appointments is at time of writing ongoing.

Establishing and maintaining judicial quality across the UPC can be achieved by (a) co-ordinating and training judges and (b) via the composition of strong judicial panels. Since 2014, much progress has been made on this front and it is expected that the judicial panels will be of very high quality.[2]

Litigation costs

Under Article 36(3) of the UPC Agreement the UPC system has the 'objective of a self-financing Court with balanced fees'. This brings great challenges. The negotiations at the UPC Preparatory Committee over fees, only resolved in early 2016, were focused on meeting the twin goals of allowing the UPC to function effectively and allowing access to justice for litigants, especially those with fewer resources, such as SMEs. In accordance with Article 36(3), the UPC fees, as finalized, will be based on a hybrid system – there will be both a fixed fee and a value-based fee set above a pre-defined ceiling.[3] The fixed fee for filing an infringement claim/counter-claim (or a declaration for non-infringement) at the CFI of the UPC will be €11,000; while a revocation claim will cost €20,000 to file.[4] These same fees will apply, as relevant, when an appeal on one of these issues is sought at the Court of Appeal of the UPC.

For infringement claims/counter claims (and claims for a declaration of non-infringement), an additional value-based fee will also

1 Powell Gilbert, 'Responses to UPC survey 2014' (March 2014), question 12.

2 See the description of UPC judicial training at www.ceipi.edu/index.php?id=14370&L=2.

3 The final fee schedules is accessible here – http://unified-patent-court.org/sites/default/files/guidelines_for_court_fees_and_recoverable_costs.pdf.

4 The fee for a counter-claim of revocation will be the same as for an infringement action, subject to a fee limit of €20,000 – as stated in the note accessible at http://powellgilbert.com/press/2016.03.04%20UPC%20note.pdf.

be levied, along a sliding scale, where the value of the case is above €500,000. For example, a case with a value of €1,000,000 will result in a value-based fee of €4,000; while a case with a value of €50,000,000 will result in a value-based fee of €250,000. For any case with a value above €50,000,000 the value based fee will be €325,000.

In addition to laying out the fees, the UPC Preparatory Committee also highlights a number of important aspects of the fees regime – points that are likely to benefit SMEs in particular (as discussed in detail further below):[5]

- 'Only one fixed fee and, if applicable, one value-based fee shall apply in an action regardless of the number of claimants, defendants or patents.'
- 'Small enterprises and micro-enterprises are entitled to pay only 60% of fixed and value-based fees.'
- 'If an action is heard by a single UPC judge, the party liable for the court fees will be reimbursed by 25%.'
- 'Withdrawal or settlement of an action will usually entitle the party liable for the court fees to be reimbursed a proportion of the fees.'
- 'Fees that "threaten the economic existence" of a party may be wholly or partly reimbursed.'

With regard to recoverable costs, the UPC will feature a 'ceiling' system with a sliding scale of values. For example, for cases with a value up to €250,000 costs are recoverable up to a ceiling of €38,000, while for cases with a value of €1,000,000 up to €112,000 may be recovered. For cases with a value greater than €50,000,000 up to €2,000,000 may be recovered. The UPC will apportion costs proportionally in the case of a partial success, and will retain the power to raise or lower the costs ceilings depending on the circumstances: it might be appropriate to raise the ceiling if the case is especially complex; while alternatively, it might be appropriate to lower the threshold if there is an economic threat to

---

[5] As stated in the note accessible at http://powellgilbert.com/press/2016.03.04%20UPC%20note.pdf.

the existence of a party involved in the litigation, such as an SME, a non-profit organization, a university or an individual.

With the UPC fees system in place, several interesting points can be noted with respect to the interview data analysed in Chapter 4. It is worth recalling that while some interviewees expressed the hope that the UPC will lead to lower overall costs for patent litigation in Europe, several other interviewees expressed the fear that the costs of patent litigation in Europe will in fact increase.

Two things are of significance here – the court fees and the private legal costs.

With respect to court fees it is worth noting that, if, as one interviewee argued, the UPC effectively moves the majority of European patent litigation from the German system to the UPC, and the UPC fees end up being higher than the current German fees, then the overall court fee cost of litigation within the EU will go up. For this reason, several interviewees argued strongly that the UPC fees ought not to be as high as the current German fees – though others stated that combined court fees of around 1–2 MS would be reasonable.[6] The final UPC fees regime, detailed above, appears to strike an appropriate balance – the fees are not broadly out of alignment with the equivalent German court fees, and the UPC fees represent a value saving when the combined current court fees of both Germany and the UK (post-April 2015) are taken into account.

With respect to private legal costs, although the absence of lengthy, UK-style oral hearings at the UPC is likely to keep costs to a relatively low level when compared with the current UK private legal costs, one point that emerged strongly from the interviews was the fear that the private legal costs of litigation at the UPC could nonetheless end up being quite high, given the wide remit of the court's jurisdiction, and the amount of resources that will need to be expounded in order to meet the short deadlines required by the court. Despite this, several interviewees expressed hope that there would be an effective, balanced costs system, with recoverable costs capped at a range of ceilings.

---

[6] As noted in Chapter 2, since the interviews took place the UK's court fees have been increased substantially, something which means that parallel patent litigation in the UK and Germany now costs more than it did in 2014. The interviewee responses must be considered with this in mind.

As noted above, the final UPC costs system does indeed include a well thought out cap on cost recovery – something that provides each side with an incentive to keep costs down, while also providing the option of raising or lowering the costs ceiling where appropriate.

The opt-out decision

From the interview data, it appears likely that initially many patentees will seek to opt out their most valuable patents (MVPs), while keeping low and mid-range patents within the UPC system. On the other hand, some lawyers are advising their clients to keep within the UPC 'strong' patents, something that could create a perception that opted-out patents are 'weak' and open to attack via revocation proceedings.

Importantly, the proposed UPC opt-out fee – expected to be set at €80 – has now been abandoned. This fee was disliked by patentees because it would have effectively meant that patentees would have to pay not to use the system.[7] For the planners/organizers of the new system, setting the fee level was undoubtedly a great challenge – they knew that if they set the opt-out fee too high, it would greatly annoy patentees; but if they set the fee at too low a level, patentees may decide to opt out their entire portfolios – which would leave very few cases at the UPC. Ultimately, the organizers have decided there is no need for an opt-out fee. For patentees, this is welcome, but it raises the possibility that there might be a mass opt out of EPs from the UPC's jurisdiction – something that would likely mean that case levels during the earlier period of the court would be low.

Forum shopping

One key argument advanced by the proponents of the UPC is that the availability of a unified court will reduce forum shopping with

---

[7] A. Johnson, 'Opt-out fee for future Unified Patent Court is (unsurprisingly) much too high', *Kluwer Patent Blog* (2015), available at www.kluwerpatentblog.com/2015/05/15/opt-out-fee-for-future-unified-patent-court-is-unsurprisingly-much-too-high.

respect to European patent litigation.[8] At the UPC, litigants will often have a choice of where to file the claim (e.g. where infringement occurs in more than one Signatory State, or if the defendant has a principal place of business in a different state to where the infringement occurs).

Interviewees noted that the UPC may give rise to an internal type of forum shopping if local and regional divisions differ drastically in their willingness to grant pan-25 EU MS injunctions, and/or to bifurcate the infringement and validity proceedings. In line with this, 'plaintiffs may select a Division which they expect to be generally patentee-friendly in its judgments and which will conduct the litigation quickly and in a manner which keeps costs low'.[9] As Sir David Kitchen argues, only a strong Court of Appeal can prevent this forum shopping risk from developing into a serious problem for the UPC system, and thus for innovative businesses in general.[10]

Patent trolls

The UPC could be more attractive to NPEs, or patent trolls, than the current fragmented European system is. Patent trolls are likely to attempt to take advantage of the uncertainty that will necessarily come with the setting up of a new, untested courts system. The possibility of obtaining a pan-25 EU MS injunction against, for example, an ICT firm is also something that could be attractive to patent trolls. Interviewees from ICT companies expressed concern that if forum shopping occurs within the system, some local/regional courts may attempt to attract business by becoming overly patentee-friendly. Conversely, a small minority of interviewees stated that the availability of forum shopping may actually increase the quality of the system, if it works as it currently does in Germany. Moreover, several interviewees from the legal community

---

[8] K. Cremers, M. Ernicke, D. Harhoff, C. Helmers, G. Licht, L. McDonagh, et al. 'Patent litigation in Europe', *ZEW Discussion Paper* No. 13-07 (2013), 1, 1–6.

[9] Hoffmann-Eitle, *The EU Patents Package Handbook: A Practioner's Guide* (Munich: Hoffmann-Eitle, 2014), 33.

[10] Sir David Kitchen, 'Introductory remarks: a judicial perspective', in J. Pila and C. Wadlow (eds), *The Unitary EU Patent System* (Oxford: Hart, 2015), 1–8, 4–5.

stated that the risk of patent troll litigation has been 'overstated'; indeed, the patent troll risk is somewhat mitigated by the presence of the 'loser pays' system at the UPC.

Nonetheless, the very existence of (a) a new and uncertain court system and (b) pan-25 EU MS remedies at that court is likely to attract patent trolls. There is not a lot the UPC organizers can do about either of these factors. Instead, in order to prevent trolls becoming an issue for the UPC, the organizers' focus on maintaining judicial quality across the system will be of critical importance.

UPC revocations

The EPO oppositions backlog is seen as a problem by patentees, but the interview data show that there is general scepticism amongst stakeholders that the existence of UPC revocation actions will help to substantially ease the backlog. Indeed, it is likely that the validity of patents will be challenged via both procedures, i.e. those who seek to challenge will both oppose patents at the EPO, which will be a lengthy process but a cost-effective one, and take action at the UPC, which will be speedy, but more costly.

Yet, if the costs of litigation at the UPC are kept down to a minimal level – and the ceilings on recoverable costs should help here – this should encourage revocation actions, which should in turn help to (partially) ease the EPO's opposition backlog. At the same time, there is a danger that patentees will lose trust in the court if patents are perceived as being revoked too easily at the UPC; as above, maintaining a consistent and reliable UPC judiciary can ensure this does not happen.

Ultimately, despite the existence of parallel oppositions at the EPO, there is likely to be a net reduction in the EPO backlog, provided that the UPC can deliver high quality, speedy decisions, something that will only become apparent once the UPC is up and running in 2017.

SMEs at the UPC

The interview data show that in the early days SMEs are likely to take a very cautious view of the UPC, given the fact that SMEs tend to be 'risk averse', and they tend to avoid litigation where possible. Moreover, the costs of the new system are likely to hit

SMEs the hardest.[11] Having said that, the system of UPC fees reduction noted above, combined with the ceilings on recoverable costs (which can be lowered further in the case of an SME), should give SMEs confidence that the new system has been designed with their concerns in mind.

Crucial for SMEs will be the quality and consistency of judicial decision making at the UPC – particularly in the context of revocations and injunctions – because the scale of the risks involved is greater for SMEs than for large enterprises and multinational corporations. As one interviewee noted, an injunction granted against an SME could be fatal to its business prospects. Ensuring consistent judicial standards are maintained across the UPC – particularly with regard to injunctions – will give all companies, including SMEs, confidence in the system.

Finally, if in the future further reforms to the UPC are thought necessary in order to aid SMEs, it would be worth taking account of the success of the UK's IPEC in recent years at attracting relatively low-value patent disputes, perhaps even in the incorporation of an SME-centred small-claims court or track into the UPC system.[12] However, in this regard, it is also worth bearing in mind the normative possibility that efforts to encourage SME litigation at the UPC might actually create incentives to litigate that were not previously there, something that might take SME energy away from more innovative activities.[13]

London's Central Division

There is a general expectation among stakeholders that the London-based court will prove to be a good thing both for the legal community in London and for Pharma more generally. London is seen as a hub of expertise in the Pharma-legal area, and the UPC will add another important institution to this environment. A

---

[11] Sir David Kitchen, 'Introductory remarks: a judicial perspective', in J. Pila and C. Wadlow (eds), *The Unitary EU Patent System* (Oxford: Hart, 2015), 1–8, 4–5.

[12] C. Helmers, Y. Lefouili and L. McDonagh, 'Evaluation of the reforms of the Intellectual Property Enterprise Court 2010–2013', *A Report Commissioned by the UK Intellectual Property Office* (July 2015), 1.

[13] C. Helmers, Y. Lefouili and L. McDonagh, 'Evaluation of the reforms of the Intellectual Property Enterprise Court 2010–2013', *A Report Commissioned by the UK Intellectual Property Office* (July 2015), 1.

building in Aldgate has now been chosen as the site of the UPC in London.[14] However, if the UK votes to leave the EU in the June 2016 referendum, it is likely the UK will no longer be in a position to participate in the UPC, and the central division will have to be relocated.

UP Observations

Renewal fees

At present, the vast majority of patentees (90%) validate in only 3–5 MS.[15] It is thus easy to over-estimate the cost savings of the UP when compared to the traditional EP. This is particularly clear when the London Agreement is taken into account. Thus, the wider protection offered by the UP must be viewed in light of the renewal fees. This is because the interview data suggest that for many businesses, particularly in the ICT and ENG sectors, the wider protection is not considered worth paying increased patent fees for. The exceptions to this are the Pharmaceutical and Chemicals sectors, where the wider coverage provided by the UP will prove to be of benefit even if the overall fees for renewing patents increase.

Regarding the specific fee level, several interviewees from the ICT and ENG sectors argued that a fee set at the 3 MS level (UK, German and French renewal fees combined) would provide a reasonable incentive to use the system – both for large companies and for SMEs. By contrast, interviewees noted that a fee set above this level may lead some companies to continue to use the existing patent routes rather than to seek to apply for UPs.

In mid-2015, the renewal fees were set at the ‘Top 4’ MS level.[16] This is higher than the 3 MS fee that most interviewees argued would be preferable in terms of encouraging uptake of the UP. Since most ICT and ENG interviewees stated that their companies do not seek protection in more than 3–4 MS, the Top 4 MS level could be seen as the ceiling for some companies’ willingness to pay (though the renewal fee level is seen as less important within the Pharma and Chemicals sectors). Even setting the fees at this Top 4

---

[14] www.gov.uk/government/news/upc-london-location.

[15] Commission Staff Working Paper (Impact Assessment) SEC(2011) 482/2 (2011), 1, 17.

[16] www.epo.org/news-issues/news/2015/20150624.html.

MS level may not provide ICT and ENG patentees with an actual incentive to use the new system, when considered from the perspective of initial financial outlay.

Further to this, when considering renewal fees it is important to consider the issue of 'selective' patent pruning, as this will not be possible with the UP. In other words, with the UP – unlike with the EP – it will not be possible to drop expensive jurisdictions from the overall patent validation portfolio. Some interviewees stated that this is a negative aspect of the UP, as it may add to the cost of maintaining a UP viz. the EP.

Having said that, there are, of course, other considerations relevant to the setting of fees. It is debatable whether a view that focuses solely on the renewal fee levels fully takes account of the direct and indirect benefits of the wider coverage provided by the UP, or the potential savings on administrative costs that could result from the use of a more efficient, simplified patenting process.[17] Indeed, there may be scenarios where the total costs to ICT and ENG firms end up being lower under the UP even with a renewal fee set at the Top 4 MS level. In terms of benefits, the IPO's 2014 impact assessment report puts forward the argument that holding a UP, as opposed to a bundle of EPs, may create the potential for better access to finance for companies as it may be seen as a more valuable asset.[18]

There are special arrangements to reduce the renewal fee costs for SMEs and similar entities based in EU member states which do not have an EPO official language (English, French or German), and the EPO has said it will continue to review SME take up of UPs as the system progresses, and may make further arrangements.[19] Overall, the Top 4 MS fee level, while not the optimal fee

[17] Intellectual Property Office, 'Unified Patent Court implementation: unitary patent – impact assessment' (March 2014), 1, 10–12, available at www.gov.uk/government/uploads/system/uploads/attachment_data/file/317641/IA_UPC_Implementation_Unitary_Patent.pdf.

[18] Intellectual Property Office, 'Unified Patent Court implementation: unitary patent – impact assessment' (March 2014), 1, 10–12. For an examination of patent-secured financing, see D. Harhoff, 'The role of patents and licenses in securing external finance for innovation', Luxemburg, *EIB Papers* 14 (2) (European Investment Bank, 2009), available at www.eib.org/attachments/efs/eibpapers/eibpapers_2009_v14_n02_en.pdf.

[19] www.epo.org/news-issues/news/2015/20150624.html

recommended by interviewees, is just within their acceptable range; and, moreover, it is lower than many patentees feared at the outset of the new system. On this basis, taking account of everything stated earlier, the UP should prove good value for money for patentees.

UP member states

There is disappointment among stakeholders that the UP doesn't cover all 28 EU MS. Moreover, until the new system covers all EU MS it is doomed to at least partial fragmentation – the exact problem the system is intended to solve. Although achieving EU unity seems unlikely in the short term given the current intransience of Spain and Poland, this is a realistic medium-term aim once the new system is successfully up and running. Moreover, given the fact that the EU is increasingly seen as a unitary market (especially by non-EU companies) it is an imperative that in the near future the UP/UPC reforms are expanded to encompass every MS.

Legal profession observations

Regarding the effect the reforms will have on the legal community, it seems that the language requirements of the UPC/UP are likely to suit English-language firms. This will be of primary benefit to UK law firms, but German law firms are likely to also do well out of the new system. Moreover, the UPC will create for the first time genuine EU-wide competition in the area of European patent litigation. The emerging view is that larger firms will benefit over smaller firms due to the amount of resources required to conduct speedy patent trials. Moreover, in the UK context the fact that the UPC will utilize more of a paper-based system, with short hearings – rather than UK-style in-depth hearings – may well benefit solicitors more than barristers. Patent attorneys (PAs) expect that there will be an increase in costs for their firms; yet, PAs welcome the fact that they will have the opportunity to represent clients in court under the new European Patent Litigation Certificate system.[20]

---

20 www.unified-patent-court.org/images/documents/Draft-EPLC-2015-07-01-final-clear.pdf.

FROM FRAGMENTATION TO UNIFICATION? ONWARDS TO 2017

The UPC and UP reforms represent the biggest changes to the European patent system since the coming into effect of the EPC in the 1970s. Of particular importance is the fact that the UPC aims to unify European patent litigation – which currently works on a fragmented, national basis – by providing a one-stop enforcement system.

Yet, even though there is much that is laudable about the new system, the problem of fragmentation of litigation will initially persist in the forthcoming UPC system in two major ways: first, not all EU member states are on board – only 25 out of 28 are UPC Signatory States, which means enforcement in Spain, Poland and Croatia will still require nation litigation; and, second, for at least the first seven years patentees who hold EPO bundle patents (EPs) will be able to opt out of the UPC system, and instead continue to use the current system of national validation and litigation.[21] Thus, the reforms will initially result in an even more fragmented litigation system in the 25 Signatory States, with the additional layer of UPC litigation on top of the current national systems.

Another aspect relevant to fragmentation is the possibility that patentees may turn away from pan-European patenting and return instead to the national patenting systems. Some companies may indeed choose to do this, but overall it seems unlikely this will be possible on a large scale. The major reason for this is that the national route is, by comparison to either the EP or UP routes, highly expensive. Nonetheless, if the UPC/UP system develops in a way that patentees do not like, it is possible that they will exercise this option once the transitional period ends and the opt-out option is no longer available – even if only for their most valuable patents.

---

[21] The situation is further complicated by the fact that the establishment of the UP falls within an area of European Union policy, and therefore signatories to the EPC who are not EU MS, including a number of countries such as Switzerland and Iceland, are not – and cannot, under CJEU, Opinion 1/09, OJ C211/28 (2011) – be part of the new system. This means that even when every EU MS is a party to the UPC, there will still be EPC MS outside the system. This is unfortunate but there appears to be no way to solve this problem at present.

On a more positive note, it is plausible that the UPC may help to create a market for cross-border patent enforcement across the 25 UPC Signatory States, while the UP may come to be seen as a much more valuable asset than either the current national patents or the bundle EPs, something that could help patent monetization. Furthermore, given the progress that has been made on the key issues highlighted in 2014 by the potential users of the UPC/UP the expectation is that, following the transitional period, the UPC will become the primary patent court for Europe, featuring litigation involving all EPs and UPs. Thus, the scheme's ambition to unify the European patent system is a realizable one in the long term.[22] Moreover, should the UPC and the UP prove to be a success, it is likely that in the future the remaining member states of the EU that are currently not taking part – Spain, Poland and Croatia – will join and participate fully in the new system.

Despite this, it is also worth sounding the cautious note that the UP and UPC reforms are unlikely to be a panacea for all of the EU's economic and innovation problems. For example, from an examination of the EPO's patent statistics, it is clear that most patent applications are filed by US and Japanese companies, with China and Korea also prominent; moreover, within the EU only Germany, and to a lesser extent France, currently compete at this world-class level.[23] As Sir David Kitchen notes, the innovation problem suffered by the UK and other EU MS will not be solved by simply putting a new patent system into place.[24] Even if it is easier to get valuable patent protection across nearly all of the EU's MS, unless there are also changes in the EU's research and development culture – with more funding for scientific and technological research being a key element – these root problems will remain for the foreseeable future.

---

[22] P. England, 'In? Out? What's it all about? Patent opt-out and withdrawal in the UPC', *Journal of Intellectual Property Law & Practice* 9 (2014), 10–17.

[23] www.epo.org/about-us/annual-reports-statistics/statistics/filings.html.

[24] Sir David Kitchen, 'Introductory remarks: a judicial perspective', in J. Pila and C. Wadlow (eds), *The Unitary EU Patent System* (Oxford: Hart, 2015), 1–8, 4–5.

Bibliography

BOOKS AND BOOK CHAPTERS

Bardehle Pagenberg, *Patent Infringement Proceedings* (2013).

Beckett, N., and J. Morton, 'United Kingdom', in N. Beckett and J. Morton (eds), *CMS International Patent Litigation Guide* (CMS, 2013), 95–100.

Bouvet, T., 'France', in M.C. Elmer and C.G. Gramaenopoulos (eds), *Global Patent Litigation* (Virginia: Bloomberg BNA, 2014), 546–89.

Cohen, S., 'Selected IP jurisdictions: Germany', in A. Jolly and J. Philpott (eds), *The Handbook of European Intellectual Property Management* (London: Kogan Page, 2007).

Freshfields Bruckhaus Deringer, *A Guide to Patent Litigation in Europe: England and Wales* (Freshfields, 2011), 1.

Hogan Lovells, *Patent Litigation Guide: Jurisdictions (France)* (2013), 1.

Hoffmann–Eitle, *The EU Patents Package Handbook: A Practioner's Guide* (Munich: Hoffmann–Eitle, 2014), 46.

Hoorneman, W., 'The Netherlands', in N. Beckett and J. Morton (eds), *CMS International Patent Litigation Guide* (CMS, 2013), 61–6.

Jolly, A., and J. Philpott (eds), *The Handbook of European Intellectual Property Management* (London: Kogan Page, 2007).

Kamstra, G., 'United Kingdom', in Global Legal Group (eds), *The International Comparative Legal Guide to: Patents* (4th edn, Global Legal Group, 2014), 194–200.

Kitchen, Sir David, 'Introductory remarks: a judicial perspective', in J. Pila and C. Wadlow (eds), *The Unitary EU Patent System* (Oxford: Hart, 2015), 1–8.

Kühnen, T., *Patent Litigation Proceedings in Germany: A Handbook for Practitioners* (6th edn, Cologne: Heymanns, 2013).

Mes, P., *Kommentar: Patentgesetz, Gebrauchsmustergesetz* (4th edn, Munich: Beck, 2015).

Moninand, J.-G., and S. Vilfeu, 'France', in N. Beckett and J. Morton (eds), *CMS International Patent Litigation Guide* (CMS, 2013), 39–44.
Pila, J., *The Requirement for an Invention in Patent Law* (Oxford: Oxford University Press, 2010).
Radcliffe, J., and M. Brown, *European Patent Litigation Strategy* (Arlington, VA: Bloomberg BMA, 2014), 1.
Schoenen, G., M. Deck and M. Eck, 'Germany', in N. Beckett and J. Morton (eds), *CMS International Patent Litigation Guide* (CMS, 2013), 45–50.
Stauder, D., *Patent– und Gebrauchsmusterverletzungsverfahren in der Bundesrepublik Deutschland, Großbritannien, Frankreich und Italien* (Cologne: Heymanns, 1989).
Taylor Wessing, *Global Intellectual Property Index* (2013), 1.
van Pottelsberghe, B., *Lost Property: The European Patent System and Why it Doesn't Work* (Brussels: Bruegel Blueprint Series, 2009).

ARTICLES, PRESENTATIONS AND REPORTS

Arnold, R., 'Case management, judicial specialisation and intellectual property litigation', *Civil Justice Quarterly* 29 (2010), 478.
Bardehle Pagenberg, 'Unitary patent and Unified Patent Court' (2013), 1. Available at: www.bardehle.com/fileadmin/content documents/broschures/Unitary-Patent_Unified-Patent-Court.pdf (accessed 4 April 2016).
Bertrams, H., 'The cross-border prohibitory injunction in Dutch patent law', *International Review of Intellectual Property and Competition Law (IIC)* 26 (1995), 618.
Bird and Bird, 'Property and contractual aspects of unitary patents and of patents in the UPC system' (23 December 2014). Available at: www.twobirds.com/en/news/articles/2014/netherlands/property-and-contractual-aspects-of-unitary-patents-and-of-patents-in-the-upc-system (accessed 4 April 2016).
Bouzanquet, A.-L., A. Bowler and A. Johnson, 'The role of the saisie in the UPC', *Bristows* (2013).
Brandi–Dohrn, M., 'Some critical observations on competence and procedure of the unified patent court', *International Review of Intellectual Property and Competition Law* 43 (2012), 372.

Brinkhoff, J., 'The enforcement of patent rights in the Netherlands', *International Review of Intellectual Property and Competition Law (IIC)* 31 (2000), 706.

Casey, A., 'Unified Patent Court (UPC) and Ireland' (2 February 2015). Available at: www.primaryopinion.com/articles/unified-patent-court-upc-and-ireland (accessed 4 April 2016).

Cook, T., 'The progress to date on the Unitary European Patent and the Unified Patent Court for Europe', *Journal of Intellectual Property Rights* 18 (2013), 584.

Cremers, K., M. Ernicke, D. Harhoff, C. Helmers, G. Licht, L. McDonagh, I. Rudyk, P. Schliessler, C. Schneider and N. van Zeebroeck, 'Patent litigation in Europe', *ZEW Discussion Paper* No. 13–07 (2013), 1.

Cremers, K., F. Gaessler, D. Harhoff, C. Helmers and Y. Lefouili, 'Invalid but infringed? An analysis of Germany's bifurcated patent litigation system', *Max Planck Institute for Innovation & Competition Research Paper* No. 14-14 (2014), 1.

Dalsgaard, S., 'The field as a temporal entity and the challenges of the contemporary', *Social Anthropology* 20 (2013), 213.

England, P., 'In? Out? What's it all about? Patent opt-out and withdrawal in the UPC', *Journal of Intellectual Property Law & Practice* 9 (2014), 10.

EPO Economic and Scientific Advisory Board, *Recommendations for Improving the Patent System* (2012), 1.

EPO, 'Business-friendly fee pattern adopted for the unitary patent' (24 June 2015). Available at: www.epo.org/news-issues/news/2015/20150624.html (accessed 4 April 2016).

EU Commission Staff Working Paper (Impact Assessment) SEC(2011) 482/2 (2011), 1.

Gaskell, G., S. Stares and A. Pottage, 'How Europe's ethical divide looms over biotech law and patents', *Nature Biotechnology* 30 (2012), 392.

Greenhalgh, C., J. Philips, R. Pitkethly, M. Rogers and J. Tomalin, *Intellectual Property Enforcement in Smaller UK Firms: A Report for the Strategy Advisory Board for Intellectual Property Policy* (SABIP, 2010), 1.

Griffiths, J., 'Constitutionalising or harmonising: the Court of Justice, the right to property and European copyright law', *European Law Review* 38 (2013), 65.

Harhoff, D., 'Economic cost–benefit analysis of a unified and integrated European patent litigation system', *EU Final Report Tender No. MARKT/2008/06/D* (2009), 1.

Helmers, C., Y. Lefouili and L. McDonagh, 'Examining patent cases at the Patents Court and Intellectual Property Enterprise Court 2007–2013', *A Report Commissioned by the UK Intellectual Property Office* (March 2015), 1.

Helmers, C., Y. Lefouili and L. McDonagh, 'Evaluation of the reforms of the Intellectual Property Enterprise Court 2010–2013', *A Report Commissioned by the UK Intellectual Property Office* (July 2015), 1.

Helmers, C., B. Love and L. McDonagh 'Is there a patent troll problem in the UK?', *Fordham Intellectual Property, Media and Entertainment Law Journal* 24 (2014), 509.

Helmers, C., and L. McDonagh, 'Patent litigation in the UK: an empirical survey 2000–2008', *Journal of Intellectual Property Law & Practice* 8 (2013), 846.

Helmers, C., and L. McDonagh, 'Trolls at the High Court?', *LSE Law, Society and Economy Working Paper* No. 13 (2012).

Herr, J., and M. Grunwald, 'Speedy patent infringement proceedings in Germany: pros and cons of the go-to courts', *Journal of Intellectual Property Law & Practice* 7 (2012), 44.

Hilty, R., 'The unitary patent package: twelve reasons for concern', *CIPA Journal* 10 (2012), 553.

Hogan Lovells, 'Property in unitary patents' (2015).

Johnson, A., 'Latest on local and regional divisions', *Bristows* (2015).

Johnson, A., 'Opt-out fee for future Unified Patent Court is (unsurprisingly) much too high', *Kluwer Patent Blog* (2015).

Kaisi, A., 'Finally a single European right for the EU? An analysis of the substantive provisions of the European patent with unitary effect', *European Intellectual Property Review* 36 (2014), 170.

Kühnen, T., and R. Claessen, 'Die Durchsetzung von Patenten in der EU', *Gewerblicher Rechtsschutz und Urheberrecht international (GRUR Int.)* (2013), 592.

Kur, A., 'A farewell to crossborder injunctions? The ECJ decisions *GAT v. LuK* and *Roche Nederland v. Primus and Goldenber*', *International Review of Intellectual Property and Competition Law (IIC)* 27 (2006), 844.

Marcus, G., 'How short can fieldwork be?', *Social Anthropology* 15 (2007), 353.

Marshall, H., 'The enforcement of patent rights in Germany', *International Review of Intellectual Property and Competition Law (IIC)* 31 (2000), 646.

McDonagh, L., 'From brand performance to consumer performativity: assessing European trade mark law after the rise of anthropological marketing', *Journal of Law & Society* 42 (2015), 611.

McDonagh, L., 'Exploring perspectives of the Unified Patent Court and the unitary patent within the business and legal communities', *A Report Commissioned by the UK Intellectual Property Office* (July 2014).

McDonagh, L. and C. Helmers, 'Patent Litigation in England and Wales and the issue-based approach to costs', *Civil Justice Quarterly* 32 (2013), 369.

Mewburn Ellis, 'Stays of UK patent litigation proceedings pending the outcome of EPO opposition proceedings' (12 November 2014). Available at: http://mewburn.com/stays-of-uk-patent-litigation-proceedings-pending-the-outcome-of-epo-opposition-proceedings/ (accessed 4 April 2016).

Moss, G., M. Jones and R. Lundie-Smith, 'Just how "anti-patent" are the UK courts?', *Journal of Intellectual Property Law & Practice* 5 (2010), 148.

Nurton, J., 'Patent practitioners call for UPC cost clarity', *Managing Intellectual Property* (2014).

Pagenberg, J., 'Unitary patent and Unified Court: what lies ahead?', *Journal of Intellectual Property Law & Practice* 8 (2013), 480.

Pila, J., 'The European patent: an old and vexing problem', *International & Comparative Law Quarterly* 62 (2013), 917.

Pors, W., 'Property and contractual aspects of unitary patents and of patents in the UPC system', *EPLAW Patent Blog* (2014).

Reddie and Grouse, 'How much more will the unitary patent cost?' (January 2013), 1. Available at: www.reddie.co.uk/M/R&G_UnitaryPatentCost.pdf (accessed 4 April 2016).

Reynolds, L., 'SPCs and the UPC: current status', *Bristows* (2015).

Rodwell, S., P. Van Eeckhout, A. Reid and J. Walendowski, *Effects of counterfeiting on EU SMEs and a review of various public and private IPR enforcement initiatives and resources*, Final Report to the Enterprise and Industry Directorate-General Directorate B1 – Development of industrial policy (2007) (Framework Contract B3/ENTR/04/093–FC–Lot 6).

Romandini, R., and A. Kliczník, 'The territoriality principle and transnational use of patented inventions: the wider reach of a unitary patent and the role of the CJEU', *International Review of Intellectual Property and Competition Law* 44 (2013), 524.

Sant, D.P., and C. de Coster, 'The unitary patent and the European Patent Court', *Bioscience Law Review* 12 (2012), 27.

Schröer, B., 'Einheitspatentgericht: Überlegungen zum Forum–Shopping im Rahmen der alternativen Zuständigkeit nach Art. 83 Abs. 1 EPGÜ', *Gewerblicher Rechtsschutz und Urheberrecht international (GRUR Int.)* 1 (2013), 1102.

Stauder, D., 'Die tatsächliche Bedeutung von Verletzungen- und Nichtigkeitsverfahren in der Bundesrepublik Deutschland, Frankreich, Großbritannien und Italien: Ergebnisse einer statistisch–empirischen Untersuchung', *GRUR: Gewerblicher Rechtsschutz und Urheberrecht International (GRUR Int.)* (1983), 233.

Swens, O., 'Patent litigation in the Netherlands and recent developments', PowerPoint presentation delivered in Munich (February, 2011). Available at: www.vondst-law.com/en/publicaties-presentaties/64/ (accessed 4 April 2016).

Thambisetty, S., 'Patent litigation in the United Kingdom: solutions in search of a problem?', *European Intellectual Property Review* 32 (2010), 238.

Tombling, A., and A. Fleuchaus, 'Creative filing strategies for the unitary patent' (31 October 2014). Available at: www.managingip.com/Article/3393022/Creative-filing-strategies-for-the-Unitary-Patent.html (accessed 4 April 2016).

Van Zeebroeck, N., and S. Graham, 'Comparing patent litigation across Europe: a first look', *Stanford Technology Law Review* 17 (2014), 655.

Véron, P., 'Patent infringement litigation in France', *Mitteilungen der deutschen Patentanwälte* 93 (2002), 386.

Véron, P., 'Le contentieux des brevets d'invention en France Étude statistique 1990–1999' (2001). Available at: www.veron.com/publications/Colloques/Le_contentieux_des_brevets_invention_1990_1999_en_couleurs.pdf (accessed 4 April 2016).

Véron, P., 'Le contentieux des brevets d'invention en France Étude statistique 2000–2009' (2010) – available at http://www.veron.com/publications/Colloques/Stats_contentieux_brevets_France_2000–2009_Veron_et_Associes.pdf.

Weatherall, K., E. Webster and L. Bently, *IP Enforcement in the UK and Beyond: A Literature Review*. SABIP Report No. EC001, SABIP (2009), 1.

West, A., S. Kusumakar and T. Powell, 'Unitary patents and the Unified Patent Court', *Computer and Telecommunications Law Review* 19 (2013), 105.

Annex: interview questions

In reading this summary of the questions and responses, it is important to note that although 26 interviews took place, there were actually 28 interviewees since two interviews were dual interviews, in which the co-interviewees largely shared the same views (they merely demonstrated different levels of expertise/experience in their explanations). Moreover, both dual interviews involved in-house ICT counsel. For this reason – and so as not to skew the data towards the one sector over others – these interviews are counted as being of 'one perspective' in the analysis given in this report.

I. INTERVIEWS 1–4

Revised Provisional Interview Questions

A. General questions for lawyers and non-lawyers alike

1 What, in your opinion, would be the perceived advantages of both the new unitary patent and the proposed Unified Patent Court system? (e.g. encouraging investment from outside Europe? One-stop shop)

2 What would be the potential benefits to businesses? Do they include competitive advantages or disadvantages in this regard?

B. Specific questions for lawyers: solicitors/patent attorneys

3 (a) As a solicitor/patent attorney, how do you see your job changing as a result of the new unitary patent reforms?

(b) What specific issues concerning the UP/UPC are of concern to solicitors/patent attorneys, e.g. the right to appear before the UPC?

The opt-in/opt-out option

4 As far as you are aware, are your clients considering the opt-out? [Provide definition where appropriate]. From the business point of view, what are the risks that you see of applying for a unitary patent viz. the current European patent system?

5 What sorts of considerations are patent attorneys making them aware of, i.e. what factors would influence their decision to opt out?

6 Alternatively, what factors would give them greater reason to opt in?

7 Are patent attorneys concerned about the practical workings of the system, e.g. how injunctions will be granted, bifurcation, etc.? Are you aware that your clients are concerned?

8 Are there any other factors that will influence your company's decision to opt in/out? [prompt on judicial composition if necessary]

Patent fees

9 The unitary patent will help inventors to protect their inventions, including potentially benefiting from licensing arrangements in all the participating jurisdictions (25) at a much lower cost:
   (i) If the fee were set at the equivalent of a bundle patent renewed in three participating countries (UK, DE and FR), do you think this would affect your clients' uptake of the unitary patent?
   (ii) If the fee were equivalent to eight countries, do you think this would affect your clients' uptake of the unitary patent? If so, how?

10 With respect to applications, do you think the unitary patent will affect costs for your firm? If so, in what areas (renewal/administration/enforcement)?

11 In your experience as a patent attorney, do clients have a demand for protection in up to 25 member states? Why, in your opinion, is this greater protection important (or not important) to your clients?

12 How important are renewal fees in your clients' patenting strategies? Compared to other factors? Why?

13 Should increasing the level of annual renewal fees be used as a way to encourage patents which are not being exploited or generating an income to be dropped from the register (so others can commercialize or innovate)?

14 What would be your ideal level for a reasonable UP annual renewal fee?

15 Would the protection provided by a unitary patent or the costs involved (e.g. no option to let protection lapse in certain countries) alter the time you might keep the patent in force?

Court fees

16 How important are court fee levels to your firm and your clients? For instance, if the initial court fee for filing an infringement claim were set at the equivalent to filing a case in four or five of the Signatory States, would this encourage your clients to use the system? Would you consider this correct, too low or too high? Will the level of fees affect spurious claims? If so, how?

17 If this court fee were set at the equivalent eight or nine of the countries, would this discourage legitimate claims from being taken?

18 The UPC fees will be made up of both fixed fees and, after a certain threshold, a value-based fee. What do you see as the pros and cons of this sort of system?

19 You were asked above about whether the level of initial court fee is of significance to your firm and your clients? How does this compare to the significance of the private legal costs involved?

20 Which sector of business, e.g. pharma, engineering, technology, do you think will benefit the most from the new system? Which do you think will benefit the least?

21 Do you think there will be a 'typical stakeholder' who will seek to use the new system?

C. Specific question for Pharma companies

22 Do you see any benefits or costs for the pharmaceutical sector in having:

(i) a unitary patent?

(ii) a specialized divisional court for pharmaceuticals/chemicals located in London?

D. Other questions (suggestions made by interviewees)

23 Is there anything else you think is of significance to the current UP/UPC debate?

Two questions were suggested during the initial pilot interviews. Both were included in the eventual list of interview questions for the full project:

- 'Does the issue of the delays/backlog at the EPO concern you? Could the fact that the UPC does not have to stay proceedings pending EPO opposition help to ameliorate this problem by effectively moving oppositions away from the EPO?'
- 'Are you aware that the potential for opt-out of the system is due to end after a transitional period (seven years, possibly extendable to 14)? Afterwards, businesses seeking a European patent will have to use either (a) the UPC system or (b) the national patent offices? How would your business approach this choice?'

II. INTERVIEWS 5–26

Final Interview Questions and Response Statistics[1]

Question 1 – General overview of advantages/disadvantages of the new system

(a) What, in your opinion, do you perceive as the advantages of (i) the new Unified Patent Court and (ii) the proposed unitary patent?

(e.g. are there advantages to the existence of a one-stop shop? Is there a need for wider protection in 25 MS rather than 3–4 MS?)

(b) Will your job as a solicitor/patent attorney change as a result

[1] The responses discussed here refer to the pilot questions as well as the final ones. Where it is necessary to distinguish between the two, this is done.

of the UP/UPC? (optional question, only for those in the legal community)

Question 1 was designed as a general 'kick off' question, to begin the interview on a relaxed note.[2] This also enabled the interviewee to flag up issues that could be explored further in the more detailed questions which followed. In other words, this first question captured whatever immediately sprang to mind for the interviewees.[3] The crucial issues raised here were discussed in greater detail with respect to Questions 2 (Opt-in/Opt-out), 3 (UP renewal fees) and 4 (UPC fees).

In this respect, it is notable that while all 26 interviewees had some initial thoughts on the UPC, the same is not true of the UP; 6 interviewees were only interested in talking about the UPC here, and any thoughts they had on the UP they left for later on in the conversation. This likely indicates that the UPC is more pressing in the minds of interviewees. Of the 11 interviewees drawn from the legal community – 2 UK PAs, 2 DE PAs, 6 UK solicitors and 1 DE lawyer – 9 gave a comment in response to the optional question on the possible effects of the new system on the legal profession.

Advantages of the UPC

With respect to the advantages of the UPC viz. the current system, the most frequently made point was that there is a benefit to having a 'one-stop shop' for enforcement in Europe; 12 out of 26 interviewees cited this as an advantage.[4] However, 9 interviewees out of 26 stated that they saw no clear advantages of the new system.

Disadvantages of the UPC

With respect to disadvantages, the most commonly cited issue was that of the fees/costs of the new system – 10 out of 26 stated that they thought the UPC would prove to be more costly than the

---

[2] Question 1 closely corresponds to Questions 1–3 in the list of pilot questions, as shown in the Annex.

[3] All solicitors and patent attorneys are UK-based unless otherwise stated.

[4] This was mentioned in the text of the question as a prompt as one 'possible' advantage, but this seems unlikely to have influenced responses – interviewees were free to state that it was not an advantage, and 14 out of 26 chose to do so.

current fragmented system of national litigation. In addition, a further 2 out of 26 interviewees expressed the view that there would be no advantages at all to the UPC if the costs ended up being higher than the costs of the current system.

Advantages of the UP

Of the 20 interviewees out of 26 who gave a view on the UP in response to the first question, the most commonly cited advantage was that of wider protection, which was cited by 9 interviewees as being advantageous (though 2 of these 9 interviewees noted that this was a benefit only for the Pharma sector).

Disadvantages of the UP

The most commonly cited disadvantage of the UP is that the (expected) high level of the UP renewal fees is likely to make obtaining and maintaining a UP more expensive than patenting in only 2–3 MS; 7 interviewees out of 20 cited this as a major disadvantage.

Question 2 – Opt-in/Opt-out

(a) *Do you think your company/your clients will use the Unified Patent Court or are you/they planning to opt out?*
(b) *What are the key issues your company/your clients are discussing in this regard, e.g. concern over bifurcation, injunctions, judicial composition.*
(c) *If your company/your clients are going to use it, how much do you think they will use it, and what patents will they opt in to the system?*
(d) *Once the transitional opt-out period ends, do you think your company/your clients will use the UPC system, or will they consider returning to the national patent systems in e.g. the UK and Germany?*

Question 2 was designed as a detailed question, focusing on whether patentees are likely to opt in their EPs to the UPC, or whether they will instead opt out of it and continue to use the current system.[5] All interviewees gave a response to this question.

Unsurprisingly, all interviewees, whether from the business and legal communities, cited the prospective costs/fees of the UPC as an important factor for determining whether to opt in or opt out of the system.[6] Almost all interviewees stated that the issue of judicial composition is a crucially important one; 15 out of 15 in-house counsel cited it as a significant factor, while 9 out of 11 interviewees from the legal community did the same.

Meanwhile, a total of 15 out of 26 interviewees stated that bifurcation is a concern: 13 in-house counsel (6 ICT, 3 ENG, 2 Pharma, 1 ICT SME and 1 Pharma SME) but only 2 lawyers. In addition, 13 out of 26 interviewees stated that they are concerned about the UPC's power to grant pan-25 MS injunctions – 9 in-house counsel (3 ENG, 4 ICT, 1 Pharma and 1 ICT SME) and 4 lawyers. A total of 7 out of 26 interviewees stated that they are definitely concerned about patent troll litigation at the UPC – 7 in-house counsel (5 ICT, 1 ENG and 1 Pharma) and 1 lawyer. A total of 10 interviewees out of 26 stated that they consider the revocation risk at the UPC to be of significant concern – 6 in-house counsel (1 ICT, 1 Chemicals, 2 Pharma, 1 ICT SME and 1 Pharma SME) and 4 lawyers. Finally, 3 out of 26 interviewees – 1 in-house ENG counsel, 1 in-house ICT counsel and 1 in-house Pharma counsel – stated that the possibility that forum shopping will occur in the UPC system is a major concern.

Regarding the possibility that patentees may choose to return to the national patent systems following the transitional period if the UPC system develops in a 'problematic' way, 23 interviewees answered a sub-question on the issue.[7] A total of 12 participants out of 23 stated that even if businesses do not like the way the jurisprudence develops at the UPC, a large-scale return to the national patenting systems is not a real possibility. Of the 12, 8

---

5 This question corresponds to Questions 4–8 in the pilot questionnaire.

6 For the UP, the level of the renewal fees was said to be a crucial issue (discussed in detail below with respect to Question 3).

7 This question was added after the first two pilot interviews at the suggestion of a pilot interviewee so the first two interviewees did not give a response. In addition, this question did not form part of the one truncated interview conducted via email.

were in-house counsel (1 ENG, 2 ICT, 3 Pharma, 1 Chemicals and 1 Pharma SME) and 4 were lawyers. Conversely, 10 interviewees out of 23 stated that a large-scale return to national patenting in Europe is a real possibility. The 10 consist of 3 in-house counsel (1 ENG and 2 ICT) and 7 lawyers. The 1 remaining interviewee – the in-house counsel at an ENG company – stated that the company had already returned to the national patenting systems of the UK and Germany due to the opposition backlog at the EPO system.

Question 3 – Patent Fees

(a) *If the patent renewal fee were set at the equivalent of a bundle patent renewed in three participating countries (UK + DE + FR), do you think this would affect your clients' uptake of the unitary patent?*
(b) *Would there be a disincentive to use the system if the fee were set at a higher level than this, e.g. 8 MS fees?*
(c) *What would be your ideal fee, e.g. 1–2 MS fees, 3 MS fees, 4–5 MS fees?*
(d) *Would you agree that annually increasing fees creates a disincentive to renewing patents that are no longer creating revenues, i.e. 'pruning of the patent portfolio'?*

The key aim of Question 3 was to discover what level of renewal fees would provide an incentive for businesses to utilize UPs. During the survey period, all interviewees gave a response to this question – 25 interviewees out of 26 referred to specific fee levels, while 1 further interviewee simply commented generally.[8]

Out of the 25 interviewees who gave a specified fee level figure, a total of 17 stated that the renewal fees for the UP would provide an incentive if set at the 2–3 MS combined fee level,[9] but not if they were set at a level above a 3 MS combined fee. These 17 participants can be broken down as follows: 10 were working as in-house counsel and 7 were in the legal community. Of the 10

[8] Question 3 corresponds with questions 9–15 in the pilot. The general comment came as a result of the one truncated interview, conducted via email.

[9] The example given in Question 3 above is the combined UK + FR + DE renewal fees (the major patent jurisdictions). The interviewee in the truncated interview was unable to provide a response to this question.

in-house interviewees, 2 were in the ENG sector, 4 were in ICT, 2 were in Pharma, and 2 worked at SMEs (1 ICT SME and 1 Pharma SME).

Furthermore, an additional 2 out of 25 interviewees – 1 in-house Pharma counsel and 1 UK solicitor – stated that in order to provide an incentive, the level of the UP fees must be set at the 1–2 MS level. Thus, a combined total of 19 out of 25 interviewees stated that the renewal fees must be set at the 3 MS level or below – the overwhelming majority. By contrast, only 6 out of 25 interviewees stated that a fee of more than 3 MS would still provide them with an incentive to use the UP. Of these remaining 6 participants, 3 were in the legal community and 3 were working in-house (1 in ENG, 1 in ICT and 1 in Chemicals). The 1 interviewee out of 26 who did not give a specific level simply stated that he hoped the fees would be 'as low as possible'.

A total of 14 out of 24 interviewees[10] who responded to a sub-question on 'patent pruning' acknowledged that selective pruning is an important factor in their discussions concerning use of the UP. The 14 included 8 in-house counsel (3 ENG, 3 ICT, 2 Pharma) and 6 lawyers.

Question 4 – Court Fees

(a) *How important are court fee levels to your firm and your clients? For instance, if the initial court fee for filing an infringement claim were set at the equivalent to filing a case in four or five of the Signatory States, would this encourage your clients to use the system? Would you consider this correct, too low or too high?*

(b) *The UPC fees will be made up of both fixed fees and, after a certain threshold, a value-based fee. What do you see as the pros and cons of this sort of system?*

---

[10] This sub-question on pruning was not included in the first two pilot interviews; in fact, it was suggested by one of those first two interviewees. The sub-question on pruning was added to the two final pilot interviews as well as to the final questions of the study. Thus, only 24 out of 26 gave a response to this sub-question.

The purpose of Question 4 was to discover from the stakeholder perspective what level the court fees should ideally be set at, and to discover what the views of the value-based system are.[11] All interviewees responded to this question. The highest proportion – 8 out of 26 interviewees – stated that they would like to see the UPC fees set at a level lower than the current fees of the German system. The 8 consisted of 6 lawyers and 2 in-house counsel – 1 ICT and 1 Pharma. A further 3 out of 26 – 2 lawyers and 1 in-house Pharma counsel – said that they hoped the UPC fees would be set at a 1–2 MS level. Meanwhile, 2 more interviewees – 1 ENG and 1 ICT in-house counsel – stated that fees at the 3–4 MS level would be acceptable. The remaining 13 interviewees – half the sample – either did not give a specific fee, and only gave general comments, or did not consider the UPC fees issue to be of importance.

Meanwhile, a total of 8 interviewees – 2 lawyers as well as 6 in-house counsel (2 ENG, 2 ICT, 1 Pharma, and 1 SME Pharma) – stated that they have a negative view of the value-based element of the mixed UPC fees system. Meanwhile, 7 interviewees said that they have a positive view of the proposed value-based system – 5 lawyers and 2 in-house counsel (1 Pharma and 1 Chemicals). The remaining 11 interviewees had nothing specific to say about the value-based system.

Question 5 – Business Sector Issues

(a) Is there a particular sector of business, e.g. Pharma, ICT, ENG, that you think will benefit more than other sectors from the UP/UPC? Why do you think this?
(b) In particular, do you see any benefits or costs for the pharmaceutical sector in having:
  (i) a unitary patent with 25 MS-wide protection?
  (ii) a specialized divisional court for pharmaceuticals/ chemicals located in London?

The aim of Question 5 was to establish whether any particular sector would benefit more than others from the new system – and, in particular, with respect to the Pharma sector, to discover what the

[11] Question 4 corresponds to Questions 15–19 in the pilot list of questions.

benefit to the sector would be from the UP or the London-based UPC Central Division;[12] 25 out of 26 interviewees were able to provide a response to this question.[13] A total of 21 out of these 25 interviewees stated that they expect the Pharma sector to benefit the most from the new UP/UPC system – 12 in-house counsel (5 ICT, 2 Pharma, 3 ENG, 1 Chemicals and 1 Pharma SME) and 9 lawyers.

18 interviewees out of 25 – 9 in-house counsel and 9 lawyers – stated that the location of the Pharma/Chemicals division in London is a good thing, both for the Pharma/Chemicals sector and for London's legal community.

Question 6 – EPO Opposition/UPC Revocation interplay

Does the current issue of the opposition delays/backlog at the EPO concern you or your clients? Could the fact that the UPC does not have to stay proceedings pending EPO opposition help to ameliorate this problem by effectively moving oppositions away from the EPO?

Question 6 sought to discover (i) the significance of the current EPO oppositions' backlog and (ii) the potential for UPC revocation actions to help alleviate this backlog; 24 out of 26 interviewees answered this question.[14]

A total of 19 out of 24 interviewees stated that the current EPO backlog is a significant problem in their opinion. Of the 19, 8 were in-house counsel (3 ENG, 2 ICT, 2 Pharma and 1 Chemicals) and 11 were lawyers. Meanwhile, 5 out of 24 interviewees stated that the current backlog is not a significant problem – all 5 were in-house counsel (3 ICT, 1 Pharma, 1 Pharma SME); 13 of the 19 who stated that it is a problem said that the availability of UPC revocations is likely to alleviate the backlog. Of the 13, 5 were in-house counsel (2 ENG, 1 ICT and 2 Pharma) and 8 were

---

12 Question 5 corresponds to questions 20–22 in the pilot survey.

13 This question was not posed during the truncated interview with the representative of the ICT SME.

14 Two participants did not answer this question. The reason for this is that this question was not in the initial first pilot interview – it was suggested afterwards by the second pilot interviewee, who gave an answer to it. Furthermore, this question was not asked during the truncated interview.

lawyers; 6 out of 19 argued that the existence of UPC revocations is unlikely to alleviate the backlog – 3 in-house counsel (1 ENG, 1 ICT and 1 Chemicals) and 3 lawyers.

Question 7 – Sources of Info

What are your major sources of info about the UP/UPC?

This question was suggested by the IPO about one third of the way through the interview process. As a result, the first 8 interviews did not feature this question; 18 out of 26 interviewees therefore answered this question. Most interviewees acknowledged that they take advantage of a mixture of formal and informal sources in their preparations. The formal sources are the primary UPC and IPO documents mentioned above. Informal sources, on the other hand, include conversations with peers, as well as blogs such as those found on the IP Kat,[15] and discussions at representative organizations. Several of the interviewees had either made representations to the UPC preparatory committee or were themselves on the committee. The interviewees were, in general, very well informed.

Question 8 – Any Other Issues

Is there anything else you think is of significance to the current UP/UPC debate?

All interviewees provided a response to this question.[16] However, most interviewees did not have anything else to add to their responses – they felt the survey had dealt with all the important issues. A number of 'other issues' were suggested by interviewees. These were as follows:

- An in-house counsel at an ICT company raised the issue of 'Amicus Curiae briefs', noting that her company would like to see 'Amicus briefs' accepted within the UPC system.

---

[15] http://ipkitten.blogspot.co.uk/

[16] This question corresponds to the final question of the original pilot interview questions.

- An in-house counsel at a large engineering firm stated that she would like to see the UK refuse to ratify the various agreements until the final details have been hammered out so that business can make plans to deal with the new system.
- An in-house counsel at a large diversified firm (with a large interest in Pharma) stated that there had been a lot of 'misinformation' about the court – particularly over supposed cost savings – and that it would have been better to spend the energy and resources devoted to the UP/UPC on reforming the EPO to alleviate the oppositions backlog.
- The in-house counsel at a large ICT firm stated that there had to be a 'lack of economic impact analysis at individual MS level'. He further noted that 'Poland is the only country that did any kind of IA and as a consequence decided to remain outside the UPC/UPP'.

LIST OF ABBREVIATIONS

CFI – Court of First Instance
CJEU – Court of Justice of the European Union
DE – Germany
ENG – Engineering sector
EP – European patent
EPC – European Patent Convention
EPO – European Patent Office
EU – European Union
FR – France
GB – Great Britain
ICT – Information and Communication Technology sector
IPC – International Patent Classification
IPEC – Intellectual Property Enterprise Court
MS – Member state
MVPs – Most valuable patents
NL – The Netherlands
NPE – Non-practising entity
PA – Patent attorney
PAE – Patent-assertion entity
PCC – Patents County Court
Pharma – Pharmaceutical sector
PHC – Patents Court, part of the Chancery Division of the High Court of England and Wales
SS – Signatory States
SWE – Sweden
UK – United Kingdom of Great Britain and Northern Ireland
UP – European patent with unitary effect
UPC – Unified Patent Court
WIPO – World Intellectual Property Organization

Index